THE COMPLEX ROLES
OF THE TEACHER

An Ecological Perspective

THE COMPLEX ROLES
OF THE TEACHER

An Ecological Perspective

SHIRLEY F. HECK
C. RAY WILLIAMS
The Ohio State University

Foreword by John I. Goodlad

TEACHERS
COLLEGE
PRESS

Teachers College, Columbia University
New York and London   1984

Published by Teachers College Press, 1234 Amsterdam Avenue, New York, N.Y.   10027

Library of Congress Cataloging in Publication Data

Heck, Shirley F.
  The complex roles of the teacher.

    Includes bibliographical references and index.
  1.   Teaching.   2.   Interaction analysis in education.
3.   First year teachers—United States—Case studies.
I. Williams, C. Ray.   II.   Title.
LB1775.H42   1984   371.1'02   83–17865

ISBN 0-8077-2748-2 (pbk.)

Manufactured in the United States of America

89   4   5   6

Contents

FOREWORD *by John I. Goodlad*   ix

ACKNOWLEDGMENTS   xiii

INTRODUCTION   xv

1. THE TEACHER AS PERSON: A CARING ROLE   1
    Perceptions of Self   3
    The Human Qualities of a Teacher   4
    Teacher Stress and Anxiety   6
    Suggestions for Dealing with Stress and Anxiety   8
    Professional Growth: A Continuous Process   10

2. THE TEACHER AS COLLEAGUE: A SUPPORTING ROLE   14
    The Need for a Support System   15
    Establishing a Climate for Facilitating Personal
       and Professional Development   17
    Principals and Teachers as Colleagues   21
    Teachers as Partners with Teacher Educators   26
    An Educational Community of Colleagues   27

3. TEACHER AND PARENTS AS PARTNERS:
    A COMPLEMENTARY ROLE   28
    The Ecology of the Family   30
    Parents Are Teachers   33
    Communication: The Key to a Successful Parent-Teacher
       Partnership   34
    Toward the Development of the Parent-Teacher
       Partnership   36

4. THE TEACHER AS UNDERSTANDER OF THE
   LEARNER: A NURTURING ROLE   50
   The Moment-to-Moment Context   51
   Understanding the Cultural and Individual Diversity of
      Students   53
   The Development of the Total Learner   56
   Creating a Learning Environment that Focuses on the
      Development of the Total Person   60
   Understanding Students: A Basis for Effective Discipline   64
   Focusing on Educational Practice   68

5. THE TEACHER AS FACILITATOR OF LEARNING:
   AN INTERACTING ROLE   72
   Creating a Problem-Solving Environment   73
   Developing the Conditions for Creative Problem-Solving   74
   Facilitating a Problem-Solving Environment Through the
      Art of Questioning   76
   Students as Problem Solvers   78
   An Interdisciplinary Focus on Instruction   82
   Becoming a Facilitator of the Learning Environment   86

6. THE TEACHER AS RESEARCHER:
   AN EXPERIMENTING ROLE   94
   Using the Classroom as a Research Laboratory   95
   Collecting Data: A Multifaceted Approach   97
   Toward Becoming a Researcher   106
   The Art of Observation   107
   Teachers as Consumers of Research   113

7. THE TEACHER AS PROGRAM DEVELOPER:
   A CREATING ROLE   116
   Educational Goals: A Basis for Continuous Program
      Development   118
   Program Development: An Integration of Theory and
      Practice   122
   Involvement in Program Decision-Making: A Professional
      Responsibility   125

8. THE TEACHER AS ADMINISTRATOR:
   A PLANNING ROLE   127
   Planning   128
   Organizing   137
   Scheduling   140

Reporting and Evaluating   142
Communicating   146

9. TRANSITION INTO THE PROFESSION:
AN ASPIRING ROLE   150
Applying for a Teaching Position: An Initial Step   153
Interviewing for a Teaching Position: The Major Steps in
    Securing a Job   155
Preparing for the Reality of Teaching: The Professionally
    Challenging and Rewarding Step   158
Substitute Teaching: A Challenging Task   165

10. THE TEACHER AS DECISION MAKER:
A PROBLEM-SOLVING ROLE   168
Teachers Are Decision Makers   169
Toward Becoming a Decision Maker   172

11. THE TEACHER AS PROFESSIONAL LEADER:
A CHALLENGING ROLE   188
The Integrating of Roles   189
Understanding the Leadership Role of the Teacher   190
Focusing on Educational Practice   193

REFERENCES   203

INDEX   209

Foreword

Schooling is largely a process of learning alone in groups. The classroom group affects the amount of attention one gets, how one responds to expectations, and one's self-concepts. But the evaluation and the rewards are individual. Everyone in a group of twenty-five may appear to be doing the same things simultaneously, but it is individual and not group performance that counts.

By the time young men and women become teachers, they are thoroughly socialized into this process of learning alone in groups. They have experienced it for sixteen or seventeen years. Further, they have experienced it in a box seemingly isolated from other classroom boxes in the building. It is a surprise, then, and often a shock to discover that being a teacher rather than a student in this box involves much more than teaching a group alone. The mesh of relationships, scarcely visible if at all to students, usually causes teachers to view and conduct their work quite differently than they had anticipated even while engaged in a teacher education program.

Shirley Heck and Ray Williams explore the nature and dimensions of these relationships in such a way as to provide an understanding of the teacher's role going far beyond the simplicity of the popular myth, "everything depends on the teacher." Of course, the teacher is crucial in what and how well students learn. But only a few are able to rise, year after year, beyond a nonsupportive culture in which relationships with the principal, fellow teachers, and parents are flawed by lack of trust and cooperation.

Heck and Williams go well beyond the insights about schools revealed by the ecological perspective from which they view the context of teaching. They draw many implications for teacher education (and it is to prospective teachers that their book is primarily addressed), but the implications for improving schools as institutions are equally clear and important. Unless the settings into which teachers come as individuals are maximally supportive of teaching and learning, neither teachers nor students will perform at the level of their capability.

I brought to these pages impressions and conclusions from studying comprehensively and in depth a small sample of elementary, junior high, and senior high schools.[1] A major purpose of the study was to gain insight into the interactions of people and things (for example, the content of the curriculum) within school settings and between schools and the surrounding community. Teachers and the circumstances within which they teach were a major focus. Not surprisingly, my conclusions served as a kind of backdrop against which to view and test the Heck–Williams perspective. Over and over, the congruence was marked. A few illustrations follow.

Heck and Williams document the service-oriented view of students in a teacher preparation program and their somewhat idealistic, professional attitudes toward children's interests and needs. But, on the job, relating personally and professionally to peers looms large as does daily survival in the classroom. Our data showed large numbers of teachers in the sample to be torn between two often irreconcilable sets of personal beliefs and values. On one hand, they saw students' interests as a major source for what and how they taught and believed that students should participate actively in decisions about their own education. On the other hand, they believed strongly in teachers being in control and being the major determiners of curriculum and instruction.

The main reason chosen for entering teaching was the service nature of the profession and a desire to teach something or help someone learn. The main reason for leaving would be frustration—with the administration and administrative requirements, to a lesser degree with peers, and to a considerable degree over students' lack of interest in learning. Teaching occurs in a particular context and is much influenced by that context.

Heck and Williams soon move away from the realities of the school environment and how teachers' interactions condition and are conditioned by these realities to help us understand how teachers can be and should be constructively proactive in the improvement of the workplace. This is a role seldom addressed in teacher education programs, dominated as they are by psychological rather than sociological and philosophical considerations. If teachers are prepared only to be technicians or even clinicians, it is unlikely that educational practices in schools will change very much. Teachers will continue to teach as they were taught as students, presumably doing the conventional and traditional somewhat better than did their predecessors.

Where we found differences among schools, these tended to be in

---

[1]Reported in John I. Goodlad, *A Place Called School* (New York: McGraw-Hill, 1983).

the quality of interpersonal relations and school-wide problem solving. We sorted out the top twenty-five percent from the bottom twenty-five percent of schools in the sample on the basis of satisfaction. The satisfaction index was derived from students, teachers, and parents: the mark they gave their school (A, B, C, D, or F), the congruence between their preferred goal (chosen from academic, civic/social, vocational, and personal) and the goal they perceived their school to emphasize, and the number of serious problems they perceived their school to have.

The top twenty-five percent of the schools so selected maintained an academic ambience; classroom climate was markedly more nurturing (the relationship between students and teachers was supportive); teachers viewed themselves as supported by their principal; teachers saw their peers as competent, hard-working professionals; principals viewed the teachers as competent professionals; parents said that teachers were accessible and that they had a good deal of information about their school. Students in the bottom twenty-five percent frequently said that the school did not provide a good education; they viewed their teachers more frequently as not helpful and supportive; teachers saw the principal as not backing them and many of their peers not doing a good job; principals saw teachers as part of the problem; parents claimed to have little knowledge of their school and regarded teachers as not very accessible. Our data showed the top twenty-five percent to be more renewing and as "taking care of the school's problems." Clearly, these schools were better places for principals, teachers, students, and parents.

For Heck and Williams, the teacher blithely teaching in an isolated classroom, insulated from the school's culture and the larger context of education and schooling is today virtually nonexistent. Consequently, teachers must be prepared for the realities, demands, and expectations of interdependence. However, simply to be adaptive is not sufficient.

Teachers should not simply adapt to environments in disarray. They should become proactive in the creation of healthy educational ecosystems. Successful businesses recognize the significant decision-making role of employees at all levels of the enterprise. This is a critical element not just in employee satisfaction, important as this is, but in productivity. It is reasonable to assume that the same is true of schools and those who work in them.

The perspective elaborated by Shirley Heck and Ray Williams is not new. They recognize the contributions to it of sociologists and social psychologists and cite contemporaries Seymour Sarason and Urie Bronfenbrenner, among others. But their application of this perspective to teachers and teacher education is unique and timely.

Each new era of school improvement seems doomed to founder on the brick put forward as the cornerstone from which to build. This is because we try to make of the one brick an entire building. We become excessively preoccupied with single elements of the whole: getting more able people into teaching, or new methods for present teachers, or more discipline, or harder subjects, or merit pay, or longer school days. For a time, "it all depends on the principal" replaced the slogan, "it all depends on the teacher," as the answer to good schools.

In spite of the holistic approach of Heck and Williams, we will try to draw from it, I fear, some simple formulas for school improvement. Alas, there are none. The problem with viewing entities such as schools in their appropriate complexity is the accompanying realization that the processes required for their improvement inevitably must take account of this complexity. This is best done close to schools—by the principals, teachers, and students who work there and the parents who have a particular stake in the schools their children attend. Improving schools one by one so that each becomes a healthy ecosystem is much more difficult and less popular than mandating excellence, but this process has a unique advantage: It just might work.

JOHN I. GOODLAD

Acknowledgments

Although we cannot acknowledge individually the many people who have helped make this book a reality, we extend our gratitude to the teachers, principals, students, parents, and board of education members who participated in our study of first-year teachers. Particular thanks are given to Dr. Loretta Buffer for her professional expertise and involvement in the study. The undergraduate and graduate students at the Mansfield Campus of The Ohio State University deserve special recognition for providing scenarios that reflect both realism and idealism in education. We would also like to acknowledge Dr. James Fox, both for his contribution to chapter 7, "The Teacher as Program Developer," and his inspiration as an outstanding instructional leader.

We are indebted to Karen Storts for her excellent professional assistance in typing the manuscript and to Dorothea Barry for her editorial contributions and encouragement throughout the writing of this book.

We are grateful to Dr. Urie Bronfenbrenner whose research, particularly his book entitled *The Ecology of Human Development*, has served as the conceptual framework for formulating the ecological perspective of our research studies and our thinking reflected throughout this book.

In the lives of each of the authors there have been those "special" educators whose achievements continue to influence us—educators who have been models through their leadership, scholarship, and commitment to excellence in education. We thank Dr. Lanore A. Netzer, Dr. Glen Eye, Dr. John I. Goodlad, Dr. Madeline Hunter, and Dr. Richard L. Wink.

Introduction

This book focuses on the dynamic interactive contexts within which teaching and learning take place. The teacher and the student are continually influenced by the significant others who share the family, school-community, and the many other social, cultural, and political contexts of which they are a part. As individuals interact within each of these contexts, behavioral changes occur. What happens to people in one situation may influence them in another. These changes are unique to each teacher and to each student. What is perceived as a reinforcing influence by one teacher or one learner may be perceived as a stressful influence by another. Because of this interactive or transactive nature of the teaching-learning phenomenon, the roles of a teacher are extremely complex and difficult.

The importance of "ecological context" is perhaps more easily understood when one compares it to a musical composition. Beneath the complexity of combinations of tones in time and space, there is a simplicity of form and sensitivity to the expressive power of the ways musical tones relate to one another. This sensitivity reflects the composer's conception of an artistic whole. The artist who performs that composition interprets it—making it an artistic rendition that reflects his or her artistry and meaning.

Similarly, teaching can be studied as a process that demands sensitivity to the multiple contexts of which both learners and teachers are a part. Teachers' specialized knowledge of subject matter, context, human development, pedagogy, and human relations helps them to understand and anticipate the reality of the teaching-learning phenomenon. It is this knowledge, as it relates to the specific teaching-learning context, that is critical for planning and providing appropriate educational experiences for students.

This book is based on our intensive case studies of first-year teachers. In these studies, the nature of the teaching-learning phenomenon was examined as it is influenced by the numerous contexts of which each teacher and each learner is a part. Our first motivation to conduct such a study came during a series of informal seminars with students enrolled in our teacher education program and during another series of seminars involving graduates of that program. In these seminars, it became evident to us that a significant shift in attitudes and behaviors was occurring between preservice teacher preparation and the actual classroom teaching that occurred during that first year. During the teacher preparation program, students experienced a high level of success and self-confidence. Their comments and questions focused consistently on the needs of children and on approaches to meet these needs. For example, "I discovered the importance of determining the unique needs and learning styles of each child and designing programs to meet these needs"; "I discovered that children sometimes have trouble communicating their feelings but those feelings are important and can't be ignored"; "Kindergarteners really put ideas together and give terrific answers—I guess I underestimated them"; "I enjoyed the challenges brought about by each individual student"; "I enjoyed learning from the children—learning their likes, dislikes, moods, and the information they shared with me."

These comments and questions were in contrast to those expressed by the same group of men and women during their first year of teaching. Then, comments and questions focused primarily on the teachers' personal needs for survival in the varied contexts. This was evident in such comments as "My greatest satisfaction of the week was being accepted as one of the group in the teachers' lounge"; "My greatest frustration was not knowing how to act with colleagues, principal, parents, and students during a threatened strike situation"; "The greatest satisfaction of the week was resolving a personal conflict with a fellow staff member." Other first-year teachers noted, "I need more time for my husband and myself"; "My greatest frustration is knowing that part of teaching carries over into my personal life." It seemed evident to us that many of the concerns being expressed by these classroom teachers extended well beyond the classroom and the school.

In our study of first-year teachers, we collected data using open-ended interviews with teachers, students, principals, teacher peers, board members, parents, and spouses of teachers. Other data sources included personal logs of the teachers and extensive videotaped observations in their classrooms. Interpretations of these data revealed patterns of both stressful influences and reinforcing influences that were operating in the teaching-learning context. These influences were reported in terms of the complex leadership roles of the teacher.

While the complex roles of the teacher are discussed separately in this book, in reality they are not discrete but occur within an integrated structure of dynamic relationships. This holistic perspective adds to the complexity of the teaching-learning process. In order to add authenticity and life to the theories being presented, we have included selected vignettes from the personal logs kept by teachers, transcriptions of videotaped classroom practices, and actual interviews with the teachers and their principals. To reach greater understanding of the larger school-community context, we have provided discussion questions to aid the reader in exploring beyond the data to other possible situations. An awareness of the complex ecological forces that affect teachers and that are affected by teachers will, we hope, help teachers to become highly sensitive, highly effective professionals—professionals who are happy that they made the decision to become teachers.

Since professional leadership spans all levels of teaching, this book is appropriate for preservice education majors in early childhood, elementary, and secondary education. It is designed as a textbook for students who have been admitted into a teacher preparation program and are enrolled in a course where the conceptions of the teaching-learning process are introduced. The text could also be used as a capstone seminar for teacher candidates. Since many current in-service teachers have not been exposed to the ecological perspectives of the teaching-learning phenomenon, this text provides a meaningful context in which these influences are discussed and extended to their particular school-community environment.

THE COMPLEX ROLES
OF THE TEACHER

An Ecological Perspective

Chapter 1

The Teacher as Person

A CARING ROLE

Within the teacher's emotional life are the forces that most powerfully affect the entire teaching process. The human, emotional qualities of the teacher are at the very heart of teaching. No matter how much emphasis is placed on such other qualities in teaching as educational technique, technology, equipment, or buildings, "the humanity of the teacher is the vital ingredient if children are to learn." Exploration of the full range and depth of feelings of teacher educators enhances our understanding of this basic ingredient. (Greenberg, 1969, pp. 20–21)

Learning, living, and becoming are continuous and interrelated. "We cannot be obliged to be 'what' we are; we must continue making ourselves what we might be" (Sartre, 1963, p. 91). This continuous process of growing and becoming was recognized by Maslow (1962), who defines personal growth as active steps toward self-fulfillment. It is a person's nature to go beyond, to improve, and to find self-fulfillment, to never rest with the present condition. The supreme goal of a human being is to be fulfilled as a creative, unique individual, developing human potentialities within the limits of reality. People seek the continuous growth and development of a self that is capable of dealing effectively and efficiently with life, both now and in the future. This growth and development is a never-ending process; when one ceases to grow, one ceases to live and begins only to exist.

In studying the role of the teacher as a person, we must consider the notion of life-span human development, that is, the continuous process of growth from conception to death. Becoming a teacher involves many developmental changes. An individual does not suddenly become a teacher; rather, becoming a teacher is a process that continues throughout one's professional career. Teachers need to understand themselves and the numerous factors that influence their own growth and development if they are to assume the complex roles involved in teaching. Fuller and Bown (1975) and Ryan et al. (1980) repeatedly refer to the notion that becoming a teacher is not a matter of learning how to teach but of personal discovery—of learning how to use one's self well.

Socrates' dictum "Know thyself" has great implications for the teacher who is in the continuous process of growing and becoming. The self is "a system of ideas, attitudes, values, and commitments. The self is a person's total subjective environment; it is the distinctive center of experience and significance. The self constitutes a person's inner world as distinguished from the outer world consisting of all other people and things" (Jersild, 1955, p. 8). The paradox, however, is that the inner world of self is influenced by the multiple contexts of which the teacher is a part. The self develops in each individual through the process of social experiences in these varied contexts.

Both past experiences and moment-to-moment experiences influence the process of becoming and growing as a person. These influences are complex and interactive. That which occurs in the family context often influences what happens at school; conversely, what occurs in the school context influences how the teacher reacts at home.

These influences are inherent in the multiple contexts of which teachers are a part, but they are unique to each person and affect individuals in different ways. For example, one's personality, which is directly influenced by the sociocultural context, may affect one's differing responses to such events as becoming a parent or grandparent; retiring from work; getting a divorce; or receiving recognition and praise from parents, principals, or peers. For some women, becoming a grandmother is the ultimate fulfillment of a lifetime; these women are proud and eager to announce to the world that they are grandmothers. For other women, however, becoming a grandmother is an unpleasant experience; these women see this life event only as a sign of growing old and prefer that others not know that they have grandchildren. These individual differences in responses to events reflect not only the person's unique self and the effects of society but also reflect the person's unique interaction with sequential developmental changes (Kimmel, 1974).

The focus on the teacher as a developing person is extremely critical, for it is the teacher who ultimately "becomes the curriculum." It is not the quality of the textbooks, the quality of the pupils or their environment, or the quality of the community, the administration, or the professional staff that makes the difference between learning and not learning for students—rather, it is the capability of the teacher as a developing person to facilitate the learner's interaction with important, ever-changing factors which he or she encounters. Many times, a student's response to a teacher is a direct reflection of the teacher's response to self. If a teacher is bored and unhappy with the subject matter or the class, the chances are great that the students will be bored and unhappy. The teacher alone must internalize and integrate learning theory and practices that motivate and provide the stimulus for learning to take place. Unless teachers understand their own unique learning processes, they will not be able to understand their students' learning processes.

PERCEPTIONS OF SELF

One important factor that influences development is the perception a person has of self. A positive self-concept or view of self provides the confidence and security to deal vigorously with life and translates to positive feelings toward others. The same is true for feelings of self-identity and belongingness. People who feel they "belong" to a particular group, whether it is formal or informal, are in a far stronger position to deal with life than those who do not. Teachers can "belong" to the formal group of the staff in a particular school or of the education association; they can also "belong" to such informal groups as the first lunch group or the group of teachers who have rooms in the basement of the building. Significant others, from a spouse to the building principal, play a crucial role in helping individuals progress through the self-actualization stages of belongingness, love, and esteem—stages that are critical to the development of a positive view of self.

Perceptions are not *reactions* to stimuli in the environment; they are more accurately described as *transactions* with stimuli. Both the inner structure—personality—and the outer structure—society—are necessary to account for human action. The point of interaction and the interdependence of these two structures result in individual perceptions (Allport, 1965). Accordingly, people react from a history of perceptual beliefs, attitudes, opinions, and experiences—experiences of love, hate, fear, anger, and compassion. The meanings and significances assigned to things, symbols, people, and events are formed by past experiences; no response reflects only the immediate situation or event.

Commenting on the philosophy of Maurice Merleau-Ponty, Greene (1978) points out that the life of reason develops against a background of perceived realities. Each person achieves contact with the world from a particular vantage point and in terms of a particular biography. All of this underlies present perspectives and affects the unique way people look at things, talk about things, structure their realities, and encounter their worlds. Because biographies differ, each person encounters the social reality of everyday life from a somewhat distinctive perspective, a perspective of which others are far too often unaware. The crucial point is that we, as conscious beings, constitute the world we inhabit through the interpretations we adopt or make for ourselves. This same view was expressed by Combs (1982), who maintains that the effect of words does not live in what is said but in how it is heard. Unless clarified, these differences in perceptions can be the source of many misunderstandings and inappropriate decisions.

Teachers who are out of touch with their own reality contribute to the distancing that often takes place in schools. Human beings who lack an awareness of their own personal reality cannot experience the mutual tuning-in relationship, the experience of the ''we'' that is at the foundation of all possible communication. They cannot know what it means to share another's experiences. Without the ability to enter a mutual tuning-in relationship, the teacher is in some manner incapacitated since teaching is, in so many of its dimensions, a mode of encounter and of communication (Schutz, 1964).

Combs (1982) emphasizes that a concern for development as a good teacher originates with the individual's self. People use self, self-knowledge, and the resources at hand to solve the problems for which they are responsible. This is easiest for teachers who feel good about themselves, who know what they are doing and why they are doing it, and who control situations rather than being controlled by them. People are capable of using themselves more creatively if the conditions that support creative responses, choices, and actions are present. These supportive conditions, according to Rogers (1967), include trustworthiness, empathy, caring, psychological freedom, and psychological safety. Human potential is increased when these supportive conditions are strengthened. Some practical suggestions for creating a supportive school environment are given at the end of this chapter and in chapter 2.

THE HUMAN QUALITIES OF A TEACHER

We have all experienced several teachers who had a special influence on our lives. A comparison of these ''special'' teachers probably reveals minimal similarity in terms of instructional techniques used, expectations placed on the students, or mode of instruction. Rather, the common characteristic is more attributable to who they were as persons, that is, their human qualities of trusting, caring, and sharing of themselves. Increasingly, the learning of "facts" can be achieved easily with good books, good TV, and good computer-assisted teaching; what cannot be done in these ways is to teach "styles" of life, to teach what it means to be, to grow, to become actualized, and to enlarge one's self. The only way a teacher can teach these qualities is to assume them. A good teacher has to be a model; it is only by being a model that one can have the courage and trust and openness to let students experiment with being. The only way to teach "actualization" is to be a person who is courageous enough and trusting enough to be vigorously and openly involved in the world and to carry that involvement into the teaching environment (Michael, 1967). Rogers (1967) identifies realness and genuineness as the most essential attributes in the role of teacher as facilitator of learning. When the facilitator is a real person—being what he or she is and entering into a relationship with the learner without presenting a facade—he or she is much more likely to be effective.

Learning to deal with one's authentic feelings is a profoundly personal process. Teachers must be willing to be vulnerable, for that is the only way that students can gain enough trust to show their own vulnerability. Teachers need to realize that it is permissible to allow students to see their humanity. They can show their own weaknesses, concerns, beliefs, and humor to students; it is possible to allow students to see the essence of one's personality and still be a stable person. Such revelations of character require courage, but they also result in much fuller relationships between students and teachers.

By sharing experiences and feelings about teaching with other teachers, teachers encounter themselves. Self-encounter enables teachers to reassess teaching styles and to determine if these styles fit their own basic philosophies of education. Through this self-encounter, teachers discover some of their own values as human beings and become aware of contradictions and confusions within themselves. Through sharing, teachers are also able to broaden the framework within which they view teaching. This sharing increases perceptions about the knowledge of other ways in which problems can be faced. There is no simple process for seeking solutions, that is, answers from others that may then be imitated by the troubled teacher as a means of dealing with his or her own feelings (Greenberg, 1969). What a troubled teacher needs is someone who listens to personal experiences and feelings without judging or giving quick solutions. A good listener can help facilitate the problem-solving process by helping an individual view possible alternatives.

A teacher's attitude and philosophy of education stem from his or her personality and definitions of the role of a teacher. Person-oriented teachers are likely to enjoy their contacts with students and to hold generally favorable attitudes toward them. Teachers who see their primary role as the transmission of knowledge will react quite differently from teachers who feel their primary responsibility is to establish a close relationship with students and to help them experience success in the pursuit of knowledge. The latter are much more likely to develop strong affective responses to students and to be concerned with their development as total persons rather than only with the more narrow range of cognitive development (Brophy & Good, 1974).

Being authentic and honest with students does not mean "acting like the students." One can and must maintain high standards of conduct and performance. Indeed, when such standards are absent, students soon lose respect for a teacher. Successful teaching demands the qualities of professionalism and leadership; these qualities must not be compromised.

TEACHER STRESS AND ANXIETY

Teaching is an emotionally exhausting profession. Teachers are continually making decisions that affect the lives of children, and they are constantly giving and sharing emotionally and intellectually. In *The Culture of the School and the Problem of Change* (1971), Sarason discusses the demanding and exhausting nature of teaching. He emphasized that students on all levels, in different ways, need, want, require, and demand *giving* from their teachers, and constant giving in the context of the constant vigilance required by the presence of many children is draining and taxing. Primary students may want the physical closeness that they associate with caring. Secondary students may want feedback—of approval or disapproval—on their beliefs and values. Sometimes the need of secondary students for attention and response is evidenced by their need to shock the teacher, to see the kind of reaction they get for their outlandish speech, dress, or behavior. Even when this giving is sustained on a high level, teachers often feel guilty because they cannot give all that they feel students need. To sustain the giving at a high level, the teacher must experience "getting"; however, sources for "getting" are surprisingly infrequent and indirect.

The role of teacher as colleague is very significant in creating a balance between giving and getting. Several studies, including our study of first-year teachers, indicate that colleagues are the best sources for the support that is so vital to a teacher's well-being. Teachers can give each other the reinforcement and encouragement that are so critical in meeting the daily challenges of the profession. The sensitive teacher will be able to "tune in" to the needs of a fellow teacher when the moment-to-moment context warrants it. For example, one of the teachers in our study had received a very upsetting note from a parent. A fellow teacher came to her and offered to take her recess supervision duties so she could stay in and relax. The first-year teacher remarked repeatedly how much the sensitivity of this teacher meant to her on that particular day.

In our study of first-year teachers, we were able to identify a number of factors that seemed to make the teacher's job easier. Teachers most often identified the following: being able to get ideas and suggestions from other teachers; having ideas accepted and acted upon by one's peers; hearing from the principal that what is being done is "good"; being involved in the staff decision-making process; having the freedom to develop one's own learning environment; and maintaining a personal support system through contact with former professors. Among the factors that made teaching more difficult were having to spend an inordinate amount of time away from one's child or spouse; perceiving that the principal was being more supportive of parents' concerns than teachers' concerns; not being prepared to handle the numerous administrative tasks required of teachers; having to spend time handling discipline problems; dealing with differences between the principal's approach to teaching and one's own; having numerous demands made on time by students and parents; and having to accept and adjust to reduced levels of school financial support. There are of course numerous other factors that facilitate or impede the work of the teacher. To expect all factors to be positive is unreasonable. However, by being aware of and sensitive to some of these more common factors, each educator is better able to get necessary support and to give the support that can make the job of teaching more satisfying for colleagues.

Similar reinforcing and stressful influences have been identified in studies of experienced teachers. In general, stress results when there is a variance between the teacher's goals and expectations and the ability to achieve these goals in the total school context. In his study of teacher problems, Cruickshank (1981) identifies five broad areas representing unfulfilled goals: (1) the need to establish and maintain good relationships with others in the schools, both staff and pupils; (2) the need to control pupil behavior; (3) the desire to relate well to adults who are important in the lives of the students; (4) the desire to be successful in terms of academic and social achievement; and (5) the need to have time for both personal and professional life.

Stress cannot and probably should not be completely eliminated from the teaching-learning environment. A certain degree of tension or stress is inevitable and necessary for creative and constructive change. But when the degree of stress becomes excessive and inordinate, it does not have a positive effect. In such situations, teachers need to identify the sources of undue stress. Hunt's article "Stress Without Distress" (1983) discusses some potential sources of stress in the lives of today's teachers. These include such factors as unrealistic expectations, internal or external pressures to succeed, economic concerns, lack of self-confidence, conflict in values, or lack of goals. Situations that cause stress for one teacher may not cause stress for another, and things that cause stress at one point in a person's life may not cause stress at another time.

In his study of teacher stress, Greenberg (1969) discovered that many teachers live with false "myths" of what a teacher should be. The discrepancy between the teacher's actual feelings and these persistent myths causes uneasiness and guilt. Myths and idealized notions about what a teacher should feel have plagued many teachers. For example, one myth is that every day is a perpetual joy; another is that a truly successful teacher will be liked by every student. Applegate et al. (1977) studied first-year teachers to determine what "surprises they encountered in their first year in the classroom." They discovered that the number of unhappy surprises far outnumbered the happier ones. The first-year teachers had begun their careers expecting to derive great satisfaction from the majority of events in the classroom, but in the first three weeks of teaching, they experienced so many problems that they began to feel happy only when no problems occurred. Their greatest source of satisfaction was just being able to cope with the situation.

According to Lortie (1975), professional jealousy is often a source of stress. The "grass often looks greener on the other side of the hall," and consequently teachers frequently compare themselves with colleagues. Often they see positive traits in others that they are unable to see in themselves. This makes for uneasiness, shyness, attempts to cover up behavior, and efforts to create an impression that one is different from the way one really is; of course, this all leads to anger and stress in its many forms.

SUGGESTIONS FOR DEALING WITH STRESS
AND ANXIETY

Since teacher stress is unique to each teacher, the initial step in dealing with stress is the identification of the problems and their possible causes. Workshops on identification and management of stress may assist teachers to explore their personal feelings about everyday teaching, to identify conditions that cause stress, and to discover coping strategies—both individually and collectively.

A support system within the school context is one of the most effective means of reducing teacher stress and anxiety. Often, just sharing concerns with other teachers and asking for their suggestions and ideas can help to relieve tensions.

Tedium has been identified as a cause of stress. Planned variation in scheduling of classes, methodologies, seating arrangements, and classroom environments can be valuable in this regard. A "change of face and a change of pace" can help both students and teachers. An exchange of students for a specific unit of study might provide sufficient variation to avoid tedium.

Time pressure is often cited as a cause of stress. To relieve this pressure, older students could be asked to help with bulletin boards and make instructional materials. Senior citizens can be tutors, help with some of the clerical work, serve as resource people, or read to small groups of pupils. Parent aides also can be used. If at all possible, teachers should try to free themselves from schoolwork over weekends. A relaxed weekend helps the teacher to come in on Monday with renewed enthusiasm and energy.

Teachers need to know and accept themselves—both strengths and weaknesses! They must be honest with themselves. For example, if they feel totally drained, they need to do something positive to remedy this situation. Teachers are influenced by the multiple contexts of which they are a part; it is often difficult to divorce personal problems from responsibilities in the classroom. Yet, it is unfair to allow personal problems to cause stress and pain for students. Teachers need to be aware of and sensitive to the impact of their personal lives on the lives of students. Physical relaxation can often help relieve tensions and anxieties—at least temporarily.

Attending a professional workshop or conference is another way to help eliminate stress. "Getting away" has a great therapeutic advantage. At a professional meeting—either general in scope or related to a specific discipline—teachers have the opportunity to meet, talk, and share problems. It is reassuring to find that others are having the same problems or are haunted by the same doubts. The professional interaction that takes place at such meetings, as well as the social gatherings that are so much a part of them, can send teachers back to their schools with renewed enthusiasm and with a more positive perspective about what they are doing in their classrooms.

Going back to school for graduate work helps many teachers gain new and fresh attitudes and ideas for their classrooms. Being a student again can remind teachers what it is like to be on the other side of the desk and how boring or exciting a classroom can be. Here again, meeting and talking with peers from other schools can show teachers that they are not the only ones facing financial difficulties, program changes, or even burnout.

Many educators find themselves in the trap of eating, sleeping, and living school with no other activities to break that routine. It is important to pursue some activities that are not related to school. A teacher's family and colleagues will find him or her a much more interesting person when the teacher has something other than school and students to talk about.

Parents of students are often identified as a cause of stress. The suggestions provided in chapter 3 may help to alleviate some of the stress in dealing with parents. Similarly, many of the suggestions in chapter 8 should help with stress caused by time pressures, planning, scheduling, and organizing. Some of the suggestions included in the following section on professional development can also help to reduce stress and anxiety.

PROFESSIONAL GROWTH: A CONTINUOUS PROCESS

Continuous professional development is a vital part of teaching. This development does not just happen; rather, teachers need to plan and pursue numerous opportunities that will enhance professional growth and development.

One way in which teachers can continue to grow as professionals is through attendance at professional meetings. The agenda for such meetings usually reflects the needs and interests of the teachers who have attended in the past—these can range from "Computer Technology in the Language Arts Classroom" to a "Make and Take" session or a "Meet the Author" group. Interaction with other teachers is another valuable characteristic of such meetings, for only from colleagues can a teacher gain first-hand knowledge of what does and does not work in classrooms. The commercial and professional exhibits often on display at conferences offer the opportunity to look at and talk about the advances that are being made in educational media, including such things as textbooks, computers, and other teaching aids.

Membership in community organizations and attendance at community meetings afford teachers an opportunity to grow professionally. Here, teachers become aware of the needs and concerns that are particular to their communities. Teachers also gain a working knowledge of community attitudes toward schools and school programs—an insight that is invaluable when they wish to introduce new programs within the school. Through local affiliations, teachers often earn the trust and confidence of the community.

A truly professional educator will subscribe to professional journals. Through these publications, teachers can become aware of the state of the art, read about ideas that have worked for other classroom teachers, and stay abreast of the research that is being conducted in their particular area of instruction. Many publications at the national, state, regional, and local levels illustrate the numerous possibilities that exist for teachers and students.

Teachers should also read in areas other than education since so much of what occurs in the classroom reflects what is occurring in the world at large. A teacher who has read any general publication, from *Newsweek* to the *New York Times,* is not surprised by the advent of the computerized classroom and all of the applications that are possible in education. Students expect their teachers to be knowledgeable about things other than mathematics or language arts; one student may want only to talk about or write about the Super Bowl; another may be totally preoccupied with the latest fall fashions as presented in *Seventeen*; yet another may be interested in the latest advances in medical technology or in the development of alternate sources of energy. A common knowledge base often enables teachers to engage in more meaningful discussions with students.

If teachers are going to read, they must reserve a special time and/or a special day during which they will *make* the time to read. It is never good enough to say, "That looks interesting. I'll put it here until I have the time to read it." The time to read never presents itself; it must be made. There are often distractions or responsibilities that can consume all of the hours in the day.

Keeping in touch with peers is an essential part of growth as a person and as a professional. Discovering what is going on in the classroom next door or the one down the hall gives teachers an opportunity to try some new approach or to begin integrating into their own course of study those parts of the curriculum that formerly seemed to have no relationship at all. Some other teachers in the building may have already tried and succeeded with a method that others have considered but were never quite certain would work. How much simpler are the lives of at least four people—social studies teacher, English teacher, librarian, and student—when the format for a research paper is being taught at the same time that the history teacher is requiring high school juniors to write one. The social studies teacher gains, for he or she is able to teach the historical importance of research, the implications of primary as opposed to secondary sources, and the importance of documentation rather than having to teach the format and procedure of writing a research paper. The English teacher profits by not having to suggest topic upon topic or to suggest that ''the Civil War'' is too broad a topic— *that* has been accomplished in the history class. English class can be utilized for the mechanics and procedures of outlining, footnoting, and creating a bibliography and polishing writing skills. The librarian, too, finds the interdisciplinary approach helpful. The topics have been limited, the framework for writing has been established, and the librarian can focus on guiding the students in their search for information. Ultimately, the students receive the greatest benefit—they are able to see that there are cross-disciplinary applications for that which they are learning in both social studies and English, and they can complete one project to satisfy the requirements of two classes. Ideally, it would be at this point in the year that the typing classes would begin their work on research papers; suddenly, many teachers and students are working together toward a common goal. How much easier the grading becomes, as well, when a given component of a research paper can be graded by the teacher who is responsible for that aspect of the curriculum.

Professional growth can also be nurtured when teachers maintain contact with the significant others who have brought them to the classroom. Teachers who stay in contact with former college professors, with their cooperating teachers from their student teaching experience, with their own elementary and secondary school teachers, and with former colleagues from other systems find themselves with a network that helps to sustain professional growth. These many professionals provide teachers with a sympathetic and familiar source of encouragement and of help—a built-in support group that complements the support group that should exist in the home and in the school. Also, contacts with professionals who work in settings that are different than their own can provide teachers with new insight about techniques that they are employing and about other possibilities that exist.

Some educators have the opportunity to serve as cooperating teachers for teacher candidates or interns attending a local college or university. Such an opportunity can provide a dynamic vehicle for professional growth. Not only will a student teacher aid the classroom teacher in assessing the methods currently in use, but that student teacher can bring a new enthusiasm and new ideas into the classroom.

Teachers grow through observing other teachers—the reason why teacher educators find such observations to be an integral part of preparing future teachers. Observations can provide opportunities to evaluate one's own teaching and to gain new knowledge and instructional skills. Classroom teachers should make the effort to observe other classes at other schools or even within the same school. Ideas as varied as new bulletin boards, a different method of arranging the classroom, or presentation of an integrated unit of study are available to teachers who leave their own "castles" and venture forth to see exactly what others are doing.

Professional growth can also come through publication. Teachers should look for the courage and self-confidence to write about ideas that they have used with success or that have completely fallen apart for them. Teachers typically find that their greatest trust rests with other teachers; only through taking the risk of trying to publish can they share with other instructors, whom they may never meet, the best and the worst of education.

Many state, county, and local resource groups—including state departments of education—are available to teachers. By making use of these groups and the materials, speakers, and research results available through them, teachers can aid their own growth while adding another dimension to their classrooms and thence to their students. Through these groups, grants and workshops are often available to assist teachers in continuing professional growth. Some workshop sessions or seminars may have direct applications to an area of specialization while other sessions are generally valuable in that they introduce new knowledge and areas of study. Regardless of the nature of a particular workshop, the potential exists for professional growth.

Teachers who offer to participate in or who are selected to work on schoolwide or districtwide committees are presented with another opportunity to grow and develop. The increased communication across subject areas, between grade levels, or among schools that comes with work on such a committee is in itself a benefit. Again, in this setting, teachers have a prime opportunity to discuss and discover with other teachers—an opportunity to grow both personally and professionally.

Since the role of the teacher as person influences each of the other roles, this personal dimension is integrated throughout each of the chapters. There is of course much more to the "personal role" of the teacher than can be included in a book of this nature. To gain further understanding of this role, the reader is encouraged to study such areas as adult human development, family studies, and human relations.

Chapter 2

The Teacher as Colleague

A SUPPORTING ROLE

Professionals in schools need opportunities for mutual exchange of information and ideas. Simply, teachers need to talk with teachers. This interaction is the life-blood of professional growth and of educational program development. (Sergiovanni and Starratt, 1971, p. 171)

Teachers can serve as powerful resources in helping each other to grow as professional educators. As teachers communicate and act, both formally and informally, they give each other the continuing social and psychological support that helps them achieve and maintain a sense of personal and professional worth. Greenberg (1969) suggests that teachers can use their colleagues to cope with their own anxieties about achieving "teacherhood." His studies show that many socializing needs are met through contacts with other persons during a normal working day. These informal social contacts often affect a person's job satisfaction and therefore must not be minimized. People who are subject to the great pressure and responsibility of teaching need the relief that comes from a forum where ideas are shared, challenged, and refined.

Staff interaction is promoted and facilitated in an environment where a trusting relationship has been established among colleagues. When teachers learn to value and trust each other in their day-to-day working relationships, the stage is set for other aspects of staff development. Through interactions with colleagues, teachers can benefit from what others know, prefer, and value. One teacher can help another to become aware of various views and practices. "In such a climate of sharing and exchange, teachers have a hand in shaping their professional lives as well as standing ready to be influenced by those who seek change" (Galloway, Steltzer, & Whitfield, 1980, p. 265).

14

In their article "The Social Realities of Teaching" (1979), Lieberman and Miller discuss the importance of professional support among colleagues. They compare the differences that often exist between teaching as a profession and other professions such as law, medicine, or even architecture. In the latter professions, the neophyte learns "with others." "The shared ordeal or joy is buttressed by a peer group, a support system, and in many cases life-long friendships. A strong sense of professional culture grows up as a result of moving from knowledge to shared experiences" (p. 57). This support system contrasts with the isolation that often characterizes the teacher's work environment.

Teaching, although often rewarding, is an extremely intense and difficult task. Teachers are required to relate to a wide range of individuals, each of whom has a unique set of characteristics, needs, and expectations. A cooperative and supportive work environment will help teachers deal with these varied expectations and the stress they cause. In a school where teachers have opportunities to interact, where they get to know each other as individuals, they have a better chance to become aware of the stressful problems that each may be experiencing. A supportive work environment may not solve stressful situations, but it can provide a tone or climate in which teachers can learn to cope realistically with problems. As a member of the teaching profession, each teacher is responsible for creating a supportive environment. Such an environment demands that a teacher be aware of the numerous interactive variables that are present in the ecological context of a school.

THE NEED FOR A SUPPORT SYSTEM

Traditionally, teaching has been viewed as that which takes place in a closed room between one teacher and a group of students. With this mind-set, many teachers find it frightening to consider an environment within which another teacher "might see what I am doing." In such a limited environment, teachers have little feedback about performance other than that received from students. They are unsure and afraid that they may be doing poor work and will be "found out." Nothing is more frightening or destructive to a professional than to perceive that peers view him or her as incompetent. Within such an environment, the teacher does not function as a strong, confident individual but rather as a tentative, isolated person. This isolation is sometimes confused with individualism.

It is vitally important that teachers become strong individuals who possess the confidence to make the informed professional decisions necessary to teaching. If they cannot function as strong, confident individuals, they will be unable to participate with other members of the educational community (principals, other teachers, specialists, and parents) in providing the optimal learning environment for students. True individualism, strength, and confidence are fostered not in isolation but in collegial interaction. Cartwright and Zander (1968) have found that people best express and most fully develop their originality and individuality within the security of a group. Similarly, Blau and Scott (1962) maintain that social interaction contributes to problem-solving by furnishing social support to individual members. Approval may be explicit in the form of verbal comments or may be implicit in the behavior of others as they nod, smile, look expectant, or just refrain from interrupting. Such social approval often reduces stress and anxieties and frees individuals to continue their dialogues with each other.

A teacher's personal and professional life cannot be totally separate. The teacher who is emotionally or physically uncomfortable is often unable to address the complex problems encountered in the classroom. Thus, a school environment that encourages teachers to do things together, to talk to and listen to each other, and to become friends is more likely to have teachers who feel good about themselves—who feel enthusiastic and optimistic about their teaching. Berne (1964) defines these interpersonal interactions as transactions or verbal "stroking." He argues that transactions, even simple greetings, can be meaningful for the persons involved. Such transactions can occur daily in the school—in hallways, teachers' lounges, workrooms, offices, and meeting rooms.

The ultimate reason for developing a support system is its influence on students. "Creating a satisfying place of work for the individuals who inhabit schools is good in its own right but it appears also to be necessary to maintaining a productive educational environment" (Goodlad, 1983). Often, the attitudes with which teachers regard each other are conveyed to students. In a building where the teachers like each other and make certain that each member of the staff knows that he or she is liked as a person and a colleague, students carry the same tone; they too find themselves liking each other and themselves. Conversely, in a building where there is little or no concern for any other professional being, students observe and play upon the feelings and the isolation they see.

Sergiovanni and Carver (1980) have devoted much of their research effort to studying the way the organizational climate of the school influences student achievement. They have concluded that improving the climate for learning depends upon improving the organizational climate of the school. "Environmental conditions have potent effects on what teachers do, how teachers relate with each other, as well as on student achievement and other gains" (p. 42). With a minimum of effort, teachers can influence positively the emotional environment of the school. To do so, they must assume personal responsibility for providing those "human conditions" that contribute to a collegial support system within the school. When there is a true concern for fellow teachers, and when people exhibit the spirit of fun that characterizes most of us, a sense of camaraderie and friendship can exist within a school building and between all of the professionals who are so much a part of that building.

ESTABLISHING A CLIMATE FOR FACILITATING PERSONAL AND PROFESSIONAL DEVELOPMENT

Sharing plays a major role in the functioning of a school as a place where teachers are truly colleagues. Sharing of ideas, of thoughts, or of teaching methods can become the impetus for a concerted effort to improve the learning environment for students. Asking a fellow teacher about a particular project, bulletin board, or approach does marvelous things for his or her self-esteem. The teacher whose self-confidence is strong is the teacher who can be creative—can take risks. This self-confidence is often developed through the reactions of fellow teachers. Thus, to create a healthy and productive teaching environment, there must be opportunities and a willingness to share information and ideas, perceptions and insights. The professional environment must be one in which teachers are regularly provided with professional feedback and encouragement from colleagues—teachers as well as administrators.

Ideas included in this section reflect activities that can help to establish an environment providing collegial feedback and encouragement. Many of the ideas and activities are drawn from our experiences; others are taken from the experiences of other classroom teachers.

Teaching includes more than what happens in a classroom or school. Teachers must try to see colleagues outside of the school setting —all it takes is someone who is willing to organize. A faculty golf outing creates a new tone of belonging and of sharing something other than students and their problems. Teams of both men and women bring a realization that each participant can do and talk about something other than school. A floating coffee klatch, one that rotates from one staff member's home to another's on a monthly basis, is another means of getting to know fellow workers in some other setting.

Those teachers' workdays that often occur before school starts, at the end of the first semester, and at the end of the school year are also opportunities for socializing. A covered-dish luncheon—either building-wide or systemwide—may find teachers sitting next to each other and talking to each other as they never have before. Such a get-together is much more conducive to friendships than having each small group wander off to have lunch in a local restaurant. Driving together to various events that teachers choose or are required to attend is another means of fostering new friendships. It can also provide the encouragement that some teachers need to attend some functions that they don't want to attend alone.

A real magic accompanies giving, and teachers are not immune to this magic. What fun it is to leave cards and notes or even flowers for some other member of the staff. This giving can be as simple as delivering a bunch of home-grown daffodils to the office secretary or leaving an anonymous valentine in the mailbox of every other member of the staff. A note to a fellow staff member recognizing a special accomplishment or that of one of his or her students works the same kind of magic. How nice it is to find such a note in with all of the memos and forms that find their way into an office mailbox. Most people never outgrow the enjoyment of having a birthday recognized with anything from cards to flowers to a birthday cake to brighten the day of all who are a part of such a celebration. A posted list of birthdays for all of the staff members in the building can help in this regard.

Teachers need to listen to other teachers. The greatest favor that one teacher can do for another is to be aware that a colleague is having a bad day and offer to help. The sensitivity that teachers have for each other will carry over to students and the classroom. Knowing that someone else in the building realizes that you are having a "bad day" can prevent the kinds of frustrations that are often taken out on students. "Interaction with others is an important social vitamin in one's daily nourishment of an expanding self-awareness" (Hamachek, 1971, p. 17).

It is important that teachers share the positive comments they may hear from students or parents about other teachers. It is never necessary to state the exact source, but a statement such as "One of my students thinks that your math class is the greatest he has ever taken" can make the rough day of a colleague much brighter. Being told that a parent has good things to say about a class or a project may be the only reminder that a teacher has had in weeks that it is worth the time and effort.

In order for healthy professional development to occur within a school, there must be a recognition of commonality, a sharing of views and values—both similarities and differences. When teachers attend conferences and workshops, it only takes a few moments to look for and to gather information that can help some other member of the staff. There is pleasure and value in both the giving and the receiving of materials that arrive with a note attached—a note that says, "I thought of you when I saw this." Students profit when those new ideas or materials are incorporated into the classroom, and teachers gain from the knowledge that colleagues have thought of them.

Teachers need to learn to offer help to other members of the staff by doing such things as covering classes or helping to chaperone a dance. Since it seems like an imposition on the friendship and the goodwill of another teacher, many teachers will not ask for that help. Usually, such a favor can be reciprocated in some way, and the sharing and gratitude that grow from these acts become a way of life in the building rather than a resented imposition. It is fine to say, "Thank you!" when another teacher covers a class, takes playground duty, or helps chaperone a dance, but why not write it as well? Both the writing and the receiving create a special feeling of caring and of being cared about.

One important factor that allows teachers to function as colleagues is a willingness to break the barriers that seem to exist in a school. Because of the feeling of autonomy that most teachers develop in terms of "their" classrooms, there is seldom as much communication or visitation between classrooms as there should be. Teachers must be willing to open their classrooms to other teachers; they must be willing to step across the invisible but real barrier that has been established at the doorway of a classroom to discuss, comment on, and praise the things that they see in another teacher's room. It is rewarding when some other adult notices the innovative bulletin board that has taken the teacher and students many hours to prepare. It is also rewarding to be invited into the music room to be a one-person audience for a song on which the choir has been laboring for weeks. When teachers take down the barriers that exist because of the physical confines of a school building, barriers between subject areas and grade levels may also fall.

Teachers should also attend or participate in a fellow staff member's co-curricular or extracurricular activities. It is important to have someone who knows how much time and effort are involved in a band concert say, "Wow! You have really done a super job with those kids. I'm so glad I came." How can anyone talk to a coach about football or basketball without ever attending a game? The girls' volleyball coach as well as the junior varsity basketball coach need to hear, "Nice game!" from someone other than parents and players. Teachers gain more than just the appreciation and goodwill of their fellow teachers; they also gain the respect of the students who participate in such activities. Students like to know, too, that teachers care about more than just that which goes on within the four walls of the classroom.

Another way of establishing a "community" spirit among teachers is to organize group participation in pep rallies or assemblies. The football team, the coach, the students, and the teachers all gain from the entertainment that results when teachers take the floor of the gym dressed as football players and cheerleaders to present their version of the outcome of the big game of the year. Students truly enjoy the entertainment value of such a skit and also enjoy knowing that teachers are human, too. In the same fashion, it is fun to discover that Santa has brought to the Christmas assembly gifts for the teachers as well as the students. Again, there is much pleasure to be had and much camaraderie to be gained for teachers and students alike when teachers have the courage and willingness to participate in the school-community in some fashion other than as instructors of young people.

Another method of establishing a professional and personal sense of well-being for both students and teachers is to find a way in which students and their work can cross the artificial boundaries between the primary and secondary buildings. One such project is to send second graders' typical Christmas letters to Santa Claus to a secondary English class for response. The primary-grade teacher might add notes to the letters regarding a student's interests or family. When the letters are answered by Santa (secondary English students), they can then be personalized for each child. What an immense amount of fun and joy is created for everyone involved in such a project. And, magically, a link in communication and caring has been established.

The religious and legal holidays around which schools pattern their calendars offer an excellent opportunity for the types of exchanges that increase camaraderie and foster high staff morale. A Christmas gift exchange can provide fellowship as well as fun for everyone—from teachers to administrators to teachers' aides; simply drawing names out of a hat and allowing the givers an opportunity to remain anonymous make the party that results that much more entertaining. Before long, staff members are found plotting from the first day of school about the gifts that will be most appropriate for any other member of the staff. Such a project fosters listening skills too, for one must know the interests and foibles of a fellow teacher to be able to purchase the most appropriate gift.

Ultimately, a sense of humor is necessary if an attitude of collegiality is to survive in a school. One must be able to be the recipient of as well as the instigator of the types of "fun" that help maintain the humanity of teachers. The librarian who closed the high school library on Friday so she could attend a conference knew when she sent an extra forty students to study hall that some form of "retribution" was likely. Monday morning, when the entire study hall of one hundred twenty students arrived at her door announcing that the study hall was closed and that they were all to report to the library, the librarian calmly found a spot for each of them — literally wall-to-wall students — and promptly gave the study hall teacher detention. For weeks, there was a great deal of laughter and speculation on the part of both teachers and students about the next skirmish that might take place. Once again, teachers and students alike felt themselves a part of the entire atmosphere of the entire school.

Ultimately, both teachers and students benefit from a supportive school atmosphere. To quote Sergiovanni and Carver (1980), "If growth is valued in youngsters, the school will need to become a growing organization for all" (p. 323).

PRINCIPALS AND TEACHERS AS COLLEAGUES

The principal of the school is in a critical position for establishing and encouraging a climate that promotes a professional partnership. When principals and teachers support each other in a spirit of collegiality, a positive emotional climate is created that pervades the atmosphere of the entire school. This climate facilitates both the personal and professional development needed to carry out effectively the complex roles of the teacher. For example, if teachers are to assume the roles of researchers and program developers, they need an understanding, caring principal who supports them in their endeavors to experiment and bring about program changes that they feel are in the best interests of students.

Support from the principal helps to build the confidence and courage that teachers need if they are to experiment with new ideas. Without this support from principals, teachers are often reluctant to forge ahead with innovative programs. Teachers need to be assured that their efforts —efforts that may result in success or, once in a while, failure—will be rewarded and supported by the principal. In an article entitled "Working Together: The Peer Group Strategy," Culver, Shiman, and Lieberman (1973) point out that the principal's traditional role is that of decision maker for the school; "yet, if he is to help teachers to adopt innovative behaviors, he must share some of this decision-making power with them. Since he is unable to tell them what to do, he must instead try to create a climate in which they can be free to experiment" (p. 93).

In a true collegial relationship, teachers share responsibility with the principal in establishing and maintaining a climate that promotes a professional partnership. Communication serves as a key to creating such a climate. Teachers should keep the principal informed about what is happening in their classrooms. They should take the initiative to share with the principal their own basic philosophies of education and the ways in which they are implementing these philosophies in the classroom. Teachers who do so will probably receive more support for their efforts. For example, one first-year teacher told how she took her kindergarten children outside to "paint an imaginary mural with water" on the wall of the school building. The principal, who was not aware of what was happening, came storming out of his office and confronted the teacher in the presence of the children. One can imagine his embarrassment when he discovered that the children were "painting" with water. How easy it would have been for the teacher to have stopped in the office before taking the children outside to explain not only what they were going to do but why. While she could defend this activity in terms of benefits such as learning how to work together, planning a logical sequence for the mural, learning to share materials, and developing gross motor coordination skills, she could have avoided problems by sharing this information with the principal. This way, too, if parents called the principal questioning such an activity, he could defend it in terms of its developmental benefits to children. Teachers cannot logically expect "blind" support from their principals. Principals can only support teachers when they know what is being done and why it is in the best interest of students.

It is important to communicate information about successful teaching experiences to the principal, the superintendent, and even the board of education. Too often, administrators are approached only about the negative things that occur in the school context; they may never have the opportunity to hear that there are far more good aspects than bad ones within the system. To say, "Boy! The kids really like that new computer course!" or "Have you seen what Mary has done with her students in Home Ec.?" creates a new awareness of program, an awareness that may not have been obvious to an administrator. Both teachers and students profit from recognition of such accomplishments.

If they are to function as professional colleagues, teachers and principals need to clarify their perceptions regarding how students learn and how learning can be facilitated. Our study of first-year teachers revealed a great variance in philosophies and theoretical understanding between teachers and principals—a variance that was the source of many stressful influences. Other research studies also show that varying expectations between principals and teachers often result in a high attrition rate of first-year teachers or the development of "coping styles" to the sacrifice of good teaching practices. Principals will usually welcome teachers with innovative ideas if they can be shown that those ideas are in the best interests of students. The following interview reflects what can happen when a principal does not understand what a teacher is doing or why. This simulated interview was constructed using data from several interviews and logs of the first-year teachers involved in our study.

Principal: Mrs. Williams, I appreciate your coming in this afternoon. It's been six weeks since school started, and I've tried to stay away from your classroom to give you a chance to get things organized. I realize that it's difficult to open school, but there are several things I would like to discuss with you regarding your classroom. I was in there the other day, and I was a bit confused about the classroom organization. I really couldn't find out what was going on. It seemed like there were youngsters running around all over the place with some studying in this area and some working over in that area. Can you explain what was happening, or was it just confusion?

Teacher: I set up some learning centers. I have children doing independent study. I pull some of these children out and work with them on certain skills. Sometimes I work with only one or two students— sometimes a small group.

Principal: It seemed to me that there was very little group instruction going on, and I really wonder if these youngsters are going to learn all that they need to learn in the first grade. Mrs. Johnson, our second-grade teacher, has a great reputation in this community for teaching youngsters basic skills, and when they come to her, she expects them to be able to do the second-grade work that is required. I am concerned that with this moving everywhere around your classroom, they won't be prepared.

Teacher: They seem to be learning quite a bit that way. I have an evaluation system that includes a record sheet covering the different activities they have completed. I often go back and ask questions about an activity. They seem to have learned quite a bit in the learning centers and the small groups.

Principal: You are, I hope, aware that the materials for this school system are adopted by the board of education. We would expect each youngster to work in the textbooks that have been adopted. I saw that your youngsters were using a lot of other materials.

Teacher: I did preview all the texts before the year started. In developing my goals for the year, I have incorporated some of the things from the textbooks with some of my own ideas and activities.

Principal: I suppose you did some of these things in your education classes at the university.

Teacher: Yes, we did a lot of that.

Principal: Those things may have been fine in college, but you know the parents in this community really expect the students to be well prepared. We provide good basic texts and workbooks in this school system, and we would expect you to use them. You said something else about the youngsters and your evaluation of them. I'm not sure I understand that.

Teacher: When I develop my lesson plans, I include specific evaluation methods that I'm going to use, either questioning or direct observation. I look for such things as a child's being able to complete an activity, or demonstrating in some way that he or she has learned the intended concepts. Thus far, the children have done very well. The ones who haven't, I've been able to work with individually.

Principal: We'll need to talk more about this. There are a couple of other things that I think we have to talk about, too. I've heard that you're not down in the teacher's lounge very much. Do you stay away from there on purpose?

Teacher: Oh no—the other staff members have been very helpful in showing me materials and sharing ideas. I quite honestly haven't had time to go down to the lounge. I've been busy at noon working on a couple of special projects with some children who needed extra attention. At recess I've gone outside to be with the children—I had a couple of children with behavior problems, and I wanted to watch them on the playground.

Principal: There are many people on our staff who have taught for a very long time, and I think they're a valuable resource for a first-year teacher. Another thing, on the playground I noticed the kids seem to hang all over you. I saw one youngster hanging on your dress, another on your coat, another on your arms. You know, I think teachers should be close to their students, but I think this friendship can go too far. Those kids should be playing with each other.

Teacher: I guess I felt that it was important that they feel close to me and get to know me in a way other than in the classroom. I think that that part of a child's development is just as important as the academic skills.

Principal: Our school system is known as a system that prepares youngsters very well academically. By the way, I also saw an activity in one of those learning centers that talked about the integration of math and science. Can you tell me about this?

Teacher: In many of my college courses, we talked about the need to integrate subject matter as it really does happen in everyday life. In science we do a lot of math: we do measurement and estimating and comparing and those kinds of things. In order to really get all of the concepts out of one lesson, I've incorporated the two subject areas together in a lot of the centers.

Principal: Mrs. Williams, I've found this discussion to be quite interesting. I have several more concerns that I would like to discuss, but we'll save them for our next conference. Again, I want to emphasize how important it is that our children have a good foundation in the basic skills. Thank you for coming in.

DISCUSSION QUESTIONS

1. Communication is the key to establishing collegial relationships. In this scenario, the principal waited for six weeks before discussing his concerns with this first-year teacher. What are some positive things the teacher could have done to inform the principal about what was happening in the classroom during those first six weeks? Why is it important for teachers to discuss their basic educational philosophies with the principal?

2. The teacher was asked to explain her interdisciplinary approach to teaching math and science. What rationale would you provide in response to this question? What might this teacher do to demonstrate that she is teaching basic skills?

3. The principal recognized the value of teachers communicating with other teachers in the faculty lounge. The teacher acknowledged that this was important but said that she lacked the time to go to the lounge. What preplanning could a teacher do in order to provide free time to relax during the teaching day? What role could parents and volunteers from the community play to free the teacher from many time-consuming clerical responsibilities?

4. The principal seemed to be very concerned about how the parents would react to the more nontraditional approach to teaching through the use of interest centers. What could the teacher do to acquaint both principal and parents with the rationale and use of learning centers in the classroom? The principal was also concerned about whether the children would be prepared for Mrs. Johnson's classroom. In what ways could this teacher use Mrs. Johnson as a professional colleague?

5. The teacher recognized the need to observe the students in different types of settings, including the playground. She also recognized the value of informal interactions with the children in terms of facilitating social development. How would you have reacted to the principal's view of this approach?

TEACHERS AS PARTNERS WITH TEACHER EDUCATORS

The roots of educational excellence are in the preparation of teachers. When teachers and university personnel work together in the interest of preparing future teachers, they cooperatively assume a major responsibility for improving the quality of the teaching profession.

A partnership of public/private schools and teacher education institutions strengthens both. Schools provide learning environments where preservice students are able to try out their new ideas under the guidance of experienced teachers. In the process of guiding preservice students, teachers grow in their awareness of the complexities of the teaching-learning phenomenon. The dictum "We learn to teach by teaching" is very applicable to cooperating teachers who are involved in the process of teaching future teachers. Lipham and Hoeh (1974) have written about the mutual value of working closely with colleges and universities, particularly with field-based experiences. "The major benefit of student teaching (however) is the exchange of ideas that occurs between faculty members and student teachers, who often bring vitality and fervor to teaching. Since the student teachers' idealism has not yet been tempered by the realities of practice, their enthusiasm can be instrumental in creating a more favorable learning climate within the schools" (p. 256).

The professional interaction between university and school personnel provides relevancy for the issues discussed in a preservice development program. In an informal conversation with one of the authors, John Goodlad[1] said that a teacher educator loses credibility as a practitioner within two years after leaving the classroom.

While we recognize that not all teachers have an opportunity to supervise preservice students, teachers as partners in education have a critical role in providing a support system for beginning teachers. Our study of first-year teachers showed that teacher colleagues had the greatest reinforcing influence. One of the teachers in our study pointed out that there were two things that helped her survive the year: "the support of a teacher colleague" and "the thought that she would experience being a first-year teacher only once!" The process of continually growing as a professional can be facilitated when teachers and teacher educators join to share ideas, identify problems and concerns, plan staff development programs based on the identified problems and concerns and the needs of specific schools, and research problems that are unique

---

[1]Dean of the Graduate School of Education at the University of California, Los Angeles, and a respected leader in the field of education.

to a particular school or classroom. School personnel often lack the necessary knowledge to compare current school practices with alternatives and to determine the precise changes that might prove helpful. Teacher educators can work cooperatively and supportively to evaluate programs. "With a thoughtfully developed agenda focused on the educational program, collaboration within the profession and between school and community and a supportive infrastructure, the schools we have will get better. All of the resources are available" (Goodlad, 1979, p. 103).

AN EDUCATIONAL COMMUNITY OF COLLEAGUES

Teachers must remember that they function only with the help and guidance of many other staff members. Secretaries and teacher aides are also a part of the school community; they need to be included in the activities, outings, and projects that create an atmosphere that sees all educators as colleagues. Noncertificated staff are an integral part of the school system. They free teachers from many clerical responsibilities so that they can perform their professional responsibilities for children. Noncertificated staff are also powerful public relations links for the school district through their formal and informal contacts with the community. "Employees who identify with the goals of the organization and exhibit pride in their work will maintain and foster a positive relationship between the school and the many subpublics that are beyond the reach of the principal, the teacher, or even the students" (Lipham & Hoeh, 1974, p. 333).

The education of today's youth is everybody's responsibility. Quality education is enhanced in a school climate in which cooperative and supportive relationships are established between all the members in the immediate school-community context. Working with colleagues is a very important part of teaching. Nowhere is there a better resource of ideas and suggestions.

Chapter 3

Teacher and Parents as Partners

A COMPLEMENTARY ROLE

Children learn in all settings throughout the day and that motivation to learn, as well as actual learning success, requires a total living situation in which parents and school work together. Parents shift from being clients, or silent partners, to becoming full partners in the education of their children. (Gordon, 1971, p. 28)

When parents and teachers serve as partners in education, they provide mutual support. Through interactive, supportive relationships between the home and school contexts, students will have a better opportunity to develop their potential. While heredity may influence the range of intelligence, the environment established by the home and school together influences the extent to which each student's potential will be attained. From birth until about age eight, rapid intellectual growth occurs. This is a period during which students spend much time in the home environment.

To help the student grow, parents and teachers need to understand both the effects of heredity and the importance of the home and school environments. Heredity and the multiple contexts of which the student is a part help to explain the behavioral changes that occur in the developing person. These two interacting forces influence what the student is, what he or she does, and what he or she becomes. In "Behavior and Development as a Function of the Total Situation" (1954), Lewin summarizes this well: "The person (P) and his environment (E) have to be viewed as variables which are mutually dependent upon each other. In other words, to understand or to predict behavior, the person and his environment have to be considered as one constellation of interdependent factors" (p. 919).

What happens in the home situation inevitably influences the student in the school situation; similarly, what happens in school influences the student at home. Although the family has the greatest and most lasting influence on the child, it is obvious that many other ecological factors influence the student, such as involvement in church, clubs, and athletics. Information about how students function in such groups and how they are affected by these groups will help both the teacher and parents to better understand a student's behavior in the classroom and in the home. Just as a teacher shares information with parents about the student's behavior in the school context, parents must provide information about a student's behavior in other settings.

By respecting and listening to what parents have to say, teachers can learn much that will help them to become better at their work. The roles of teacher and parent must complement each other. Lightfoot's extensive study of the partnership of parents and teachers as educators (1981) led her to conclude that education will only be successful when trust, accountability, and responsibility are shared among families, communities, and schools. An awareness of the significant role of families does not diminish the school's role of accountability for teaching. In fact, once school personnel begin to value the significant place of families in the educational process, they will feel more responsible to the communities they serve and the children they teach. When education is seen more holistically in terms of styles of learning within families, the school can and should be designed to take into consideration the values of community life.

The school must understand and share with parents the benefits of parents and teachers working together. For example, research shows that when parents and teachers work as partners in education, students' IQ scores, verbal achievement test scores, social and study habits, visual and tactile skills, and school attendance all rise. In addition to these results that influence student development, the parent-teacher partnership has positive gains for both parents and teachers. Studies show improvement of parents' self-images and of their confidence in themselves as parents. Teachers develop a greater empathy and appreciation for the difficulties parents encounter in child-rearing; conversely, parents develop a better understanding and appreciation of the role of teachers (Goodson & Hess, 1975; Gordon, 1971; Lightfoot, 1981; Outland, 1977).

Home and school experiences can be complemented, enriched, and extended when parents and teachers share information about a child's specific needs, interests, and goals. Parents' perceptions of a child outside the classroom often differ from the teacher's perceptions of the same child in the classroom. Remarks from parents such as "I don't know how you put up with my child," or the opposite view, "I can't understand why you're having problems with my son; he's so good at home," have implications in terms of the teacher's understanding of a student's basic needs. These differences in perceptions were highlighted several years ago in a special NBC television program reporting the results of a study of teen-age suicide victims. The majority of these victims were perceived by their former teachers as being well adjusted and academically successful. They seldom, if ever, gave teachers or administrators any problems. This contrasted significantly with the perceptions of the parents, who often reported that their children seemed to be moody, lonely, and not interested in out-of-school activities. This kind of information from parents, if shared with the teacher, could help the teacher to better understand the child as an individual so that appropriate help could be provided in both the school and the home environments.

THE ECOLOGY OF THE FAMILY

The family is the most significant influence on the student's development. Educational goals and instructional activities must be adapted and developed with sensitivity to each student's family background and experiences. Educators need to expand their definition of teaching beyond the classroom and move toward viewing teaching as setting the stage for learning. If the stage is set, individual differences in the family and school contexts can be accommodated. It is important that teachers welcome, accept, value, and utilize information from parents when making decisions about students and their development (Gordon, 1971).

Ecological factors such as housing, nutrition, educational level, employment, income, neighborhood, and available support services affect the family and its interaction with the world. According to Chilman (1971), communication problems may be the result of differing ethnic or national origins of parents and teachers. Many teachers, for complex reasons of their own, fail to appreciate the fact that cultural roots go deep and are entangled in the matrix of the family over generations. Teachers must not only understand the complexities of the heritage and the prejudices that may lie within it, but must also be careful not to impose their own values on their students. They need to be sensitive to and accepting of the values that children bring to the educational setting. Educational decisions need to be built on these varying family values.

Children today are encountering changes in the family unit. These changes include greater separation from the adult world and communication barriers that are caused by such factors as increasing numbers of women in the work force, divorce, and geographic mobility. These changes often result in the presence of fewer adults in the home environment and are often stress-producing for family members. Stress is inevitable and is experienced by adults and children alike. Although children may not understand the sources of stress, they have an intuitive knowledge that it exists, and they are aware of changes that result in their home environments because of it. A student might not understand the financial difficulties the family is facing; that student does understand, however, that he or she cannot have new shoes and that his or her parents are unhappy about some situation that exists. It is critical that teachers help students learn to cope with stress. The ability to cope depends on many factors: personality, temperament, cognitive development, problem-solving ability, age, and past experience.

Through coping with their own stress and through their own reactions to stressful situations, teachers show most effectively how to handle difficulty. A teacher who breaks out into a cold sweat, who snaps at the children, and who cannot function normally when the principal steps into the room is communicating more than a negative attitude toward the principal. That teacher is demonstrating to the class that stress can reduce a person's effectiveness. How, then, will these students react themselves when confronted by the principal or by some other stress-producing event?

A major stress-producing factor in our society today is the significant rate of divorce. The traditional two-parent family unit may provide comfort and security, but these feelings are often shattered through divorce. Research shows that serious psychological, behavioral, and academic problems often characterize children of divorced parents. These include increased aggression and hostility toward peers and siblings, negative reactions toward either parent or both parents, depression, fear of rejection, concerns about who will take care of them, guilt over fantasies of causing their parents' divorce, lack of ability to concentrate, daydreaming, and difficulty in progressing academically. Yet, in the United States little or no attention has been paid to the school needs of children from single-parent homes (Brown, 1980).

Although teachers are not able to do anything directly about divorce, they need to be aware of the symptoms of distress so that they can help students make satisfactory adjustments. In times of distress, such as divorce, students need to be able to rely on someone to help them deal with feelings of insecurity, fear, rejection, and helplessness.

Since, except for the home, the school is the most continuous institution in a pupil's life, the teacher can help bridge the gap. The teacher can provide the needed structure in a student's life when the family seems to be torn apart, giving students opportunities to talk about their concerns and to help remove the "what ifs" from the stress situation. Many times teachers help students just by letting them know that someone is aware of what they are experiencing.

One way to help students cope with the stress of divorce is to give them books that deal with the subject—especially from a child's point of view. By reading fiction that has been written about a situation similar to their own, students may find an outlet for their fears and doubts. They are more apt to talk about someone else's problems than they are to talk about their own; there is some safety from vulnerability in transferring problems and fears to an imaginary character. Some available books in paperback are *Taking Sides* (Klein, 1974); *It's Not the End of the World* (Blume, 1972); and *My Dad Lives in a Downtown Hotel* (Mann, 1973). Another method to aid students coping with a divorce could be through the establishment of interest groups or support groups composed of students who have had similar experiences. Who could be truly more understanding of the situation than another person of the same age who has had the very same experience? These groups could meet before, during, or after school with no particular structure except to meet the needs of a peer who is attempting to survive the same difficulty. Parents often feel guilty about a divorce and welcome any outside assistance for their children.

The teacher is in a good position to introduce some of the social realities into the curriculum. For example, in studying the family as a unit in society, the class should discuss all of the different kinds of families, not only the stereotypical two-parent family. There are families with many children, few children, and no children; some families include grandparents, some have two parents, and others have only one parent. Students could role play different types of families and show the positive points of each, increasing both understanding of their own family structure and understanding of their peers' situations. Students could also role play the sibling structures that exist in the various homes, thus gaining a new awareness of what it would be like to be an only child, the youngest child, the oldest child, or one of ten children.

In an article entitled "What Teachers Can Do About Childhood Stress," Chandler (1981) suggests several ways to help students. The major emphasis is on providing a classroom environment in which the teacher nurtures the student's feelings of competence. A predictable environment reduces stress for some students; teachers must be aware of this and must be predictable in their day-to-day reactions to given situations within the school context. Students need a feeling of ownership of an individual space. Even in the open classroom, they need privacy. Chandler suggests that if the class schedule changes from day to day, it should be posted on the board each morning. Students also need to know what their limitations are. These elements are the boundaries that make the students' physical and psychological worlds more manageable and secure.

PARENTS ARE TEACHERS

Parents are the primary educators of their children. They are the foundation, the starting point from which almost everything else happens. Often, however, they do not perceive themselves as teachers. They need to be reminded about how much they "taught" the child before he or she came to school and how much they will continue to teach their child throughout life.

Parents serve as teachers primarily through their day-to-day actions, their reactions, and their interactions within the family context. However, teachers can help parents to become more effective teachers by sharing with them their specialized professional knowledge regarding human development and ways to foster it in the home environment. As children develop, they discover and create meaning from the experiences with people and events they encounter. Parents as teachers have a fundamental responsibility to provide a context within which children are encouraged to explore and discover meaning from a variety of learning opportunities. Tyler (1981) discusses the importance of schooling in both home and classroom as a basis for discovering meaning. He defines schooling as helping human beings to understand themselves and find meaning in every facet of living. Therefore, it is important that the meanings of schooling be deepened for and by all involved— teachers, students, administrators, and parents. Educators and parents alike must recognize that the home exists as a learning environment. Only through this recognition and the encouragement of the home learning context can the school context begin to gain in relevance and importance.

The context of the home helps form the child's attitudes and motivation. It provides the child's first interpretations of life. It provides the atmosphere in which the child forms his or her style of life. The child absorbs, internalizes, and personalizes experiences with parents. Perhaps the most critical area in which parents serve as teachers is in the development of the child's self-concept, which begins forming in infancy. Parental consistency helps the child develop the sense of security that is essential to the development of a positive self-concept. The infant also perceives the parents' attitudes toward each other and uses these perceptions when forming his or her own self-concept. Purkey (1978) points out that parents must first show respect for and confidence in a child before he or she can develop self-respect and self-confidence.

What vocation could be more demanding than the responsibilities of parenthood? While the medical profession has made progress in educating parents about the physical care of children, who assumes the responsibility of helping parents understand children's socioemotional and cognitive development? It is the responsibility of teachers to help parents understand these developmental concepts. Educators must be teachers not only of children but also of parents. Parents want what is good for their children but *often* do not know what that is. Even in documentaries on child abuse, guilty parents express a great love for their children but admit they do not know how to relate to them. Like teachers, parents make mistakes in dealing with children. As parents work with teachers, they might gain support and advice in dealing with the problems they are experiencing in child-rearing.

Teachers can also encourage parents to reinforce what is being taught in school. With increased class sizes, this individual assistance to students is very valuable and necessary. In this way, parents share a vital role with teachers. With the pupil as a common bond, parents and teachers have an ideal framework in which to share the joys, the frustrations, and the perspectives of guiding a student to self-awareness. With support from the school, parents can become better teachers while simultaneously teachers learn from parents.

COMMUNICATION: THE KEY TO A SUCCESSFUL PARENT-TEACHER PARTNERSHIP

Students respond to expectations and function best when there is communication and cooperation between home and school. Establishing a relationship where the home and school can communicate in a warm and supportive manner will have significant benefits for all concerned. But it is very difficult to set up a forum in which ideas and information can be exchanged. Teachers are frequently unwilling to admit that they do not have all the answers to the world's problems. They often seem afraid to ask for the advice and the opinions of the parents with whom they are working. Teachers may perceive that the autonomy of their classroom is being threatened by the appearance of parents. Teachers are accustomed to being the authority figures in the classroom; they may not want their authority threatened by a parent who may have some concern or question with which they cannot deal.

Just as teachers' concerns often inhibit the development of a parent-teacher partnership, so too, parents' concerns have their impact on establishing a cooperative relationship. For some parents, school may rekindle bad memories of previous failure or conflict with teachers; others are turned off by the professional jargon of the schools; still others fear being rejected. Parents whose life-styles differ from the mainstream life-style of society may feel guilty or insecure about interacting with teachers. Divorced parents often fear discussing their children's problems with teachers because of their own guilt feelings of having failed their children. Wolfgang (1977) studied this problem and found that a statement that is only mildly critical or suggests that the child has a problem is amplified in the ears of a divorced parent. Immediately, that parent attempts to place blame and guilt. If teachers directly confront parents with the problem as they see it, the parents' ability to accept the teachers' speculations will vary with their capacities to handle the guilt and anxiety that they feel. Most parents do not care to assume the entire burden for some real or imagined failing on the part of their children, and they will place blame instead on the teacher, the school, or the entire educational system. Alienation of the parents in this way further reduces the possibility of parents and teachers working as partners in education. Too often, the student loses again, for he or she begins to adopt the negative feelings that the family has toward the school. Soon the alienation is a complete one.

Gordon's writings in his books *Parent Effectiveness Training* (1970) and *Teacher Effectiveness Training* (1974) can be used to facilitate communication. Rather than offering solutions to specific problems, he offers a system to help people deal with problems in general. His philosophy is based on the premise that what goes on among parents, teachers, and students will be determined more by the quality of their relationships than by any other factor. Teachers should serve as good role models when communicating with parents; they should show genuine interest, avoid being defensive, and listen to what the parent is saying. The unpredictability of parents' reactions during a conference makes it even more imperative that teachers develop effective communication skills. They need to be active and sensitive listeners as well as processors of the information parents provide. Questions that are designed to clarify can provide invaluable information about students and their behavior in the home-community environment.

Teachers provide the key link between the home, the student, and the school. By working together, parents and teachers can provide each other with a wealth of information to use in making a school a positive experience for the student and for other family members. Also, since public education is supported directly and indirectly by the parents, parents have a right and a responsibility to become involved. Through having their advice and knowledge solicited and used, parents will continue to support the schools, both financially and ideologically.

TOWARD THE DEVELOPMENT
OF THE PARENT-TEACHER PARTNERSHIP

Teachers and administrators can use a variety of approaches to foster a partnership between parents and the school. Parents who are sending a child to school for the first time have many fears and anxieties. One way to alleviate these fears would be to have a "New Parents' Tea Party." This practice could inform parents of the experience their children will have throughout the coming year. It would familiarize them with the child's learning environment and acquaint them with the professional adults with whom the child will be working. It would also be an excellent opportunity to recruit room parents, parent aides, or other volunteers. Finally, it allows the parents to meet other parents who share similar fears and anxieties.

On the secondary- and middle-school levels, arrangements could be made to have parents pick up their children's schedules for the new school year. At this time, during both daytime and evening sessions, the parents could follow their children's schedules through an abbreviated school day. Ten-minute class periods would be sufficient for meeting teachers, seeing the physical plant of the school, and gaining first-hand knowledge of the course of study being followed by their children.

A procedure for greeting parents, students, and teachers new to the community or the school system is to establish a school-based "Welcome Wagon." Retired teachers, volunteer parents, and/or students could be the ambassadors. Families often move into the community at the beginning of the summer, and they may be unaware of the local facilities available to them. Library hours, recreational facilities, social functions, and the best shopping areas are a few "insider's" insights that could be shared. These insights would give the newcomer an early sense of belonging and a realization of the cooperative spirit that exists between the community-at-large and the school.

Increased contact with parents increases the success of any educational endeavor. According to Gordon (1971), participation in educational decision-making is one of the most effective and desirable ways to involve parents. In American education, there has been a long tradition of involving parents in the activities of the public school through participation in various parent groups such as parent-teacher organizations, band and athletic boosters, and mothers' clubs. Although there is inherent worth in the work of these organizations, these parental groups have not been involved in the decision-making process to suggest meaningful programs. (This topic is dealt with further in chapter 7.) A school Advisory Committee with extensive parent representation could hold great potential in this regard; reciprocal participation of teachers in these community groups could further enhance the flow of creative, varied suggestions.

A survey of community interests would provide information ensuring that topics discussed at PTA or building meetings would be of primary interest to those attending. All too often, parents coming to a meeting are not interested in the topics to be discussed and never return. Some ways to obtain feedback are school-developed questionnaires, talk sessions, telephone inquiries, service club discussions, and editorials. A suggestion box in each school building and in the administrative offices may encourage people to write comments, suggestions, or criticisms that they are afraid to verbalize.

A committee of students, parents, and teachers could study problems and make recommendations, or students and parents could be placed on existing teacher/administrator committees. When parents and students are involved in the planning process, program content and other aspects of the school will usually reflect needs that they experience and thus give the program a sense of realism and ensure support for its implementation.

A recent advisory committee study illustrates the benefits of this process. A committee composed of parents, school board members, and teachers studied the food service program of a mid-Ohio school district. Committee members first compiled a list of questions and concerns representative of their interests. Questions in hand, they set out for the three buildings housing grades kindergarten through twelve. The committee members interviewed food service personnel and surveyed students and staff members in each of the three buildings. Each member of the committee also ate lunch at each of the three buildings. The cooperative study produced some positive results: increased communication at all levels and through all sectors of the school and community; a realization that the same menu did not work for all three buildings; and an increased understanding of the quirks of preparing that much food for that many students on a daily basis.

There are many ways in which the schools can enhance communication between the school and the community. The school can invite community service and professional groups in for mini-tours of the school facilities. These tours could bring community members up to date on programs and new equipment or just let them see "how things have changed since I was in school." All areas of the community should be included: business people, professionals, and nonparents. People who "talk for a living"—such as beauticians, barbers, and bartenders—should be included; they sometimes represent the single most effective grapevine system in any community. If each person who attends such a tour is impressed and tells a friend who tells a friend, the ripple effect could be tremendous, even at the end of the first year of such a program.

Monthly informal "talk sessions" are another way to get and to keep parents involved. These sessions could involve teachers and parents, administrators and parents, or even students and parents. The opportunity would be there to share information and to listen to concerns, building unity and goodwill. Perhaps these sessions could and should be held outside of the formal school setting, thus allowing for expression that is not stifled by the "institutional" home territory of the school officials.

School system participation in an evaluative self-study is an excellent way to encourage community participation. When the system undertakes self-study, community members, parents, and students as well as faculty and staff members are assigned to committees investigating all aspects of the school. The areas of study may range from specific curriculum areas to the physical plant with an opportunity for the school to draw on the expertise of the community members.

Senior citizens should be made aware that it is still "their" school, too. "Gold Card Passes" providing free or reduced admission to events ranging from basketball games to the annual band concert could be given to senior citizens. If there is an organized senior citizens' group in the community, a standing invitation to school functions could be issued; transportation to and from these events could be provided by staff or parent volunteers.

Volunteer programs involving parents or senior citizens in classrooms can take many forms: creating new materials; providing instruction to large or small groups; tutoring small groups or individuals; supervising playgrounds or lunchrooms; accompanying students on field trips; performing clerical duties; recording grades or filling out forms or records; working in the library; and organizing learning files. The needs and abilities of volunteers should be considered when assigning tasks, and all parents should be given the opportunity to be involved. There should be the chance for parents and other community members to share the wealth of knowledge that they have accumulated throughout their lifetimes. How much more interesting a history lesson could be with the addition of someone to give students the "You Were There" viewpoint. Emphasis should be placed on the benefits to children and parents, not merely on the free time created for teachers or on the benefit to the school.

Parents' observations in the classroom, followed by a parent-teacher discussion, could prove valuable in exposing parents to the school curriculum and all of its ramifications. Small study group meetings in the home to explain what is going on in school might prove less intimidating than individual sessions. This also could be accomplished through outside speakers who reflect the wishes, expectations, and needs of the parents.

Personal contact with parents is not possible as often as it should be; however, an established schedule of contacting a specific number of parents each week would make this task less intimidating. The teacher might call a parent each week with some positive report about his or her child. Too often, there is communication between the school and the home only when there is a problem. Positive comments need not and should not be limited to academic progress. Sometimes a student's social progress is more important to both the student and the parents.

Each day, the teacher could write a "Happy Gram" to one student. At the end of a few weeks, each student would have received one. "Success Cards" can also be sent for a job well done or for a helpful deed. All students, from five-year-olds to eighteen-year-olds, love getting special acknowledgment and are more likely to repeat the performance when it is appreciated or praised. Students need encouragement, and parents do too; "Positive Parenting Certificates" can encourage parents to become involved. These are awarded to parents who demonstrate observable behaviors of supporting their children and the teachers in making the school and the home better places for everyone. Also, any progress by students instills in parents the belief that they as well as their children have been successful.

Teachers in lower grades should summarize the day's work with children just before they go home each day. Too frequently, the answer a parent gets to "What did you learn today in school?" is "Nothing!" Perhaps a recap of the day would modify this answer. Students might also keep a daily diary that could be taken home at the end of the week. In the upper grades, five minutes at the conclusion of each class period could be reserved for a synthesis of the day's work. Students could volunteer or be called upon to state what they learned or were supposed to learn today. This gives the students an opportunity to review the lesson or the concepts, and also gives the teacher an accurate impression of whether or not the day's objectives were reached.

Home visits can enhance the involvement of parents. For children in the elementary school, a home visit before school starts allows the teacher to gather valuable information about children, their home life, and their siblings. It also provides the teacher with a time to relate information to parents. Teacher, parents, and children are able to discuss the educational goals they hope to achieve during the year. McCarthy and Houston (1980) recommend that the home visit be kept ⌐n a rather light level, that serious discussions be avoided. The visit is an opportunity to work toward the trust and understanding that will form the basis of the teacher's relationship with the child and the eventual relationship with the parents. The child should be encouraged to participate or to play nearby where he or she can watch and listen to the friendly interactions between teacher and parent.

Educators need to share with parents professional knowledge regarding appropriate learning experiences for their children. Almost any school outreach approach to promote parent-child interaction at home with academic activities will improve student achievement. Programs that involve parents as active teachers of their children will provide a type of social reinforcement in which increased attention is given both from the school to the parent and from the parent to the child. These programs create a sense of excitement, commitment, and enthusiasm in everyone involved. Results of a study by Rich (1976) indicated a significant rise in reading achievement when academic activities were sent home to the parents from school every two weeks. Furthermore, parents willlingly participated in the activities with their children and often expressed their appreciation to the school for these instructional opportunities. One school district compiled a calendar with specific parent/student activities for each day of the year. Again, parents were very receptive to this idea and reported that the children would inquire about the activity of the day. A program of "parents as tutors," with appropriate instruction and support from the school, can be of value both in school and at home.

Teachers have a duty to make the student and the parent aware of out-of-school activities that may be suited to student needs. The teacher has knowledge not only of the interest, needs, and talents of the pupil but also of available resources and opportunities. For example, a student who is obviously gifted in art should be afforded every opportunity to attend appropriate workshops and exhibits; teachers should have this information and should supply it. A creative writer who shows his or her poetry to the teacher should be encouraged to enter that poetry in competition and should have the opportunity to see it in print. Again, teachers have access to this information—information that parents may not have. It is the responsibility of the professional educator to make the student aware of the possibilities and, if necessary, to introduce the child to them. A dimension of warmth and safety for students and adults alike is created when parents and teachers serve as partners in education.

Many high schools have 'successfully adopted a program of "Enrichment Week" or "Mini-Course Week." In such programs, three days to a week are set aside for community members to teach and for students to learn subjects that are not a part of the regular curriculum. The woman who has a cake-decorating shop may teach a class in her specialty. The insurance salesman who ties his own fishing flies may teach a course that culminates in a fishing trip to the local pond. The best resources for any job entry skills course are local professional and paraprofessional people. Students want to know about the world of work from the people who are in it, and this is an opportunity for those people to share the knowledge and expertise they have gained through many years of experience.

The school newspaper adviser and the yearbook adviser should always be alerted when community members are taking part in instruction. These school publications are a great forum for fostering and continuing this type of community involvement in the schools.

Workshops for parents could provide an opportunity to discuss summer homework or ways to reinforce the curriculum. They could also allow time for making activities to use as reinforcement for various concepts. These could be areas in which students are having difficulty or areas that they particularly enjoy doing. Parents are always asking, "What can I do?" Get them together. Show them! Tell them! Give them a chance to use the skills, knowledge, and creativity that they have gained and that they have to share.

Almy and Genishi (1979) suggest that teachers collect vignettes to share with parents. For example, each student might receive the attention of a detailed observation each week or every two weeks, perhaps with the place for observation specified, such as during the math class. This plan does not exclude recording other observations that provide information about a student's problems or progress. In observing an open classroom in England, one of the authors noticed a teacher wearing an apron with pockets displaying each letter of the alphabet and a name card for each child alphabetized accordingly. As the teacher observed a student's behavior, she would record her observations with a few words so that she could recall the incident at the end of the day when she noted more details about the observations. Another teacher used the same idea with a pocket chart pinned on the bulletin board. An index card file box could be used for the same purpose.

School personnel and family members often do not know where to get help in solving certain problems or in improving various areas of family and school life. A "Family Resource Book" could be developed that lists the available services or how to use existing resources. The family-school relationship can be strengthened by identifying community agencies that provide mental health care, homemaker services, economic assistance, social support, and other preventive and rehabilitative services. Data gathered could be shared through school newsletters, parent-teacher programs, and in-service education.

Teachers should also provide information to the media. Events that may seem routine in the classroom often seem innovative and interesting to the community. The local newspaper is an excellent public relations resource. Some newspapers have established or would be willing to establish a page to be set aside for students' work once each week. Poems, sketches, short stories, and letters to the editor could find their way into publication through such a program. Again, there would be high visibility for the program, the accomplishments, and the concerns of the students and of the school. Many magazines are also willing to publish students' drawings, ideas, and creative stories, while local radio and television stations may be willing to carry human interest stories and announce important events.

Some teachers have found that a monthly newspaper compiled by the students is an effective means of communicating with the parents. This newspaper might include such things as students' stories, helpful teaching ideas for parents to use with their children at home, and a letter from the teacher as well as artwork and illustrations created by the students.

Parent-teacher conferences involve the mutual sharing of information. In discussing parent-conference procedures, McCarthy and Houston (1980) suggest that the teacher begin on a positive note. Since many parents are quite anxious, they can be helped to relax if the teacher first describes their child's areas of competence and some of the activities in which the child has been involved. If the student is having a problem, such as fighting with classmates, the teacher may seek advice from the parents: Does fighting occur in the home environment? How does the parent deal with it? When appropriate, students should be involved in conferences.

Almy and Genishi (1979) describe some of the characteristics of a successful parent-teacher conference. A good conference is purposeful.

When formulating the statement of purpose, it is good to consider whether the goal would seem acceptable and reasonable if the roles of the teacher and parent were reversed. To preface the goal with statements like "I find I can help children more if I have information about their interests, their ability to make friends, their interest in school, and their home environment" makes the questions less threatening to parents.

A good conference is a two-way process; a twenty-minute criticism by the teacher on the faults of the student cannot accomplish anything positive. Fewer but broader open-ended questions are more effective than specific, narrow ones in helping parents perceive that their feelings and opinions are genuinely respected. Through active listening, teachers can take clues from parents and follow-up with clarifying questions. There should be a balance of talk between parent and teacher. To personalize the conference, teachers should share specific examples of the particular child and not talk in generalities such as "Your child is doing very well in math." A discussion of the appropriate next steps for parents, teacher, and student is critical to a good conference. All parties must remember that not all problems can be solved through one conference; further data and observations may be required. Follow-through after a parent-teacher conference is as vital as the initial communication session. Telephone calls, written notes, or brief visits to the home show genuine concern, clarify issues and directions, and encourage parents, children, and teachers to do their best.

Teachers must follow up on all problems that parents call to their attention and resolve complaints as soon as possible. A problem that seems insignificant to a teacher may seem momentous to the parent or the student; otherwise, there would not be a problem or complaint to a teacher. It is the little problems that, left unattended, build into larger ones.

Teachers must be enthusiastic. They can show their genuine interest through their enthusiasm. Parents should be treated with the same respect with which the teacher would want to be treated. Parents are as individualistic as students, and a teacher must assess each particular situation and deal with it accordingly. Viewing the parent-teacher relationship from a position of strength will certainly promote more growth than will focusing on the negatives. In assessing this relationship, parents and teachers can learn about their needs and make plans to strengthen their skills for helping each other and ultimately helping the child.

Numerous parental influences were described in the daily journals of the first-year teachers studied. In order to help the reader become aware of the varied situations that arise between teachers and parents, we will present excerpts from the journals. Each excerpt is followed by a commentary compiled by a college student, but the reader is encouraged to generate approaches to solving the problem. In the role of decision maker (as discussed in chapter 10), the teacher needs to be able to make informal decisions intuitively and spontaneously, not only in teacher-student relationships but also in teacher-parent situations. We hope that by reading through these scenarios, the reader will become more sensitive to the numerous factors that must be considered in the decision-making process when communicating with parents.

Scenario 1

A parent told a colleague of mine that she was going to send me a positive note since it must be rather defeating for a teacher only to receive negative notes. Wouldn't you know it, the very next day after she made that statement, she sent in a note — nothing positive — but told me her son lost five Mickey Mouse pencils and would I please watch the children's materials more closely. I about died! First I wrote back when I got the note. It made me so angry! I wrote that it took fifteen minutes of class time, and knowing how lackadaisical her son is, I asked him to open his desk and look for his pencils. Sure enough there were two of them. I asked him to go to his book bag and check that — sure enough, there was another one. Then he told me he gave one to someone else. So I had wasted my time, and what made me angry is that it is not my responsibility. Children have to be responsible for their own things. When are the parents going to say to their children, rather than write a note to the teacher, "Johnny, you keep track of your pencils. Mrs. Jones has too much to do with twenty-eight children. She cannot keep track of everyone's pencils, everyone's scarves, everyone's gloves, everyone's boots." But instead they blame the teacher, and I think that is wrong.

By the end of the day, I tore up the note I had written to the mother. I felt better after I cooled down. I made a vow, and I hope to stick to it, that from now on rather than read parents' notes in the morning and be upset over these petty little things, I'm going to read them in the evening when the children are gone, or right before they go home in case I have to answer them. That way I won't be upsetting myself.

REACTION TO SCENARIO 1

Problems that seem petty to the teacher may seem major to parents. Simply send a note thanking the parent for bringing the problem to your

attention. Tell the parents you will check into the problem, and ask them
to let you know if it persists.

A teacher cannot wait until the end of a day to read notes from
parents. The note may contain something that needs immediate attention or an explanation about a matter that the teacher needs to be aware
of at the beginning of the day (such as a death in the family).

Scenario 2

My colleague got such an annoying note this morning. A little girl in
her room had her sweater on, and I guess she had worn it out to recess.
When they got back inside, the room was overheated and so the teacher
asked her to take off the sweater so that she wouldn't be too warm. The
girl had a cough, and she thought that if she were overheated it would
get worse. My colleague got a note from the father today saying that his
daughter was up all night coughing and that if the teacher can't take care
of her in her class, he would like her to be in another class. He said that if
she gets any sicker, he would send her the doctor bill because she had
the girl take her sweater off. It just went on and on like this. Just an
absolutely absurd note. It ruined my colleague's day. It is unbelievable!
So we both decided we will not read these notes until after school is over.

REACTION TO SCENARIO 2

Do not judge parents too quickly. A sick child can be an exhausting
and even frightening experience for parents. Try to put yourself in their
situation. The parents who made the complaint had been up most of the
night and were probably very tired. Next time a student has a cough or
seems a little under the weather, ask if there are any instructions from
home or maybe give the parents a quick call. Many times a student
leaves home healthy but develops a problem during the day. Give the
parents the facts and let them make the decisions.

Scenario 3

I have a little boy whose mother keeps sending me notes about
finding his pencils and do this and do that. She's always taking the child's
side. She feels the other children are picking on him, but actually this
child is turning out to be quite a bully—mainly, I think, because his
mother is behind him. The child has been using some poor language at
school and I told him to go home and tell his mother what he said. He
said this morning, "Well, mom didn't punish me." I am debating whether

to write a note to her. You can be very intimidated by people like that. I've heard that she has been very sassy to some other teachers and really upsets them. I hate to let a parent, or a child, get away with something because I am afraid of the parent, but sometimes that can happen.

REACTION TO SCENARIO 3

Teachers should not have students relay messages; the message can change on the way. Then if parents do not act as the teacher feels they should, it leaves the teacher in a corner. Do not rely on a note; call the parent or ask for an appointment. This is a more open means of communication and it leaves the student out as a messenger. It is a fact of life that most parents will back their child. This is a relationship that the teacher really does not want to break down.

There are all types of people in this world. The teacher should not be too quick to cast blame. The language that the student used could be what he hears at home.

Teachers need not be intimidated by parents if they have a philosophy and a rationale to back their actions in the classroom. Is the problem really that important? There are many actions in a classroom that are better ignored. A teacher must be careful not to be too picky. If there truly is a problem, he or she should approach the situation with "I am concerned about. . . . " Instead of just talking to the mother, make an appointment to see both parents. Even if you do not solve the problem, you may discover why there is one.

Scenario 4

Today was the first day back after Christmas vacation. It's good to see the children again. They seem to be happy to be back and are very enthusiastic. Our day was super; the only thing that I would consider disappointing was that I had put quite a bit of money and time into the children's Christmas gifts for their parents and I thought that at least one parent might send a note saying, "Thank you" or "What a cute gift." But they didn't, and I think that surprised me. The other first grade teacher told me before Christmas that she was making paper plate angels in which no amount of money was invested. I was surprised because I had wooden plaques done. I had bought all sorts of expensive wood for the plaques, had varnished them, and had put a hook on the back for parents to hang them. We made ecology plaques. I estimated that it cost me around $2 to $2.50 apiece times twenty-eight kids, and I also bought wrapping paper and bows for all of them to wrap their presents in, while the other teachers had their little gifts wrapped in paper bags. So I really went to some expense. I guess I can see why, after a few years, teachers don't go to so much trouble over different things for the children. The parents either don't seem to appreciate it or perhaps have so many things on their minds that they never think to thank the teacher. Otherwise it was a really good day.

REACTION TO SCENARIO 4

The gift is not from the teacher; it is from the students. Ask the children to bring in money to cover expenses. The class could brainstorm ways to earn this money. The students could also be responsible for bringing in the boxes, bows, ribbon, and wrapping paper. If it is not possible for them to bring in these items, then perhaps the teacher should choose a less involved or cheaper project.

Parents may not be aware of the time and effort that goes into a project. In many cases what the teacher considers cute and nice, the parents may not.

Teachers cannot do a project because they expect thanks. It is really nice to be thanked, but people are so busy that they do not think about it or just forget. Teachers have to do projects because they enjoy doing them with the students. Many times a teacher's thanks are in the enthusiasm and excitement shown by the pupils participating.

Scenario 5

I wonder why parents never call about the good things. They are worried about the students' affective area and we, as teachers, strive to meet the students' needs, emotional as well as educational. In our building, the principal has us send happy notes home to two children per week. I do that as a matter of course, because I believe in that type of reinforcement; but I wonder when the community is going to realize that even though it doesn't reward teachers financially, it could at least support them emotionally. I guess that would be my biggest complaint about this profession. All I hear is that teachers are overpaid; after all, they only work a few hours a day, they have summers off, and their job isn't that difficult. I can't think of a job that I've ever done that's been more difficult, more demanding, has more frustration, more responsibility, and pays so little. Yet the public won't even admit that we work hard. And that's a very difficult idea with which to come to terms.

I had two parents come in before school who wanted to talk about little things, such as their children not going out to recess because of colds. That's such a hectic time of the day for a teacher — before school starts. It seems like the students all have something they want to discuss as soon as they come in the room, and you get a few parents and a few lost lunches. It's really a hectic time. But it was a good day today.

REACTION TO SCENARIO 5

Teaching is a profession that people choose because they enjoy doing it, not because of financial or emotional rewards. Life in today's society is so fast-paced that we may think kind thoughts but too often forget to write or verbalize them. It is nice when someone gives us praise, but it is also unrealistic to expect it all the time.

Perhaps the emotional needs of teachers can be enhanced through a support system with colleagues. Staff interaction and mutual support can help to minimize the pressure and responsibility that teaching entails.

The time before school starts can be very hectic. It can be difficult to have a meaningful discussion with a parent who stops in. Tell the parents how much you appreciate their concern and their taking the time to stop in. If the parents need more than a couple of minutes, give them your free times and make an appointment.

Perhaps the mornings could be made less hectic if one did more preparation at the end of the previous day. When the students leave, get the next day organized; put work on the board, and be sure lesson plans are in order.

Scenario 6

Today one of the parents came in and registered a complaint with my principal about my incompetency as a math teacher. I made an oversight at the time I was teaching her child fractions. While I admitted to the principal that it was an oversight, I didn't feel that it necessitated a charge of incompetency. I called the parent involved and tried to deal with her. She was very upset about the situation. She had hoped my principal would not have handled it in this manner. She just wanted to have the principal move the child from my math group. I don't know how she planned to do it, and I feel that the principal handled it the best way that he could have. However, she didn't see things that way, and I think, deep down inside, felt bad that I had been involved in a situation like this as a first-year teacher. By the same token, I also felt that she was very patronizing of my position as a first-year teacher and really was not willing to listen.

REACTION TO SCENARIO 6

It is very upsetting when a parent goes to the administration with a problem about which the teacher is not even aware. The problem, at this point, is out of the teacher's hands. The principal should ask if the teacher was contacted concerning the problem and should suggest that the parent start there and come back to him if necessary. A positive note is that at least the parent voiced her complaint to the school and not the the community. There are always parents who take problems straight to administrators. Teachers must do their best and be satisfied with themselves.

Teachers must keep their administrators aware of what is happening in their classrooms, particularly as to new programs and any potential problems.

Teachers need to be professional when dealing with a problem. They should admit when they are wrong, try not to make excuses, and tell parents they are glad the error was brought to their attention. Teachers need to open channels of communication with parents as soon as possible and to keep them open. Open communication should eliminate many problems. Teachers should make sure parents understand the programs in which their children are involved.

It is important for parents to feel free to question. There may be problems within a program that a teacher cannot see. Perhaps a parent may have an idea the teacher had not thought of. These criticisms and suggestions could result in a better program.

This chapter has emphasized an interactive, supportive relationship between the home and school contexts. Both parents and teachers make decisions that affect the lives of children and therefore are active members of the educational team. When they work as partners, students will have a better opportunity to develop their potential. Furthermore, students respond to expectations and function best when there is communication and cooperation between home and school. The key to any successful school community is the presence of understanding adults who are able to facilitate the exchange of ideas and information, help students develop their talents and interests, and enable them to be spontaneous — yet teach, guide, nurture, and discipline.

Chapter 4

The Teacher
as Understander
of the Learner
A NURTURING ROLE

The ecology of human development involves the scientific study of the progressive, mutual accommodation between an active, growing human being and the changing properties of the immediate settings in which the developing person lives, and this process is affected by relations between these settings, and by the larger contexts in which the settings are embedded. (Bronfenbrenner, 1979, p. 21)

Numerous environmental forces influence a student's behavior. As he or she interacts with the environment, behavioral changes occur. These changes are unique to each student; what is perceived as a positive influence for one may be perceived as a stressful influence for another.

One cannot understand fully the things a person does or does not do without understanding the contexts of which that person is a part. Breidemeier and Breidemeier (1978) define this context as the structure of opportunities, pressures, and constraints by everything and everyone in the person's environment. The basic phenomenon of any environment is that human beings are interdependent. Whether their interpersonal relations are competitive, cooperative, or conflicting, people are influenced by other people. Similarly, students are influenced by others who share their life space. They are affected by highly integrated and complex components of the natural and man-made worlds. These include the family context, the school-community context, and the many social contexts such as clubs, athletic teams, and church groups.

Within these multiple contexts, the child's self-image is formed. Snygg and Combs (1959) claim that all behavior is determined by and pertinent to each situation. Therefore, individuals behave according to their perceptions of the situation and the self at the moment of their actions.

A person's total appraisal of self—including such factors as appearance, background and origins, values, attitudes, and feelings—is built through social contacts and experiences with other people in multiple contexts. What happens to the student in one context may influence the student in another. For example, the student who is successful on the basketball team may transfer feelings of self-confidence and acceptance by peers to relationships with those who share some other aspect of the school context. This is why it is so important for students to be involved in experiences in which they can succeed. To help students see themselves as successful people, a teacher needs to help them set realistic goals—goals that are consistent with their abilities, needs, and interests. Through successful experiences and through opportunities to interact with the environment, students gain greater control of themselves in the environment and, to a great extent, begin to control things in that environment.

The student's environment includes the people, places, and events encountered either directly or indirectly. Often students are confused about their environment—an environment with seemingly contradictory expectations and with events over which they have little control. They need help in sorting out this confusion and alternatives from which to choose when faced with inconsistencies. Value conflict is inevitable in a pluralistic, democratic society. Students must confront diversified values in order to develop a conceptual approach to cope with reality. To help in this regard, teachers can provide opportunities for the students to explore the interrelationships between events and people around them. Teachers can involve students in decision-making processes that deal realistically with their environment and, ultimately, with the larger societal context.

THE MOMENT-TO-MOMENT CONTEXT

The larger societal context also influences the moment-to-moment context in which a student lives. International conditions, social and political leadership, technology, customs, mores, and traditions that people accept as part of their culture are some examples of forces that directly or indirectly influence education in our country. Furthermore, the American family, a major factor in the education of children, is threatened today by both internal and external pressures. Child abuse, adolescent suicide rates, drug abuse, juvenile delinquency, economic problems, high unemployment, and social mobility can all profoundly affect children and their families. While these general influences have always been recognized to affect education, less recognition has been given traditionally to the specific influences in each student's unique world. For example, while unemployment influences education generally, a pupil whose parents have been unemployed for months or even years will be influenced more specifically than one whose parents have maintained stable jobs. Insecurity, concern for basic needs, and bad feelings about self that result from unemployment may cause a change in life patterns for an entire family. Parental inability to cope with these problems directly influences the children; conversely, children's inabilities to cope with these changes can affect the parents.

Both past and present experiences affect behavior. The student who interacts with the teacher one moment may be quite different from that same student interacting at another moment. Factors that influence these moment-to-moment changes range from the obvious to the very subtle. The rather obvious factors include the illness of a parent or grandparent, the loss of a pet, a birthday celebration, or a special shopping trip. Some of the more subtle influences might include a student's perceptions of the manner in which the teacher says, "Good morning," the fact that a student's friend chooses another friend for an activity, and praise or lack of recognition by the teacher or parents.

The teacher must be acutely aware of the myriad of factors that affect each student—the obvious and the not so obvious. This information, gathered through observations or interactions, must be considered in making professional decisions that are designed to meet the individual needs of students. As noted in chapter 3, a student's parents serve as a valuable resource for providing information about the contexts of which the student is a part. To help the student grow, both parents and teachers need to understand that student as he or she relates to these multiple contexts.

Although the family has the greatest and most lasting influence on a student, many other factors obviously are important, such as involvement in church, clubs, and athletics. Information about how the student functions in such groups and is affected by them will help the teacher to understand more fully behavior in the classroom as well as in the home. Just as a teacher shares information about the student's behavior in the school context, parents must provide information about the student's behavior in various social settings.

It becomes the responsibility of teachers to attend school-related activities in which students may be involved. Teachers thus gain first-hand knowledge about pupils, parents, and the relationships that exist between them. Such activities and the behavior of both parents and students in this context often indicate aspects of the student-parent relationship that are not readily obvious in other contexts. How revealing to watch an uncoordinated high school freshman struggle on the basketball court; it quickly becomes apparent that she has neither the interest in nor the ability for basketball. How revealing, too, to watch the mother and father exhort from the sidelines: "Shoot the ball!" or "Oh no! How could you miss that shot?" The dissatisfaction of the parents with their child and the unhappiness of the student assume a new meaning from this perspective.

Teachers who accept this responsibility of observation in multiple contexts gain a new awareness of their students and their personalities. Too often, students who do not gain success or even recognition in the school context may be outstanding in some other situation. A young man who appears to have no grasp of concepts within the structured mathematics classroom may be winning recognition through the Future Farmers of America as the student who produces the greatest yield from his soybean project. A young woman who is incapable of completing a language arts assignment or of compiling a notebook of her work could be receiving blue ribbons for the scrapbook she has created as a 4-H project at the county fair. Any sixteen-year-old who is able to memorize and execute complex football plays for Friday night's game is certainly able to learn the necessary theorems for a geometry class. Without taking the time and making the effort to view students in co-curricular and extracurricular settings, teachers miss an opportunity to gain deeper insights about those students and their needs.

The time involved in gaining such insights is far outweighed by the advantages inherent in attaining them. Students are aware of the effort involved and appreciate it when teachers take interest in the total person. Teachers also gain additional common ground about which they may communicate with their students.

UNDERSTANDING THE CULTURAL AND INDIVIDUAL DIVERSITY OF STUDENTS

If teachers are to truly serve as understanders of students' behaviors, they need to comprehend, accept, value, and affirm respect for all people regardless of sexual, racial, cultural, ethnic, religious, and physical differences. Respect in the belief of the equality of people is vitally necessary because of its importance to the total social and academic development of all students. Teachers need to view each student as an unique individual who possesses a rich cultural heritage. This view of teaching is not, however, what Persell (1977) found as she reviewed hundreds of studies regarding multiculturalism. Her findings indicate that race and social class influence teachers' expectations. Policies were often made on false assumptions about low-income and minority children. The view that these students do not achieve in school and in life because of deficiencies in their home environments and that individual inequalities in educational achievement are genetic in origin dominate teachers' perspectives. What a teacher perceives as a deficiency may be a value that is part of the traditional culture of the student—a value that needs to be recognized and legitimized in its own right.

With a better understanding of the cultural traditions and values that are brought to the learning situation by both teacher and students, the teacher may incorporate this information into the structure of the learning environment. For example, some students live in a culture in which spontaneous movements and verbal responses are encouraged as a basic form of learning and living. When they are put in a situation where the teacher does most of the talking and punishes such spontaneous responses, students have very little opportunity to participate along their traditional family lines. One teacher's behavior that particularly confounds this situation is the prevalent use of factual questions that elicit a single word response. This type of dialogue does not encourage or include any information from the students other than correct or incorrect answers. Students do not feel in control or personally responsible for their learning. Nor does such a dialogue give an opportunity to experience success on difficult tasks—it is more a matter of who is called upon to answer. Those who are not called upon to answer do not have the opportunity to discuss the processes they used. Recognition of students' efforts is necessary to encourage continued problem-solving.

If teachers are to understand the multicultural contexts and develop the skills and attitudes needed for teaching in a pluralistic society, they must learn about the history, culture, and current problems encountered by racial and ethnic minorities. Without this knowledge, they cannot appreciate and affirm cultural differences. With a knowledge of their own cultural values and prejudices, teachers become more sensitive to subconscious reactions to students and situations. Most prejudice springs from deep-seated beliefs that are a result of ignorance of diversity; this ignorance often is directly related to upbringing and may be difficult to recognize and remedy. However, until teachers are able to subvert their own prejudices, they will not be able to approach students with the sensitivity and respect that are so much a part of building the same sensitivity and respect in students.

Children are not born with prejudices; rather, these attitudes emerge as they interact with their environment. Although it is impossible to control the influences of all of the multiple contexts in which the student is involved, the teacher is in a strategic position to create a school context in which pupils learn to understand, accept, and affirm cultural differences and values. The teacher, as person, serves as a mediator of culture throughout the day. Recently, this has been referred to in the literature as the *hidden curriculum*, the unintended implications of content, teacher behavior, and the numerous encounters and transactions that students have with teachers, peers, and others in the school context. Much of the hidden curriculum has to do with values, even in subject areas that are often considered to be "value-free" such as science and mathematics. Teachers need to be aware of and sensitive to the influences of the hidden curriculum.

In addition to an awareness of the hidden curriculum, teachers can plan instructional activities throughout the formal curriculum that will enhance a greater understanding of and appreciation for cultural diversities. Literature serves as an excellent means for discussing the ways in which people are basically alike. Once students see the likenesses of people, teachers can focus on the differences, such as physical appearance, emotional stamina, and creative talent. The teacher could have the students find things about themselves and others that are unique. Building on the positive nature of being unique forms the basis for eliminating prejudices. Teachers can also emphasize the important contributions of people of all races, creeds, sexes, and ethnic backgrounds through their teaching in all areas of the curriculum.

Due to our society's mobility, teachers are very likely to have students from diverse cultural backgrounds. After identifying the racial and ethnic groups represented in the classroom, the teacher could designate one week as "Cultural Awareness Week" for each group. The students could work in small groups to study their cultural heritage, interview their parents and grandparents, construct displays, and give presentations about contributions made by each ethnic and racial group. Parents and grandparents of various ethnic and racial backgrounds could speak to the class and answer students' questions. Since specific cuisines are often associated with specific ethnic groups, each group could treat the class to some culinary speciality during the week it presents its report. If students are to grow in their appreciation of cultural diversity, they need to have some knowledge of the unique contributions that various groups have made to the development of our nation.

THE DEVELOPMENT OF THE TOTAL LEARNER

Teaching is a human relationship. To be successful, teachers need the most accurate understanding of people and their behavior. As discussed in chapter 1, teachers must understand themselves in order to truly understand children. Teachers also need to be aware of the influence their behaviors have on children. Each of us can behave only in terms of what we as individuals believe; therefore, what teachers believe about the nature of students will have a most important effect on interactions with them.

For example, teachers must be aware that a student's self-image is partially dependent upon communication with the teacher. Consciously or unconsciously, teachers communicate trust, acceptance, authenticity, or lack of these qualities. Students are very sensitive to these characteristics, and their own perceptions of self are often influenced by them. Teachers must remember the importance of presenting themselves as authentic, positive people who experience the whole gamut of human emotions—joys and sorrows, hopes and fears, satisfactions and dissatisfactions, promises and problems. Authentic people do not deny the existence of problems but accept them as a part of daily living. Teachers who are not able to accept and deal with problems as a natural part of life will find it difficult to concentrate efforts on providing the positive atmosphere that helps to nurture self-confident students.

Teachers who are optimistic and enthusiastic are excellent role models. This does not mean that a teacher is constantly "happy"—rather it denotes a mature attitude toward accepting problems and pursuing possible solutions. One of the most lasting values for students is the habit of being optimistic and enthusiastic. These qualities cannot be taught but are rather "caught" in an atmosphere permeated with optimism and enthusiasm.

A teacher's consistency is another very important quality that influences a student's level of security and confidence. Children come to depend on adults who demonstrate a consistent pattern or way of living. In fact, students prefer adults who are consistently negative over those who vacillate in terms of emotions, expectations, and standards. If students can rely upon consistency in response—a consistency that is impossible in teachers who take out their personal frustrations on the students—then they will be able to gain the self-confidence that comes with being able to do things that are consistently correct or incorrect.

An understanding and acceptance of self is vital to understanding young people. At the same time that people grow in understanding of self, they grow in understanding of others. An awareness of the general developmental needs of students and the specific needs of an individual student is integral to the role of the teacher as understander of students. It is not our intention to develop a lengthy treatise on these developmental needs since numerous books related to human development are available; rather, our purpose is to focus on how the many areas of human development are integrated and mutually interrelated.

The learner's affective, emotional characteristics influence cognitive development. There is no behavior pattern, however intellectual, that does not involve affective factors as motives (Piaget, 1970). Similarly, physical growth, development, and maturation all contribute to social integration and personal integrity. Mastery of physical skills can influence students' perceptions of their self-sufficiency, self-confidence, and self-image. These are the same qualities that influence academic achievement.

Learning that involves the whole person, emotionally as well as intellectually, is the most lasting and pervasive. Erikson (1963) studied the affective and social needs of the individual. He theorized that internal feelings develop in stages, each stage producing a positive or negative feeling about self. The human personality develops according to steps that are determined by the person's readiness to approach, be aware of, and interact with a wider social horizon. There is an intricate balance between the individual's maturation and society's expectations. As a child goes through these predetermined stages, his or her current understanding and perceptions of self and what society expects change. The societal role structure and a person's reaction to this structure are very complex. The psychological development of the learner is directly related to the influences of society's expectations — expectations that differ according to various age levels. For example, expectations for the degree of responsibility and self-direction of an elementary school child differ from the expectations placed on middle school children. Teachers at each age level need to provide learning opportunities that serve as building blocks for successive stages of development.

Just as attitudes influence cognitive development, physical development is highly significant to the pattern of social development and maturation. Erikson (1963) points out that mastery of a skill such as walking helps to make the child feel a part of his or her culture. The resulting cultural recognition — in addition to the physical mastery — contributes to the child's self-esteem. Teachers need to be aware of this interrelatedness when planning various physical activities. The student who has achieved proficiency in some motor ability is more likely to be chosen as a leader in athletic and social activities. Those not chosen often suffer a loss of self-confidence and may experience some degree of frustration. This is but another example of how one context in which the student is involved influences the same student in another context. Bronfenbrenner (1979) compares development to a set of concentric circles in which each circle is related to all of the others. At the center of the concentric circles is self. The other circles represent the multiple contexts within which the individual interacts — either directly or indirectly. These multiple contexts influence the child's process of growing into and becoming a total person. Factors that influence this growth for one child may differ for another child as each progresses through the various stages of development.

Piaget (1970) defines the various stages of change as the universals of every being's development. These stages involve progress toward increasing complexity. Each successive stage integrates critical formal aspects of previous stages into a more articulated organization of thought. The rate at which students progress through these various stages differs as a function of both biological and environmental influences. Movement from one stage of development to another is predominately based on maturation, which cannot be accelerated by an attempt to "teach" the tasks. Often parents and teachers do not realize this and place unrealistic pressures on students to advance from one stage to another. While it is easy to accept the fact that not all children walk at the same age (even with the greatest desire and encouragement from parents), teachers and parents seem to forget this maturational difference when it comes to such things as cognitive, social, and moral development.

Even at seventeen and eighteen years of age, students reflect this wide variety of maturational levels. While some students are ready for all of the responsibilities and emotional responses required by the "dating game," many others feel threatened by the idea of relationships with members of the opposite sex and prefer the relative stability and safety of remaining close to their friends. Although some high school students prefer the freedom of independent study, many are unable to accept this freedom—even to choose the courses that they are to take. Most students at this level have ceased to blindly accept the precepts of their parents and have begun to develop their own standards and beliefs; some, however, remain on a level at which they are capable only of echoing the beliefs to which they have been exposed for eighteen years. Both teachers and parents must be responsive to students' individual rates of development. Appropriate learning experiences, adapted to this wide range of developmental levels, need to be available for exploration as maturation continues. With a thorough knowledge of human development, teachers can assist parents in planning learning experiences that take into consideration their child's personal levels of readiness.

Elementary-school-age children depend on the use of their environment for concept formation. Both the classroom and home environments should contain a rich variety of concrete materials that support development at all levels. Physical experiences are the building blocks from which concepts are extracted. The concrete physical world that the child comprehends should always be the starting point for new learning. This holds true for all age levels even though the degree of concrete experiences will vary according to age level. Younger children need more concrete and semiconcrete experiences; older students also need both concrete and semiconcrete experiences, but to a lesser degree.

Concepts are often hierarchical, or progressively dependent, in nature. If students truly understand a concept, they will be able to relate it in a meaningful way to other concepts they know. The role of the teacher is to provide experiences in which students have the opportunities to explore, formulate, evaluate, study patterns, and examine and discuss related concepts. If a student is having difficulty learning a specific concept, perhaps it is because the expectation is not consistent with his or her present stage of cognitive development. The teacher's professional responsibility is to ensure that students are not asked to do what is developmentally inappropriate. To this end, a teacher must be aware of the numerous factors that influence the student's stages of development.

Learning tasks that require cognitive processing beyond or beneath the capabilities of a student are unfair as well as detrimental. Piaget (1973) suggests an optimal balance between what students already know and their ability to reorganize this knowledge to include new information about the environment. Expectations that are beyond or beneath a student's immediate reach run the risk of interrupting that balance. The ideal of education is not necessarily to teach the maximum but to help students learn to learn and to help them maintain the desire to continue to develop as lifelong learners.

Learning, living, and becoming are continuously interrelated. Learning starts as soon as a person is born and continues throughout life. The child's evolving world is truly a "construction of reality" rather than a mere representation of it (Piaget, 1973). Bronfenbrenner (1979) views the child's world as "his emerging perceptions and activities," not as a mere reflection of what he sees. These perceptions have active, creative aspects. Students need to bring personal meaning to an experience if they are to obtain information from it. The teacher plays a key role in stimulating and assisting the student to create this "personal context" for the information that is presented. Discussion with others helps to create meaning by building connections between what is new and what is already familiar. Britton (1970) illustrates this with the example of putting a notice of a scheduled event on the school bulletin board. As students talk to each other about the implications of the notice, they are each "creating a personal context" while helping each other to do so.

While teaching often occurs in a large group, learning is always a very personal and individual act. Teachers must penetrate beyond the likenesses of group members to the differences between individual learners. All students are the total of their life experiences. It is this information that helps teachers respond to the question "Why would I have students do this?" For example, children cannot be expected to share, take turns, and listen to each other talk when their behavior is impeded by their own egocentric functioning. It is only through an understanding of why students behave as they do that teachers will develop more appropriate learner-oriented strategies for their classrooms.

CREATING A LEARNING ENVIRONMENT THAT FOCUSES ON THE DEVELOPMENT OF THE TOTAL PERSON

The school years are crucial in the development of positive attitudes toward self, others, and society. Students need to be aware of and accepting of themselves in order to live with other students and with adults, to learn from their environment, to enjoy the present, to prepare for the future, to create, to love, to learn to face adversity, and to behave responsibly; in a word, to be total human beings. If the working world needs people who possess these qualities, teachers need to make both programmatic and instructional decisions that will foster the development of these characteristics. For example, aesthetic needs can be enhanced by experiences that encourage exploration, analysis, curiosity, and discovery; the esteem needs can be fulfilled by providing successful experiences that promote feelings of adequacy. Experiences that foster a positive self-concept and lead students to a more complete understanding of self are necessary if they are to progress toward self-actualization, which Maslow (1962) defines as "becoming all one is capable of being."

The ideal learning environment is one in which students work *with* rather than depend upon the teacher—an environment in which the pupil assumes the basic responsibility for learning but uses the teacher as a guide, a consultant, a resource person, and many times as a "navigator" for the learning effort (Hunter, 1979). There are many ways the teacher can facilitate affective, social, moral, and cognitive growth and development in schools. The social environment of the school itself offers numerous firsthand problem-solving situations, and these should provide the subject matter for discussion of moral problems. Kohlberg and Turiel (1971) emphasize the importance of having students deal with problems that are real to them—that is, problems that are appropriate to their levels of development—so that they can conceptualize, interpret, and become morally involved. They see engaging learners in conflict as a means of helping them move to the next higher stage of moral reasoning.

While teachers are becoming more and more aware of the interrelatedness of such factors as self-concept with academic achievement, peer relations, and behavior problems, they often do not detect the student who may have a low self-concept. The adviser/advisee concept, as formulated in the Individually Guided Education Model developed at the University of Wisconsin, is valuable in this regard. This concept is also strongly endorsed in the guidelines of the National Middle School Association. The program requires a five- to ten-minute conference between the teacher and each student on a weekly or bi-weekly basis. This gives students an opportunity to discuss their behavioral and academic goals and concerns. Teachers can gather and process valuable information about students through this personalized conference, and studies have shown significant differences in students' attitudes toward self and others subsequent to involvement in the adviser/advisee program.

Individual or small group conferences have also been used successfully at the secondary level. Students are placed in advisory groups with a teacher of their choice, one with whom they feel the greatest rapport. These small groups meet frequently, sometimes as often as once a day, for a specified period. The groups explore values clarification exercises, discuss individual academic problems and needs, and help members build positive self-concepts through the initial common factor of esteem for a particular teacher. Students are provided with a specific, scheduled, predictable time during which they may discuss and begin to solve their problems. This program is similar to conducting teacher-pupil conferences. Genishi (1979) emphasizes the need and value of teacher-pupil conferences. She maintains that a teacher cannot teach successfully nor can the researcher investigate fully unless both consider what students themselves experience and think. Observations of and interactions with students are invaluable in this regard.

Another technique for gathering information about students' experiences, attitudes, and values is an open-ended interest questionnaire. Such a questionnaire might include such statements as: "I enjoy playing with friends who . . ."; "I have a special interest in . . ."; "My favorite activity is . . ."; "I like to read books that . . ."; "My favorite school subjects are . . ."; "I like homework projects that . . ."; "I like a teacher who . . ."; "I get upset when. . . ." Information from a questionnaire of this nature can help teachers create an environment that reflects everyday life and some of the social and physical realities that pupils confront outside the school environment. As teachers grow in their understanding of students' current needs, of their past experiences, and of how these experiences influence their viewpoints and motivations, they will be able to personalize instruction to meet the unique needs of specific learners.

Just as the learning environment needs to reflect a basic understanding of the integration of social, emotional, and cognitive development, physical development needs to be considered. The relationship between physical development and social development exists at all age levels but is perhaps more evident outwardly in the middle school. This is often attributed to the variance that exists in the onset of pubescent growth spurts. The early maturing girl and the late maturing boy seem to suffer the most during this period of transition. Social experiences provided in the middle school should be appropriate for the middle school student and must not simply emulate those of the senior high school.

The curricular and co-curricular program for middle school students should provide physical activities based on the needs of all students. Intramural activities rather than intermural activities are advocated; many students at this level cannot accept the emotional strain that comes with intermural competition. The development of healthy relationships between people needs to be emphasized and meaningfully integrated into the curriculum. The middle school program should focus on a sense of planned gradualism; the program needs to satisfy the learner's need for more independence while continuing to offer the assurance of sound adult guidance (Alexander & George, 1981).

The student's desire for independence and need for dependence serve as a constant internal conflict for many middle school children. During these years, students need acceptance from teachers and parents who are truly "understanders of their behaviors" more than they need direction. This need is also apparent at the high school level. When an eighteen-year-old faces the reality of graduation and the responsibilities of adulthood, he or she begins to long for the simplicity and comfort of being a child. The doubts that become apparent at this stage of students' lives are compounded by their fear of asking for help from the adults that surround them. These students are constantly reminded of being adults, and they do not want to show what they feel is weakness by asking for advice and guidance.

Students learn *from* each other and *with* each other; therefore, the learning environment should provide opportunities for students to interact. Peer interactions facilitate concept development. Through informal, exploratory play and through guided learning activities, students confront opposing ideas, reconcile differences, explain positions, try out ideas, integrate existing concepts, and stimulate new reflective thought. Britton (1970) refers to these interactions as expressive speech that makes possible a new series of teaching/learning events. Each speaker alternates speech with silence. In listening to others, students generate further speech. The silences themselves create the possibility of discovery of learning in a way that might not occur in independent learning. What one person says may spark discovery in another which, when discussed, may form a starting point for someone else. Collectively, the group is doing more than each student could do individually.

Classroom activities such as group discussions, decision-making exploration, and investigation encourage student-student relationships and the development of human relations skills. Learning centers, simulation games, and debates allow students to interact and also promote higher cognitive and moral reasoning. Interaction enables students to experience the opinions, wants, and needs of others. Role-playing provides opportunities for learners to interact morally with their environment. Moral principles cannot be dictated but rather are fostered within a natural social environment. To help them plan meaningful educational experiences, teachers may want to list the basic educational goals and then reflect on the opportunities and learning experiences afforded the student to develop these goals. For example, if an educational goal is to help students learn in a group and to solve group problems, then the curriculum needs to reflect opportunities to work in small groups — to discuss, debate, argue, and finally arrive at consensus.

The teacher must help parents see the relationship between the activities that involve the child in the learning process and the basic cognitive goals and understandings. Prior to initiating a unit of study, it would be helpful for a teacher to send home a newsletter listing basic concepts and the activities that are planned to help in the development of these concepts. Such a newsletter can help parents recognize the relevancy of such activities as role-playing, construction activities, simulation games, field trips, media productions, and use of resource people. Parents also need to understand the difference between rote learning and concept development. When understanding is reached through exploration and guided discovery, the result is meaningful learning that can be generalized to other situations. When students are involved in discovering ideas that lead to concept development, they are also learning how to learn, using the higher-level thought processes of analysis, synthesis, and evaluation.

UNDERSTANDING STUDENTS:
A BASIS FOR EFFECTIVE DISCIPLINE

Several philosophical notions that permeate this book are integral to maintaining effective classroom discipline. These include the teacher's knowledge of the ever-changing developmental needs of children, a sensitivity to the influences of the numerous contexts in which the student resides, an awareness of the moment-to-moment influences affecting each pupil, and the need to create a physical and emotional environment that reflects the individual needs of the students. When these conditions exist in the classroom, discipline problems are minimized. There is no such thing as a problem-free environment, nor should there be. Problems are an inevitable part of living; without problems to be solved, little learning takes place. However, instead of the teacher providing solutions for the students, students need to be guided in developing or selecting their own solutions—thus developing the critical life-long skills necessary to solve problems.

Effective discipline takes into account the individual needs of students. As teachers enter the classroom each day, they must be sensitive to the needs of individuals and of the class as a whole. Each day there will be students who feel like working and others who do not, and students who have just had a positive experience and those who have had a negative one. Based on the specific needs of students on a particular day, a teacher may need to adapt the instruction. On a September afternoon during the last class of the day, students are probably not very interested in the study of simple sentences when half of them are football players or cheerleaders, ready for the biggest game of the season. There are days when wandering off the subject matter is the best decision—at other times, it is important to follow a prepared lesson plan. This is where the quality that Hunter (1971) refers to as the "use of self" plays an important role; use of self is the ability of a teacher to use personality and judgment in conjunction with the science of teaching. This use of self differentiates the artist from the competent technician in the profession. It takes into account the sensitive characteristics of the learner and teacher that are so responsive to the environment that they can vary from day to day—or even from moment to moment.

Developmental changes affect the behavior of students in the school setting. Teachers need to judge a student's behavior on the present, not solely on the past record or on the perceptions of other teachers. Too often, students do not have a chance; teachers have a preconceived notion about their abilities or behaviors, and they are burdened with living up to that notion. A boy who is told on the first day of school, "You sit back there in the corner and don't cause any trouble in *my* class" will quickly respond to that attitude. He will feel that since he has already been punished, he might as well misbehave as he has in the past.

Since students' behaviors reflect their perceptions of themselves, teachers should try to understand each student's self-perception. Unlike adults, students often consider themselves as either good or bad at something; they do not view themselves objectively on the basis of both strengths and weaknesses. They frequently fail to understand that it is all right to be good at some things and not so good at others. Teachers need to help students develop the attitude "I'm great because I am!" not "I'm great only when I get 'A's,' " or "when I help the basketball team win," or "when I'm elected class president." Too often, value is associated with outstanding achievement. Those who are not able to achieve begin to feel negatively about themselves and tend to minimize their overall value.

Students may view themselves as being good or bad based upon their relationships with their peers. They usually think that they are "bad" when they get into disputes; they fail to realize that they may be justified in their feelings. Teachers must help students understand their feelings and help them realize that at times it is all right to be angry. It is not the anger that is wrong; it is the way in which the student resolves a dispute or shows anger that may be inappropriate. The sensitive teacher focuses on the "good" or "bad" of a student's behavior and is not judgmental about the "good" or "bad" of that student's emotions. If teachers do not aid their students in understanding this distinction, students may begin to repress the emotions that they do not understand rather than finding a way of expressing these emotions in an appropriate fashion.

The notion of context, discussed throughout this book, must carry over into any plan for handling discipline problems. Teachers must understand that students' abilities, traits, and values are always in a state of change and development. The contexts in which a student exists can change in many ways. For example, family stability may be in a state of flux—this can affect a student in all of the contexts of which he or she is a part. In making decisions concerning classroom discipline, the teacher must remember that the student is reacting to more than a single event. A girl who is tardy may have been hiding in the restroom, crying about the fight that she had with a parent before coming to school that morning. The boy who verbally lashes out at the teacher may in reality be lashing out only because he is not feeling well—he needs to vent his frustrations on someone. Again, teachers must have knowledge of more than the moment-to-moment context of which they are a part; they must be aware of the multiple contexts, both inside and outside of the school setting, that affect students.

A positive emotional environment reflects the teachers' beliefs that pupils learn best when they are developmentally ready; when they feel confident that they can learn; and, when they are learning something that is meaningful to them. When these conditions exist, motivation is enhanced. Many discipline problems exist because of a lack of motivation to learn.

An emotionally positive environment helps to facilitate the development of a positive self-concept. It is free from threat of failure yet challenging; it is an environment in which students are respected and their ideas are heard and tried; it focuses on strengths rather than weaknesses; and it encourages self-expression. Such a supportive environment does not just happen. Teachers should be aware of the numerous factors that contribute to a supportive environment.

Purkey (1978) has written extensively on the role teachers play in creating a supportive environment. He describes good teaching in terms of the nature of the invitation to learning that teachers extend to students. These invitations include messages—verbal and nonverbal, formal and informal, intentional and unintentional—that are consistently transmitted to students and inform them that they are able, valuable, and responsible. Invitational teaching increases the probability of student success in the classroom. Factors that enhance invitational teaching include challenge, control, freedom, respect, success, and warmth. The sensitive teacher knows how to balance these factors within the moment-to-moment context of each student.

The sensitive teacher is also aware of helping all students feel that they are a very valuable part of the class. The classroom belongs to each learner! Teachers should display work of all students, not just the best work. Classroom responsibilities should be shared by all students. Students are very perceptive—they know when they are not being treated fairly. They value the authenticity and fairness of the teacher. They want and need honest reinforcement, praise, and respect. Teachers who communicate poorly with students will not gain the respect they desire. A teacher's disrespect for students opens the door for students to behave the same way toward others. The teacher who screams at students will often find a classroom filled with screaming students. If positive behavior is communicated, then students are more likely to behave positively.

Pupils are influenced more by the home than by any other factor. After the home, schools probably exert the next greatest influence on how students see themselves and their abilities. Therefore, it is crucial for teachers to be sensitive to the myriad of factors that affect a class. They must be able to sort and evaluate this information and use it in making informed teaching decisions. There is no "right" answer; what works once may never work again. Teachers must be aware of the changing data in the teaching/learning environment and adjust their decisions accordingly.

Maintaining order in the classroom is as much a part of the teaching-learning process as anything else. In order to allow students to learn and in order to maintain some pattern or scheme of learning, teachers must establish and maintain some form of classroom order. This does not necessitate total silence, nor should it bring to mind visions of thirty students, eyes forward and hands folded on the desk, raptly and unquestioningly drinking in all that the teacher has to impart in the way of knowledge. Active participation, discussion among peers, and movement may be prerequisites for any number of valid learning styles and situations; for example, a biology lab, an art class, or a time during which students are using learning centers each require movement and discussion. There are occasions when strict silence and physical inactivity are also a necessary part of education; one cannot picture twenty-five high school seniors successfully taking a final exam as they talk and wander about the room. The classroom management system actually employed should, of course, reflect the teacher's style and needs.

In their book *Solving Discipline Problems: Strategies for Classroom Teachers* (1980), Wolfgang and Glickman present an eclectic approach to discipline using a continuum ranging from teachers' reactions that allow predominately pupil-controlled behavior to those that consist of teacher-controlled behavior. They review books and articles that reflect several approaches on this continuum.

Effective discipline is the establishment of a learning environment in which the children have the freedom to learn and to choose and yet one in which there is control. Models that tend to support the balance between freedom and control include the following: Glasser's reality model, described in his book *Schools Without Failure* (1969); the social discipline model of Dreikurs and Cassel, discussed in their book *Discipline Without Tears: What to Do with Children Who Misbehave* (1974);

the transactional analysis model as presented by Berne in *Games People Play* (1964) and by Harris in *I'm OK—You're OK* (1969); and the values clarification model that Raths, Harmin, and Simon present in *Values and Teaching* (1966). While these books outline various approaches to solving discipline problems, solutions to specific problems cannot be prescribed. Only the teacher will know which of the methods best accommodates each particular situation. As a professional decision maker, the teacher has the general knowledge of the developmental needs of students, an awareness of his or her own needs, and sensitivity to the moment-to-moment contexts in which each child resides. It is this knowledge that should serve as a basis for making effective professional decisions about discipline problems.

FOCUSING ON EDUCATIONAL PRACTICE

Understanding students within their multiple contexts is critical; however, the real challenge for the professional teacher is taking action and making decisions that are based on that knowledge. We hope that by reflecting on the following scenarios, the reader will begin to develop the ability to translate theoretical understandings of learners into meaningful practice. The scenarios included in this chapter are transcriptions from actual classroom settings of first-year teachers.

Earlier in this chapter we emphasized that while teaching may occur in a larger or smaller group, learning is always a very personal act. To meet pupil needs, teachers must be committed to individualized instruction. Students need to be provided with the means of pursuing learning at a rate that is comfortable yet challenging. They must be guided toward the achievement of their own needs, not the needs of their fellow classmates. Individualized instruction does not imply students working alone all of the time. Instead, it means that instruction is paced for personal success and that students often work in small groups and sometimes even in large ones. They work with aides, tutors, parent volunteers, an older peer, or the teacher. Rather than isolating students, individualized instruction aims to teach them how to work with others in different settings for various purposes. Scenario 1 was selected to illustrate the teacher's awareness of this fact and her ability to deal effectively with meeting various needs.

Scenario 1

The teacher is reading a story to a small group of children. Other students are busy working together on various projects. As the teacher starts reading the story, she is distracted by several children who are not in the reading group. She announces to the whole class that she does not want any interruption while she is working with the small group. The small group is very attentive when the teacher reads the story, and children not in the reading group are also listening. The teacher's voice is very expressive, yet soft and calming. She shows the book as she reads the story. More children come over to listen. One child interrupts and asks a question about his mathematics worksheet. She says, "I'm sorry, but I'm working with this group—goodbye!" The child leaves without becoming defensive. Upon completion of the story, the teacher encourages comments and sharing of ideas. She is attentive to the pupils and encourages respect for each child's turn to talk. The children are given a follow-up activity related to the story. The teacher then goes over to the child who had interrupted the story to find out what problem he was having in mathematics. While the teacher is talking to the child about his problem, she puts her arm around his shoulder. The child looks up at the teacher with a smile and says, "I figured the problem out by myself." The teacher very expressively says, "Great! Tell me about it."

DISCUSSION QUESTIONS

1. What evidence was there that the teacher was truly an understander of students' behaviors?
2. What are some techniques to encourage children's respect for each child's turn to talk?
3. What are some possible follow-up activities to a story that has been read?
4. What are your reactions to the teacher's comment to the child who interrupted the class? Why was it important for the teacher to go over and see this child after the story was completed? What does this tell you about the role of the teacher? How would you have responded to a child who interrupted you?
5. Would you have allowed the children who were not in the specific reading group to stay and listen to the story?

Earlier in this chapter, we emphasized that individuals move through the various developmental stages at different rates. The teacher's responsibility is to ensure that students are not asked to do what is developmentally inappropriate. In order to meet these varying levels of readiness, small group or individual instruction is often planned. Scenario 2 was selected to illustrate the complex factors that need to be dealt with if small group instruction is to be successful.

Scenario 2

The teacher is engaged in math instruction with three students. The other students are involved in either peer-teaching, learning center activities, independent activities, or a small group simulation game. Students are free to move around the room. The teacher's attention is continuously diverted from the three children with whom she is working. She is surrounded at the small table by other children who need help. Children argue over who is next to get the teacher's time and attention. The teacher repeatedly says, "Just a minute" to the children wanting her attention. She constantly switches her attention from the math instruction to the children working at the interest centers or in small group activities. The three children at the table become discouraged when the teacher starts to help them but is interrupted by other children.

DISCUSSION QUESTIONS

1. What methods of classroom management might facilitate fewer interruptions by students in need of individual attention while the teacher is instructing the small group?
2. How could student frustration be eased or minimized for the students who are not working directly with the teacher?
3. What behaviors in this scenario do you feel are acceptable and unacceptable?
4. How would you deal with the continuous interruptions? What are some potential causes of these problems?
5. In order to plan interest center activities that children can do independently while the teacher is engaged in small group instruction, what does she need to know regarding children's behaviors and levels of cognitive development?
6. What are some social factors the teacher should be aware of in planning small group activities that do not require teacher supervision?

The scenarios and discussion questions in this chapter are a basis for developing an understanding of the complexity of the moment-to-moment teaching-learning phenomenon. We hope that the reader will have numerous opportunities to observe actual classroom situations. However, videotaped scenarios from a classroom setting, although not as good as live observation, can be a valuable tool. The following general questions related to the role of the teacher as understander of students' behaviors could be used to analyze and discuss actual or videotaped classroom observations.

1. What evidence was there that the children were at various levels of social development? How did the teacher respond to these variances? What contextual factors could influence social development?
2. What evidence was there that the learning environment was adaptive and responsive to the students' individual rates of cognitive development?
3. What evidence was there of the teacher's awareness of the affective development of the child?
4. What were some of the possible cognitive, socioemotional, affective, and psychomotor objectives of the instructional activities observed?
5. In listening to the students' ideas, how did the teacher build on them?
6. In what way was the teacher a primary source of facilitating higher-level thought processes?
7. What five discrete child behaviors (both positive and negative) did you observe? Choose one behavior and write a paragraph or scenario describing how you would handle that behavior if you were the classroom teacher. Focus on the type of information you would need about the total school-community context.

The teacher's role as understander of students' behaviors is what distinguishes the teacher as a professional from the teacher as a technician. To understand the unique needs of the total student, the teacher needs an awareness of and a sensitivity to the ecological influences inherent in society in general and in the particular home-school-community contexts within which each pupil functions. This knowledge is gained through reading the professional literature, observing and analyzing student behaviors, talking with students, working closely with parents, and working with professional colleagues. The effective teacher is constantly searching for and gathering data as a basis for making professional decisions—some conscious, some unconscious— that affect learning. As teachers strive to understand student behaviors and the factors that affect these behaviors, they will be able to make informed decisions and thus provide appropriate educational experiences for each learner. These educational experiences are explored further in chapter 5, "The Teacher as Facilitator of Learning."

The Teacher as Facilitator of Learning

AN INTERACTING ROLE

The goal of education, if we are to survive, is the facilitation of change and learning. The only man who is educated is the man who has learned how to adapt and change; the man who has realized that no knowledge is secure, that only the process of seeking knowledge gives a basis for security. Changingness, a reliance on "process" rather than upon static knowledge, is the only thing that makes any sense as a goal of education in the modern world. (Rogers, 1967, p. 2)

Life is a fascinating world of activity for young people. They are born seekers who keep the task of "finding out" always before them. They deserve to be supported in school with experiences that will widen their world as they grow. The natural environment becomes a continuous stimulus for new learning. These are notions that have emerged historically from the educational and human development literature. As Rousseau's revolutionary ideas on man, society, and education became known, they began to influence succeeding generations of educational scholars. Illuminated and inspired by the writings of Rousseau, Pestalozzi dedicated his life to the elevation of all persons. Driven by a boundless concern for children, especially poor children, he committed himself to the cause of improving the human condition through education. He argued that education should aim at the harmonious development of the personality. Similarly, Dewey believed that education must begin with a psychological insight into the student's capabilities, interests, and habits and that educational decisions must be made with reference to these same considerations. In his pedagogical creed, Dewey (1900) emphasizes that education is a process of living and not a preparation for future living. The school must represent life—life as real and vital to students as that which they experience in the home, in the neighborhood, or on the playground. Through educational experiences that reflect the realities of life, uncertainty and ambiguity become a challenge—a challenge that is a fact of everyday living.

We live in a highly complex and rapidly changing society. We are faced by an increasing number and variety of problems that demand creative and far-reaching solutions. To meet this challenge, our children must be provided with an education that prepares them to solve problems and make decisions. Throughout education, learners must have opportunities to confront and address the problems of everyday life. One of the most critical responsibilities of teachers as facilitators of learning is to create an environment that promotes critical thinking and problem-solving skills. These skills must be integrated into all subject areas.

CREATING A PROBLEM-SOLVING ENVIRONMENT

A creative learning environment is not designed to teach students what to think but rather to show them how to think. A stimulating environment motivates students to become critical thinkers through the processes of reading, living, and experiencing. Through discoveries and explorations, students develop a more complex frame of reference from which hypotheses can be formulated and tested and from which creative ideas can emerge. It is important that the home and school provide an environment that challenges students to become problem solvers and decision makers, that integrates understandings, skills, attitudes, and appreciations with significant real-life themes. A greater emphasis on understanding concepts and relating them to life experiences makes learning more relevant to daily life.

A classroom can be an environment that causes students to grow and become excited about learning. Smith (1975) defines learning as "a process the child himself can manage—providing that the situation he tries to make sense of is potentially meaningful to him and he has access to the right kind of information at the right time" (p. 225). Such a classroom setting might be thought of as a learning resource center or a laboratory, and the teacher might be seen as a resource person. The role of resource person implies that the teacher provides a variety of ideas and materials from which the learner can examine a range of choices.

Raths, Wasserman, Jonas, and Rothstein (1967) maintain that the student will take the responsibility for learning if the educational diet is rich in experiences associated with a variety of thought processes. They warn, however, that if teachers are to be concerned with teaching for thinking, they will discover that it takes more than diversified activities to bring it about.

Teachers must create a climate that permits freedom for thinking beyond the classroom — a supportive environment in which students feel free to take risks, make mistakes, question, explore, and disagree. The educational environment can be designed to facilitate problem-solving. Instead of a "problem-free," sterile environment, a setting with situational and simulated problems can provide opportunities that encourage problem-solving, decision-making, and research. Perhaps the most important aspect of learning exists in the learner's freedom to manipulate the environment. Learners are not simply recipients of instruction. Their thinking, feeling, and reacting are of great importance. Students should be actively engaged in creating and recreating their environment. The processes they use — such as setting their own purposes and suggesting and choosing among alternatives — constitute learning itself. The capacity to remold the environment and the reality of its meaning represents the highest of intellectual development (Bronfenbrenner, 1979; Goodlad and Tyler, 1979; Piaget, 1970).

DEVELOPING THE CONDITIONS
FOR CREATIVE PROBLEM-SOLVING

The teacher's role is to create the conditions within which problem-solving and creativity can occur. Because problem-solving is a quality deeply embedded in the human personality, it must be nurtured and reinforced. Thus, the main function of the creative teacher is to maintain certain physical, psychological, socioemotional, and intellectual conditions within the classroom so that creativity will be free to rise to the surface where it can be reached and developed. To encourage creativity, teachers must be capable of fostering curiosity, independence, and self-reliance. Rogers (1967) describes those personal attitudes as genuineness of the facilitator, a willingness to be a person, and the ability to be and to live the feelings and thoughts of the moment. It is his belief that when this realness includes a prizing, a caring, a trust, and a respect for the learner, the climate for learning is enhanced. When the teacher exhibits sensitivity and accurate empathic listening, then indeed a freeing climate, stimulative of self-initiated learning and growth, exists. Many of these qualities are discussed in chapter 1.

Teaching that takes into account the attitudes, cultural experiences, development, and viewpoints of students provides a means of motivation and a basis for future learning. Both teachers and learners are "carriers" of pressure, prejudice, optimism, pessimism, and other attitudes that enhance or discourage creative thinking. As facilitators of the learning environment, teachers should be constantly aware of these influences. They have an unique opportunity to counteract unhealthy influences and to construct healthy ones. They have the power to affect their students' lives for better or for worse since, to a great degree, students become what they experience.

Creative thinking and problem-solving cannot be taught by simply having learners watch someone else perform or by merely giving critical information. Learning comes through doing. Learners instruct themselves, and teachers are responsible primarily for providing constructive feedback, for encouraging students to think beyond the obvious, and for providing the guidelines and parameters within which problem-solving can take place. The abstract thinking that is often necessary for solving difficult problems cannot be communicated to students by a definition but only by arranging diversified problem-solving experiences.

Although problem-solving involves critical thinking, there is little attention given to these skills in today's schools. New programs for the gifted and talented focus on critical thinking skills, but the majority of students are not given opportunities to develop these skills. Problem-solving should be integrated into every aspect of the curriculum. Simply telling learners that problem-solving is important is not effective. Rather, educators must help learners to discover for themselves that critical thinking is important for societies in general and for each of them in particular. Rogers (1967) defines the facilitation of learning as transforming a group into a community of learners where individuals enthusiastically explore new directions and ideas dictated by their own interests; curiosity is unleashed, and everything is opened to questioning and exploration; everything is recognized as existing within the process of change.

Students should be encouraged to examine how critical thinking, or the lack of it, has affected their lives and the lives of others. The literature is replete with examples to illustrate the impact of decisions made throughout history. There were people who were great in the sense that they faced crucial problems and worked intelligently, often against great odds, to solve them. Once students leave the classroom, they seldom encounter a textbook or workbook problem; what they do encounter are real-life situations that need to be addressed.

Active involvement in the learning process increases the opportunity for students to discover for themselves many concepts and generalizations that they would otherwise have to accept secondhand; involvement promotes independence in searching for and finding or generating needed information and ideas, in learning how to learn. The discovery of meaning takes place within people and cannot occur without their involvement in the process—this is the human side of learning. It is in this regard that the role of the teacher as facilitator of the learning environment gains significance.

The background and intellectual maturity of students bear upon their readiness for new concepts and skills. The scholarly works of Jean Piaget furnish an excellent developmental base for understanding how learners assimilate concepts. Learning begins with concrete objects and situations where the student is given experience involving spatial or numerical attributes and representations and is guided into making generalizations that form concepts. This type of concept development provides more permanence of learning and transfer of a deeper insight into one's environment.

An excellent strategy for determining concept development is to ask students to verbalize, and perhaps record on audiotape, the thought processes they use in arriving at solutions to various problems. This provides the teacher with information not only about "what" was done but, more importantly, "how" and "why" a pupil arrived at a particular solution. As students explain "why," the teacher learns whether they truly understand the concept or have just memorized and applied a meaningless formula as an approach to solving problems.

FACILITATING A PROBLEM-SOLVING ENVIRONMENT THROUGH THE ART OF QUESTIONING

Questioning is one important mode for creating an environment that stimulates problem-solving. This mode can be used to guide and challenge students through the "search" or "inquiry" process. Questioning can also serve as a teaching strategy that draws out specific relevant details, helps learners sense relationships, facilitates their reasoning processes, tests their knowledge, and challenges their thinking (Jarolimek & Foster, 1981).

Numerous studies have assessed the relationships between the teachers' levels of questioning and the students' development and application of problem-solving skills. There is evidence that when teachers ask higher-level questions, student performance improves. Turner and Durrett (1975) found that exposure to higher-level cognitive questions in the home and school setting produces at least temporary gains in scores on certain problem-solving measures in young children. Specifically, the study indicated that young children generate a significantly greater number of similarities between familiar objects after being exposed to higher-level cognitive questioning in their daily nursery school activities than they do after being exposed to lower-level cognitive questioning. Seeing similarities is the basis for establishing relationships — the building blocks of concept development.

The value of divergent questions is discussed in recent studies of the dimensions of learning and, in particular, the hemispheric processes of the brain. It would appear that the left hemisphere has resident verbal, numerical, linear, rational, and logical functions and that the right hemisphere has resident visual, spatial, perceptual, intuitive, imaginative, and imagery functions. American education has stressed the rational, verbal, logical skills of the left hemisphere and ignored the visual, intuitive, imaginative functions of the right hemisphere— functions that are so important to creative problem-solving. Learners approach tasks in different ways; one student seems to grasp things intuitively and another in an organized step-by-step approach (Languis & Kraft, 1975).

The process approach to learning takes into account both the intuitive and logical modes of learning. The approach must be multifaceted to account for and meet the needs of all students. The types of questions teachers ask have a relationship to hemispheric brain functioning. Of the four types of questions—cognitive, convergent, divergent, and evaluative—the first two are asked by teachers of their pupils over 95% of the time (Blosser, 1970). When open, divergent, and evaluative questions with many possible solutions are posed, the right hemisphere will become involved in the learning process, thus promoting the scientific approach — the development of critical problem-solving techniques in all facets of living.

Rowe (1978) did extensive studies related to questioning and, in particular, to the wait time following a question. She concluded that rapid questioning does little in inquiry-based studies to stimulate a student's depth of thought or to produce a high-quality explanation. With increased wait time, students begin to increase their roles as problem solvers and decision makers; they start structuring the learning situation; and they begin to evaluate and to value their thoughts and those of others.

While the teacher's role as questioner is integral to the inquiry process, so too, the role of students as questioners and problem "creators" is important. In a developmental approach to learning, the student is looked upon as an active participant. All students should be encouraged to ask questions — not only the conventional "how" and "what" but also "why." As noted, this requires a classroom environment in which students feel free to question, take risks, hypothesize, and make mistakes. The teacher must interact with the students and develop activities that promote questioning. The environment must make students feel the need to ask questions and feel comfortable in asking them. Supportive responses from teachers and honest acceptance of divergent viewpoints can encourage students to ask more questions and become actively involved in learning.

Students tend to ask more questions when they are given opportunities to use concrete objects on their own or within small groups. They need to be allowed time for trial, time for error, and time for learning from their errors.

STUDENTS AS PROBLEM SOLVERS

Problem-solving is not separate from the problem solver. After a careful review of the literature on problem-solving and a year of observing over seven hundred intermediate grade children in problem-solving situations, the staff of the Mathematical Problem-Solving Project concluded that willingness, perseverance, and self-confidence were three of the most important influences on problem-solving performance (Webb, Moses, & Kerr, 1977). Students often arrive in class with attitudes that block them from freely using their creative abilities for learning. To overcome these fears and anxieties, they need a positive, supportive environment with a teacher who has an optimistic view of students, faith in their potential, and trust in them as creative problem solvers and who provides the freedom and encouragement to develop as problem solvers. The teacher plays a critical role in helping students gain confidence in themselves and in their ability to solve problems. It is interesting to note that Colgrove's studies (1967) demonstrate that the mere suggestion that a person has the reputation of being an original thinker creates a mental set that upgrades his or her problem-solving performance. The teacher's verbal and nonverbal approval, recognition, and encouragement are significant in this regard.

Within a creative and supportive classroom environment, numerous approaches can be used to help learners become problem solvers. The best educational incentives are those that are internalized, those motivational strategies that satisfy curiosity and enable students to derive both satisfaction and a sense of accomplishment from their experiences. Successful experiences are critical in developing and maintaining healthy pupil attitudes toward learning. Students who experience considerable failure lower their levels of aspiration; success, however, builds confidence in one's ability. Increased confidence, in turn, results in higher levels of aspiration. Successful problem-solving experiences should be an important part of the total curriculum.

Problem-solving, which is essentially a creative activity, cannot be built exclusively on isolated ideas or the low-level recall of facts. Bloom's (1965) taxonomy of educational objectives could be used to plan activities that emphasize critical thinking. The list of processes included in the taxonomy can be used to brainstorm corresponding activities. In *Values Clarification: A Handbook of Practical Strategies for Teachers and Students* (1972), Simon, Howe, and Kirschenbaum present a wide variety of activities that can be used in classrooms of any level—primary through secondary. The activities explore problems from decisions about one's life work to changes that could or should be made in one's life; problem-solving and critical-thinking skills can be developed and an awareness of the multiple solutions to situations can be considered through such class and individual exercises.

Children's books provide illustrations of many of the critical-thinking skills. Examples can be found in such books as *The Great Gilly Hopkins* (Paterson, 1978), which discusses the problems of a foster child, and *Roll of Thunder, Hear My Cry* (Taylor, 1976), which deals with the problems encountered by black Americans during the Depression. Besides dealing with contemporary problems, many of the novels for adolescents approach these problems from a realistic point of view. *The Great Gilly Hopkins* does not end idealistically with Gilly reunited with her mother —a mother who has never really wanted her—nor does it end with Gilly returning to the foster home in which she found people for whom she could finally care and who cared for her. Rather, she remains in a setting that is not, initially, the one which she desires.

In both fiction and nonfiction, we find accounts of how people have gone about the business of solving problems. Some of the problems are important, some unimportant; some are simple, others are complex. Some attempts to solve problems are successful while others fail. In any case, we find an underlying assumption reflected in many books: if people develop and exercise their potential for critical thinking, they thereby increase their control over themselves and their environment. In discussing with learners the books they read, we can help them recognize the role played by critical thought in their own lives as well as in those lives about which they read. Recently, the paperback book publishing houses have begun listing selections by topic—topics such as divorce, foster homes, death, and dying. This facilitates the purchase of books that deal with those areas in which students are most interested from a very personal viewpoint.

The "simulation games" often used in social studies or science can provide rich opportunities for developing problem-solving skills. These simulations present problems that are open-ended and range from ecological studies to reenactment of the great battles of civilization. This openness is especially beneficial when one considers that many of the problems facing both students and adults in their world of reality involve more than a single answer. Positive effects from using discussion have been found at all grade levels; it is particularly valuable for students who are weak in reading comprehension or independent study skills. In addition, discussion enhances the development of communication and listening skills.

The daily newspaper is an excellent means for applying problem-solving skills to local, state, national, and international problems. Environmental, cultural, social, and technological issues can be studied in terms of their problem-solving implications. Some newspapers have presented workshops that emphasize their application and use in any area of the curriculum. Consumer concerns such as comparison shopping through advertisements, vocabulary study (through reading of the various types of articles), and letter-writing skills presented through "Letters to the Editor" can be explored and amplified for their applications in the classroom. For example, environmental and energy issues can be related to production, distribution, and use of energy. The problem-solving skills of describing, comparing, contrasting, analyzing, and evaluating can be reinforced by debating controversial dilemmas such as the need for nuclear energy versus the hazards of waste disposal, the economy of strip-mining of coal versus preservation of our natural landscape, and the demand for lower school taxes versus the high cost of good education. The interpretation of symbolism can be explored through political cartoons; students can investigate the use of particular symbols for particular concerns and can study the use of caricatures for representation of various political figures.

Numerous problem-solving skills can be used in publishing a student newspaper or magazine. Such a publication might include a "Dear Science Challenger" column in which students respond to problem questions submitted by other students; the new invention of the month; scientific breakthroughs; classified advertisements; editorials on the value of reading; and a science experiment corner. In addition to seeing the relationship of math, science, and reading to everyday problems and situations, newspaper-publishing itself can be a situation requiring problem-solving skills. Basic understanding of costs, timing, communications, production, distribution, and labor is essential to successful publishing. These conditions create natural problem-solving experiences.

Role-playing and creative dramatics can provide a means for developing problem-solving ability. By assuming a variety of roles in a contrived situation, students can learn to make decisions similar to those they might encounter in their present or future experiences. The use of creative dramatics to support learning is predicated on the idea that material is not really learned until it is assimilated in such a way that it influences the consciousness of the individual—both the thought processes and the feelings. Role-playing permits students to assimilate the material and to use it to create previously unthought-of solutions to problems.

Situational problems that arise in the school environment provide an excellent opportunity for problem-solving. Shields (1980) reports on one fourth grade class that tried to solve a continuing logistics problem in the school cafeteria. In the classroom she studied, students worked on the various aspects of the problem for six weeks. The culmination of these experiences was a set of proposals to improve service in the cafeteria. As a result of the work, the administration implemented several changes and the students were anxious to attack other problems they found around the school.

Mathematics, integral to all disciplines, is one area within which students should learn to solve problems. It is quite important for students at all age levels to encounter situations in which mathematics might be useful and to try their hands at formulating useful problems. Stevenson (1975) suggests that students be given problems that have no answers, that have many answers, that contain irrelevant data, or that are without sufficient information. Younger children tend to focus on irrelevant attributes of a problem situation, thereby making errors. Separating information that is relevant from that which is irrelevant to the problem emphasizes not only reading skills but also organizational skills. Secondary students gain insight regarding the day-to-day applications of mathematics through courses such as business math and practical math; these students study a range of skills from check-writing to balancing a budget and calculating net pay. All students need and want to know how deductions for income tax and Social Security are going to affect their take-home pay.

The teacher's role is to assist students in developing problem-solving abilities that include observing, drawing inferences, establishing facts, formulating hypotheses, testing hypotheses, and evaluating results. These processes are basic to all aspects of the curriculum and not exclusively to mathematics and science. When pupils identify problems in any area of the curriculum, teachers should avoid answering the questions directly. Rather, they should help students to find sources of information, ask more questions, develop possible answers, perform experiments and demonstrations, and otherwise discover solutions. The possible solutions should come from the learner. For practice in this area, students can be presented with pictures that depict a problem situation. They can develop a theory as to what problems exist. Similarly, a story can be initiated, and the students can be asked to develop a theory about a story's possible ending had it been written fifty years ago, today, or perhaps fifty years from now. By having their abilities to make and evaluate problem situations sharpened, students begin to realize that generalizations must be supported by evidence. Hence, one may be justified in holding a theory today that may need modification tomorrow when new evidence appears.

The ability to solve one's problems and the problems of society is crucial to the individual and to the future of our world. Through "discovery learning" and problem-solving, students can explore, formulate, evaluate, study, examine, and discuss patterns. When understanding is reached through exploration and guided discovery, the result is meaningful learning. When students are involved in discovering an idea, they are also learning how to utilize higher-level thinking. To help each learner develop these important abilities is the central task for all of education. Those who teach must assume a leadership role in facilitating a learning environment that promotes creative problem-solving.

AN INTERDISCIPLINARY FOCUS ON INSTRUCTION

An interdisciplinary or thematic approach to teaching provides many opportunities for structuring and analyzing real-life problems and implementing the ideas discussed in the previous section. Knowledge and skills that students bring with them can be related to the present and the future through an interdisciplinary focus that places learning in its natural setting — a setting where ideas are integrated and interrelated. Much work remains to be done in curriculum development to make problem-solving an integral part of the classroom experience. Continuing efforts to emphasize critical thinking and problem-solving in the total curriculum naturally go hand-in-hand with attempts to bring genuine applications to the classroom. The two efforts reinforce each other, and both are essential for problem-solving in our schools. The world of today and tomorrow demands that teachers assist students to gain deeper understanding and facility in using and applying knowledge. In order for this to take place, it must be continuously demonstrated to students that the information they are learning is interrelated and will continue to be of practical value to them. Greene (1978) refers to this as a "network of relationships" and feels the curriculum should offer the possibility for students to be the makers of such networks. To achieve this, teachers need to stimulate an awareness of the educational context and to aid in the identification of thematically relevant ideas.

SAMPLE ACTIVITY PLANS

Although social studies themes lend themselves very naturally to an interdisciplinary unit, virtually any discipline can be used. For example, a group of students was asked to create an integrated unit around the play *Treasure Island,* which was being performed in the local community. In response to this assignment, the preservice students developed a number of activities designed to integrate the academic disciplines. The following are a few examples of the representative interdisciplinary activities developed.

SOCIAL STUDIES

1. Tracing the evolution of the compass from the ancient Greeks through the pirates to the present day. Then constructing crude compasses as the early sailors did.
2. Examining the mapping of the sea by the pirates and by other early sailors. Discussing the advantages of using latitude measurements. Then making angle-measuring devices and finding the latitude of their homes or their school.

LANGUAGE ARTS

1. Writing a story in which they set off on a space adventure in search of some "treasure."
2. Creating a business venture (as individuals or in groups) and naming that venture after some character from *Treasure Island.* Then discussing the advantages of advertising for their business and creating a media campaign including radio, television, newspapers, and billboards to promote the business.
3. Writing a paragraph describing one of the characters in *Treasure Island.* Then using the thesaurus and changing all the adjectives to synonymous ones.

SCIENCE

1. Discussing the specific nutritional concerns for sailors on a long sea voyage, especially the need for fruit (Vitamin C) and fresh water. Then examining the methods for drying fruit to take on a sea voyage.

2. Studying the types of wild animals that might live on an island like *Treasure Island* and describing the type of habitat each animal might need.

MATHEMATICS

1. Explaining the speed with which the ship will travel during a calm day, during a stormy day, during a calm night, and during a stormy night. Examining a captain's log of the weather and having them determine how long it would take to sail from one point to another.

2. Making a pirate hat strictly from geometric shapes. Then computing the entire area of the hat they have drawn.

HEALTH

1. Discussing malaria and other tropical diseases. Discussing the advances that have/have not been made in treating these diseases.

2. Studying and providing responses to the following problem: Ben Gunn lived on goats' meat, berries, and oysters. Is it possible that he was a healthy man? (They should employ their knowledge of vitamins, minerals, and the four food groups.)

ART

1. Designing and creating a string art picture of a pirate ship or of a parrot or some other aspect of *Treasure Island*. The teacher may want to give younger children the design for the sails and allow them to do the stringing only.

2. Creating and then wearing their own pirate costumes for a *Treasure Island* day.

MUSIC

1. Students who have more advanced backgrounds in music could write both the music and the lyrics to a pirate song, using correct timing, proper notation, and the division of measures.

2. Older students may want to produce their own filmstrip or slide/

tape presentations, illustrating their favorite scene(s) from *Treasure Island*. Students might create or find their own appropriate background music for the presentations.

The Creative Classroom Environment: A Stage-Set Design by Heck and Cobes (1978) contains an interdisciplinary strategy that both preservice and in-service teachers have used successfully. In this plan, the classroom is perceived as a regular theatrical setting. When the curtain opens for a play, the audience becomes aware of the time, place, and setting of the play through action, stage scenery, and properties. Similarly, simple representations can be used in the classroom at all grade levels to create an illusion of time and place, thus creating a more naturalistic setting for simulated problems. The ultimate development of the classroom as a stage-set design is, of course, a learning environment where bulletin boards, chalkboards, instructional centers, and arrange-ment of furniture can reflect the time, place, or concept being studied. For example, the Olympic symbol of unity, posters of Olympic events, international flags, and the symbolic torch are sufficient to set the stage for an Olympic theme. Like the scenographic elements that support actors in their efforts on the stage, setting the stage provides additional stimulus to students in researching and role-playing many of their learn-ing experiences. They thus learn to apply problem-solving to many unstructured and unexpected situations.

Teachers need not be artistic to design the creative learning envi-ronment. They can manipulate the environment with free or inexpensive materials in order to make a specific unit of study come alive. Crude cardboard can be used very effectively. A first step might be to locate illustrations that depict the era or setting of the unit being studied. Good resource materials for this activity include encyclopedias, basic his-tories, brochures from travel agencies, picture files in the public library, and juvenile books or slides. A second step in drafting the design might be to make cutouts from the original illustrations so that when seen in isolation and out of context, they will cause the learner to think about the original illustration. For example, Big Ben evokes thoughts of London, or a skyline evokes the image of a large city. Such illustrations can be created using an overhead projector to make a line drawing, an opaque projector to make a silhouette drawing on any type of material including cardboard, paper, or wood, and a slide projector to show pictures of the desired image. By using any of these three techniques, one could elimi-nate the precise scaling process used in theatrical stagecraft. In many cases, a mere outline of the image is sufficient to evoke the total picture. For younger children, the teacher might provide much of this environment; older children could be given the problem of developing their own setting unique to a specific area of study.

To illustrate the interdisciplinary approach using the stage-set design, we will describe a unit on the Island of Nantucket. The unit was prepared and implemented by teachers enrolled in a workshop concerning curriculum integration.

In order to create a classroom setting depicting the Island of Nantucket, the entrance into the classroom was used to simulate the ferry platform. The children who operated the ferry were responsible each day for reporting the weather, graphing the wind velocity, selling the tickets for the ferry ride, and keeping a journal of expenditures and receipts. Nets with shells, plastic lobsters, and crabs were placed along one wall of the classroom. In another area of the room, tourist shops were built. The students had to determine the main products sold on the island before setting up the shops. They sent letters to the Nantucket Chamber of Commerce and the American Automobile Association (AAA) for information about the island, its history, and points of interest. The students hung baskets of cranberries around the tourists shops, and from cardboard they constructed marshes, bogs, and seaside homes with a weathered look around the room. The window side of the classroom was ideal for a lighthouse, seascapes, and sailing ships. Within this simulated setting, role-playing, reading, experimenting, and discovering were stimulated.

In addition to teacher-designed scenery, there is a wide range of ready-made materials available to fit a variety of possible "set changes" for a unit of study. Through the use of both original and commercial resources, classroom teachers from kindergarten to grade twelve can implement the creative stage-set design.

BECOMING A FACILITATOR
OF THE LEARNING ENVIRONMENT

In becoming facilitators of the learning environment, teachers must begin with a knowledge of students, understanding of their behaviors, and an awareness of the many interacting forces that influence the teaching-learning phenomenon. The role of a teacher can be compared to that of a performing artist. Teachers have an "audience" of students to address, a classroom "stage" on which to perform, an educational message to communicate, and a "human instrument" to play the role. They perform both for and with the audience by facilitating the development of desirable understandings, attitudes, and skills. The instrument is, of course, the teacher as "self." A goal that is common to both teachers and performing artists is to convey enthusiasm; if teachers convey interest and excitement about the subject matter, the audience will catch some of that enthusiasm and respond in like fashion. Teachers are, in many ways, ultimately entertainers.

As teachers gain more knowledge about how pupils learn, they will experiment with new and better ways of creating and facilitating a learning environment that is responsive to the needs of students. A retired primary grade teacher who had been nominated year after year as the "Teacher of the Year" attributed her success to the fact that she was always willing to try out new ideas gleaned from the professional literature. If they worked, it was fine; if they did not work as well as her previous ways, she trusted her professional judgment and felt free to reject the ideas. Her example illustrates two very important factors in the professional development of teachers as facilitators of the learning environment: Teachers must remain flexible and open and willing to experiment and to evaluate new ideas.

Facilitating a learning environment requires numerous administrative skills such as planning, organizing, scheduling, decision-making, observing, and evaluating. These skills can help teachers deal with the various complexities of the classroom and thus improve the learning environment. The skills are discussed at length in chapter 8.

In our study of first-year teachers, we identified both reinforcing and stressful influences as they related to the role of teacher as facilitator of the learning environment. Some of the *reinforcing* influences included the following: observing student growth in the development of social skills; time to interact with students; ability to use divergent questioning skills for promoting discussions; use of diversified learning activities; ability to promote student self-direction and decision-making; use of various learning modes such as peer teaching, independent work, and small groups; and seeing academic progress.

The *stressful* influences included lack of time to get around and meet the individual needs of students; inordinate amounts of time spent on record-keeping to the sacrifice of "actual teaching"; lack of teacher aides to assist with some of the nonacademic responsibilities; difficulty in giving clear directions; interruptions by students who were not involved in the direct small group instruction; lack of time to design activities to keep other pupils constructively busy while the teacher was working with one small group; and parental observation in the classroom when the students seemed to be out of control.

We identified both the reinforcing and stressful influences on the role of the teacher as facilitator to help the reader become more conscious of the numerous factors that affect a teacher's effectiveness. The basic premise of this book is that teacher education cannot provide answers to specific problems teachers encounter since problems are unique to the moment-to-moment context of each situation. Furthermore, there is no such thing as one single answer to any given problem. Rather, teachers need to develop a repertoire of ideas from which to select the most appropriate solution to a specific problem.

Through analyzing the potential reinforcing and stressful influences in the following three scenarios, we hope the reader will begin to develop the ability to select and apply theoretical principles to the unique situations that arise on a daily basis. The ability to do this distinguishes the teacher as a professional from the teacher as a technician. The scenarios and the follow-up questions are included to help teachers explore far beyond a specific context to a wide range of possible classroom situations and potential reinforcing and stressful influences. The purpose of analyzing the scenarios is not to criticize the teachers described but to help teachers develop creative problem-solving approaches to the complex context that teachers and learners share. The scenarios selected for this chapter address many of the factors presented concerning the role of the teacher as facilitator of the learning environment.

As stated earlier in this chapter, the role of the teacher as facilitator of learning is to provide students with many educational opportunities and the freedom to choose from various alternatives. With many opportunities for growth and responsible independence, each pupil will gradually accept more responsibility for his or her own learning. While both opportunity and freedom to choose from numerous alternatives help to foster self-direction and responsibility, the teacher plays a vital and critical role in the development of these self-directed qualities. Teachers need to be aware of each learner's level of readiness to deal with freedom. They must balance the degree of guidance with each student's level of development.

Scenario 1

The teacher and learner together are preparing a written contract that includes specific educational goals and the instructional activities designed to achieve them. Some of the activities are assigned by the teacher; for other activities, the child has the freedom to select from the given list of choices or is encouraged to suggest other activities that will help to achieve the specific goals. Contracts are usually issued on a weekly basis. The child signs the contract as an agreement of the activities for which he or she will assume responsibility. During a contracting session, the child also shares the work accomplished during the previous week. Numerous problems arise among the children who are not getting the teacher's immediate attention. Although the ultimate goal is to help the children become self-directed in their learning, the teacher needs to be aware of the numerous dynamic influences of the total environment in which the children are involved.

The teacher was developing and discussing contracts with individual students. The other children moved from one learning center to another. Children were working in small groups, in peer teaching situations, or independently. The atmosphere was designed to encourage independence, responsibility, and trust of children in making some instructional choices. The teacher informed one student that she must finish the teacher-directed task before beginning her choice of open art in the art studio. Another child was roaming around the room aimlessly. The teacher told her to get a library book. The student said she didn't want to read. The teacher informed her that the teacher has some choices and the students have some choices; however, in this situation, the child had no choice. She threatened to take the child's recess period away if she didn't comply. The child cooperated and got her book. A short time later, the teacher asked the child if she would like to read the book to a classmate. The child responded positively to this invitation.

After the teacher had spent twenty minutes contracting with individual students, the children became restless and began interrupting her with questions. She called the whole class together to discuss the apparent problem of interruptions. One child said, "But there's nothing to do." The teacher gave several suggestions and asked the children for their ideas. Two children thought of making "letter cookies" since they were working on number formations. They proceeded to make plans for baking the cookies. One child still moaned that there was nothing to do. He was given the choice of working *now* or staying after school. Another child came to his rescue and said, "Let's play the math game together." This was a math activity prepared by the teacher for the math learning center. The teacher proceeded with the contracting activity for about ten to fifteen more minutes. She had trouble locating a child's individual contract folder. After looking desperately for it, the child found it inside his math booklet. The teacher asked the child how it got there and then reviewed with him the system for filing his papers.

DISCUSSION QUESTIONS

1. While the classroom environment encourages independence, responsibility, and trust of children in making some instructional choices, what evidence is there that the teacher sets expectations and enforces them?

2. What were the advantages of having the teacher call the whole group together to review the rule about not interrupting her while she was contracting with individual students? In what other ways might this have been handled?

3. When the two children decided to make "letter cookies," what inferences could be made regarding the classroom environment?

4. What are your reactions to the teacher's comment that the child work *now* or stay after school?

5. How would you respond to a student's refusal to join an activity or complete an assignment?

6. What types of teacher preparations are required for arranging interest centers so that teachers can be freed to spend time contracting with individual students?

7. What characteristics of an effective facilitator of the learning environment did the teacher demonstrate in this scenario?

8. What are some reasons why the children became restless? What implications do they have for pacing instruction and scheduling?

9. How should the teacher prepare for effective contracting with children?

10. What evidence was there that the teacher involved the children in the problem-solving process?

In Scenario 2, the teacher attempted to use a questioning strategy to stimulate discussion as a follow-up to a filmstrip on the nervous system. While questioning is one strategy to challenge the learner's thinking, this scenario demonstrates that other factors need to be considered in order for questioning to be successful.

Scenario 2

Thirty children were randomly seated on a carpeted floor in a large room. Children were causing disturbances while the teacher attempted to set up the filmstrip projector. She reprimanded a child by saying with a loud voice, "I'm tired of it!" Meanwhile, another child operated the filmstrip projector and recorder. The teacher stopped the recorder when she realized that the audiotape was not on the correct side. While the child changed the tape, the teacher directed review questions about the filmstrip. These questions were not prepared in advance and essentially required recall of facts. She encouraged sharing of ideas, comments, and questions. When the filmstrip resumed, the children didn't seem as attentive as before. The filmstrip was quite long. The teacher directed a follow-up discussion at the end. She then asked the children to bring in any examples of optical illusions they might have at home.

DISCUSSION QUESTIONS

1. What instructional strategies did the teacher use to make the filmstrip meaningful to the students?
2. What learning theories are reflected in the teacher's instructional procedures? What other strategies could have been used?
3. What are some examples of analytical, synthetical, and evaluative questions related to the nervous system that could be used to promote critical thinking and problem-solving?
4. What preliminary preparations could the teacher have made to prevent the initial disturbances among the children?
5. In what way did the teacher involve children in the learning environment?
6. What are the advantages and/or disadvantages of giving students a list of questions prior to viewing a filmstrip?
7. What are some higher-level research activities that could be used for a unit on the nervous system? (Refer to the higher-level problem-solving processes included in the earlier part of this chapter.)

In the earlier part of this chapter, we emphasized the value of teacher interactions with students and the need to develop a climate in which learners feel free to question, explore, and take risks. The teacher needs to interact with the students and develop activities that promote questioning. The environment must make students feel the need to ask questions and feel comfortable in asking them. Supportive responses from teachers can encourage students to ask more questions and become actively involved in learning. Although teachers are often convinced of the philosophical value of interacting with students, there are numerous constraints on the amount of time they have during the course of the day to do this. Scenario 3 demonstrates some of these pressures and constraints.

Scenario 3

The teacher was writing on the chalkboard as the children entered the classroom. She turned briefly to some of them and asked how their weekend was and continued to write on the chalkboard without stopping to listen to their responses. A child gave her a note from her mother. The teacher read the note and immediately went to the principal's office. When she returned, one of the parents was waiting to see her. Shortly afterward, a colleague came in and requested some supplies for her classroom. As the teacher talked to her colleague, a child came in with wet shoes and socks. She expressed concern about the wet socks and got a dry pair. The principal made some daily announcements over the loudspeaker. The teacher then continued with the initial activities of the day. These included very structured and routinized activities: one child read the calendar; another marked the weather on a chart. Three children were asked to share something with the class while the teacher proceeded to do the attendance and hot lunch count. She did not pay attention to what was shared and did not ask for follow-up questions. One child wanted to share his object; however, the teacher said he would have to wait until recess. The teacher reinforced good behavior by comments such as, "I like the way you're being quiet."

DISCUSSION QUESTIONS

1. Time pressure is often a problem for teachers. The hot lunch count, attendance cards, and milk count frequently must be sent to the principal's office within the first fifteen minutes of class. What are some ways of doing this rather than when children are sharing things with the class?
2. Why is it important for the teacher to be a good listener and questioner during the sharing time? What are some benefits of sharing time?
3. How could morning activities, such as the calendar date and weather, be varied?
4. What are your reactions to the way the teacher responded to the child with wet socks? What characteristic of an effective facilitator did she demonstrate in her concern for the child?
5. What preparations could the teacher make to free herself for interaction with the children as they enter the classroom?

While the scenarios described above reflect actual classroom settings, they cannot portray the numerous factors that affect the total learning context. We hope that the reader will have numerous opportunities to observe actual classroom situations or to view videotapes of classroom settings. The following general questions related to the role of the teacher as facilitator of the learning environment can be used to analyze and discuss actual or simulated classroom observations.

1. What types of instruction are portrayed: expository, inquiry, discovery, independent, experimentation? Why do you think the specific type of teaching was selected?
2. In what way does the classroom environment promote independence, problem-solving, and student self-direction?

3. How did the teacher respond to the students' questions?
4. What questions related to the observed instruction could be used to promote higher levels of thinking?
5. How do pupils interact with the teacher? Are the interactions primarily teacher-initiated or student-initiated, or is there a balance?
6. How do the students interact? What leadership qualities do they display?
7. What practical life experiences or activities could be used to help students apply the concepts they learned?
8. What community resources (human and material) could be used to enhance the instructional unit?
9. How could questioning strategies increase the amount of student interaction during group instruction and decrease the amount of teacher talk?
10. What can be learned about the management of the physical environment of the classroom?
11. How could the classroom be designed using the stage-set design approach described in this chapter?
12. What are the advantages and/or disadvantages of integrating several subjects such as math, science, social studies, and language arts into an instructional unit?

Enrichment, freedom, and responsibility are encouraged within a creative classroom environment. Enrichment is achieved through the numerous small group activities that are designed to help students become critical problem solvers; freedom is achieved by offering numerous alternatives from which the students can choose. Enrichment and freedom foster responsibility. When these characteristics exist, the classroom becomes a place where students discover the joy of knowledge, the potential of ideas, and the fun of growing. Although the emphasis is on the free and happy experience of discovery and active involvement in the learning process, the creative classroom is structured and disciplined to make the most of the few short years when young minds are most receptive to ideas and, therefore, to learning. The role of the teacher is critical in facilitating an enriched environment in which ideas are challenged, discovered, and refined.

Chapter 6

The Teacher as Researcher

AN EXPERIMENTING ROLE

If teachers are successfully to assume their responsibilities in the improvement of schools, not only must they understand research and development activities under way but they must be actively involved in these activities. Theirs is an unique contribution, without which improvement efforts are often either irrelevant, impractical or both. (DeVault, 1970, p. 4)

In general, the word *research* implies a "search" for truth. More specifically, educational research is a search for theories and practices that will help teachers create an effective teaching-learning environment for all students. Excellent teachers have always recognized the need for research as a basis for improvement of educational experiences for students. The role of teachers as researchers is a very natural one considering that teachers, because of their daily observations and interactions with students, are in a key position to gather data constantly over a long period. This cumulative information is meaningful in assessing the curriculum and other issues involved in the teaching-learning phenomenon. From their observations, teachers can make general inferences, hypothesize relationships, experiment, test out their ideas, and make decisions based on their conclusions. These are the basic steps of any research. In generating this type of first hand knowledge, teachers can bring about appropriate changes in the environment or in general teaching practices. Through experimentation, teachers can develop a strong rationale for the decisions they need to make, thus gaining more confidence in themselves as professional decision makers.

Teachers are involved throughout the day in making decisions that influence the lives of students. The quality of these decisions is often based on the adequacy and accuracy of information available. Effective decision-making requires basic knowledge of the foundations, methodology, knowledge related to the specific classroom setting, and the ability to diagnose the numerous factors that operate simultaneously in the classroom. Research can provide the comprehensive information needed for decision-making.

While decision-making is at the heart of teaching, no decision is better than the motivation used to carry it out. Changes in practice are more likely to occur if they are a result of inquiry in which teachers have been involved and for which they see some value. Just as motivation and relevance increase when students are involved personally in the learning process, so too, motivation for bringing about change increases in teachers who are actively and personally involved in solving problems through research. Through internalizing the outcomes and the process of research, teachers become more aware of the areas of teaching that are effective and those that need change.

USING THE CLASSROOM AS A RESEARCH LABORATORY

By following the basic principles of research, teachers turn their classrooms into living laboratories where hypotheses are tested and where relationships that contribute to the improvement of teaching are uncovered. Traditionally, research and evaluation have been done by professionals who function outside the classroom. However, any suggestion that the "place" of evaluation or research is in the hands of the external scholar would be most unhealthy (Scriven, 1977). Internal research and evaluation are just as necessary as external research and evaluation. If change is to take place, the teacher as an internal researcher-evaluator must be convinced of its worth.

With a focus on internal research, teachers become an integral and vital part of the research process. Instead of just filling out questionnaires, they assist in designing them; instead of just opening their classrooms for observation by outside researchers, teachers serve as partners in gathering and interpreting data. Teachers' daily observations of and sensitivities to children and the ability to relate and integrate these observations through their knowledge of human development and learning place them in a strategic position to contribute to the research process.

Dewey (1900) often spoke about this role of the teacher as researcher. He emphasized that he and his staff did not have any "ready-made principles" regarding the best education for youth. Instead, they began by looking at the problems and questions, and together they searched for solutions. One of the greatest benefits of involving teachers as researchers is that a more holistic perspective can be developed. Throughout this book, the focus has been on the ecological influences, within and beyond the classroom, that affect the moment-to-moment context. Instead of examining only one particular outcome or behavior, teachers can study the complexities of the larger teaching-learning phenomenon. Because of their cumulative knowledge of individuals over a longer period of time, teachers can begin to assess the relationships between previous events, conditions, and situations and those of the moment. Just as the Gestaltist finds more to the whole than the sum of its parts, the teacher who shares the teaching-learning context with the student can find more to describe about the student than can any external evaluator—who often comes into the classroom with preconceived ideas of what variables to study.

Hinely and Ponder (1979) emphasize the need to focus on the total environment instead of on selected predetermined variables. They feel there is a significant change in traditional classroom research that focused on predetermined ideas toward a search for understanding the complex phenomena that occur in classroom settings. The classroom environment plays a large role in shaping the behavior of the students and teachers who actively construct their own meanings for the events that occur there. Therefore, the students and teachers should be valued as potential and vital partners in the research process.

The classroom as a laboratory provides various sources for gathering data about student behaviors. These include such things as student conferences, pupils' writings, the nature and quality of student interactions, group discussions, interest questionnaires, conferences with parents, cumulative records, achievement test scores, and comparisons of work samples over a given period. None of these sources, taken individually, provides sufficient data for making educational decisions. Rather, the teacher needs to assess all of these sources to see if general patterns of behavior emerge. For example, if a parent informs the teacher that his son complains of a stomachache each morning as an excuse for not coming to school, this may alert the teacher to observe more keenly what happens to the boy at school. If the teacher observes that he is not welcomed or accepted by other students or that he stands alone on the playground, the teacher has another piece of information about the student. Through group discussions and individual conferences, the teacher might discover further information about the student's attitudes toward school.

Many times factors that may seem external to the specific problems can influence the pupils' perceptions and attitudes toward school. These factors might include the comparisons students make between themselves and others. For example, a girl's real reason for not wanting to attend school may be that she is very conscious of the fact that her clothes are old and out of style, that she has to walk to school alone while the neighbors' children get rides from their parents, that her lunch is very meager compared to that of the other children who share the table with her, or that her small, used pencils and crayons contrast with the new ones of her peers. By gathering data in a chain of events from various sources, the teacher can begin to see relationships between the child's attitudes about coming to school and her self-perceptions. Even though the teacher cannot change the student's economic situation, awareness and sensitivity can be of value in making certain decisions that influence the student. For example, to help a boy who is uncomfortable when he arrives at school, the teacher might select him to be responsible for some task such as taking the hot lunch count down to the principal each day. A decision as simple as this one indirectly tells the child and his peers that he is perceived by the teacher as a responsible, trustworthy person. The teacher, in modeling acceptance of and trust in the child, may influence his peers toward accepting him. The teacher might also want to inform the principal about this child's situation so that the principal can also reinforce the child's feelings of acceptance. Teachers need to become aware of the multiple sources for gathering data within this holistic framework. The next section describes some of these sources of data that are available daily to the classroom teacher.

COLLECTING DATA: A MULTI-FACETED APPROACH

The collection of data about students must be an ongoing process that involves multiple factors and various methods. Teachers should use a combination of approaches that focus on the multiple contexts of which the student is a part. These approaches might include observations, interactions, communications with parents, adviser/advisee conferences, work samples, tests, and records of each student's progress. Each of these approaches is discussed briefly in this section.

Observations of a student and his or her actions and reactions both inside and outside the classroom can reveal important aspects of the student's personality, development, and academic or social progress. The way in which a student works by himself or herself may or may not indicate that student's ability to work alone. A student who is able to remain on task when working alone may be revealing several things. He or she may be exhibiting confidence in the ability to solve problems or to grasp the concepts that are being studied. A student who cannot remain on task or who is distracted by the sights and sounds of others may not be demonstrating an unwillingness to work; rather, he or she may be exhibiting a need for support and encouragement from others or a lack of understanding of the concepts or knowledge involved in the task. Decisions regarding the organization of students for small group, individualized, or teacher-aided instruction can in part be based on observations by the teacher.

Observing students in their interactions with their peers can also reveal their level of social development. Understanding not only the quantity of such interactions but also their quality can lead teachers to a better understanding of students. A student who "buys" attention or friendship with candy, parties, or possessions may be making a statement about his or her own self-concept and self-worth. Those students who are chosen first and those who are chosen last to participate on teams during recess or gym class are being labeled by their peers, and teachers must take note of this. Choice under these circumstances may indicate either physical prowess or social development; the first child chosen for a team may be the one who is best liked rather than the most coordinated.

Observations are sometimes important in pinpointing students' physical difficulties. A student who constantly squints at the words written on the chalkboard may be communicating a need to the teacher. The same is true for the student who constantly asks that oral instructions be repeated or who never seems quite able to follow instructions as they are given.

Interacting with students is another important way in which teachers collect data. Students respond to events in school from their past experiences and from their understanding of what happens around them; the manner in which students respond to a teacher is based not only on the context of that momentary encounter but on the numerous other contexts of which they are a part. Teachers can gain understanding of students' perceptions from these interactions and can respond accordingly. A student may push a teacher's understanding and patience to the limit; the student may, through word and deed, seem to demand physical isolation or punishment as the only means of changing behavior.

Teachers' interactions with students may be facilitated by a series of probing questions. Students' interactions may also be facilitated by a teacher's willingness and ability to trust and to be open with them. Through such interactions, students reveal beliefs, concerns, and goals that should and must be incorporated into the instructional plan for each individual.

As suggested in chapter 3, communicating with parents is another essential source of data about students. Through in-home visitations, parent-teacher conferences, and publication of and response to newsletters, teachers discover a plethora of information about their students. Only through understanding of the ethnic, socioeconomic, and cultural attitudes of the home environment can teachers understand the drives and the motivations of students. And it is only through understanding these varied and multiple backgrounds that teachers can begin to educate students about the multiple contexts of other people. The attitudes of students toward school, teachers, themselves, and others can be placed in a more appropriate perspective when teachers communicate with parents about these factors. Communication as a method of gathering data about students can be accomplished by the formulating and asking of appropriate questions, and such questions may become the basis of parent-teacher conferences. Information about attitudes and beliefs might also be gathered through carefully constructed questionnaires completed by parents.

Through the use of an adviser/advisee conference, teachers can gain additional knowledge and insight about students. For such a program, the teacher regularly sets aside a specified time to meet with each student in the class. This is a time for discussion of concerns, social or academic progress, or interests that the teacher and the student share. This conference time is ideal for individual work on values clarification and on the establishment of an individualized course of study. The time parameters of the secondary classroom and the limits imposed by the sheer number of students involved may restrict the opportunities for establishing such a program; however, those times set aside for individual conferences about writing assignments may be utilized for adviser/advisee concerns. The fact that student writing often reveals attitudes and beliefs may aid the teacher in opening a discussion about the content as well as the mechanics of a writing assignment. Book reports, history papers, and mathematics and science projects can be discussed in individual conferences.

Student work samples provide another primary source of data. These work samples are revealing not only through content but also through their precision and neatness. A paper, for example, written on the topic "What I Would Buy If I Had a Million Dollars," can provide a teacher with many different perceptions and with a great deal of information about the author. Students' attitudes about money, themselves, or family and friends may be apparent in the ways they would spend that million dollars. The writing assignment also shows grasp of organization and of mechanical skills of language arts. If students have difficulty seeing, there may be evidence in the paper of consistently transposed letters or of cramped handwriting. Any assignment that requires students to put pencil to paper can reveal much more about them than their knowledge of particular concepts or ideas.

Testing of students can be a valid source of information if the results are interpreted by professionals who are knowledgeable about testing and who have a thorough understanding of pupils and educational practice. Test scores should be viewed in their relationship to other indicators of student ability and progress. Viewed in isolation, such results indicate only a particular student's performance on a specific test on a given day; viewed as an integral part of a student's academic and social record, such results can gain real significance.

Although standardized tests are valuable sources of data, they are only one source. Their results are not infallible. Circumstances within the multiple contexts of which the student is a part influence the reliability or lack of reliability of the test results. Factors that might influence test results include the pupil's health; the emotional environment on the specific day on which the test was taken; the student's home life, including the language spoken and the nature of the setting (urban or rural); the student's perception of the test directions; and the anxiety level due to time constraints on various sections of the test. In analyzing test results, the teacher's professional judgment of the learner's ability and progress is extremely important. If a great discrepancy exists between test results and the teacher's professional judgment, further data should be collected. In many cases, the professional judgment of a competent teacher is more accurate than the test results.

Teacher-written tests may provide additional information about students and their grasp of concepts. Test results, when taken into consideration with other information concerning the pupil, reveal many aspects of the student's education.

Tests that are administered intermittently to all students in the system can be viewed in relationship to each student's own past performance on the test battery. In general, grades involve value judgments on the part of the teacher. As professionals, teachers need to trust their judgment, which includes both analytical and intuitive knowledge about students and their moment-to-moment environment. Grades may indicate success or lack of success in meeting the requirements and skill levels for a particular grade. They may also reflect any number of the multiple contexts of which the student is a part. Grades might be affected by a change in the home environment such as a divorce, a remarriage, or the death of a parent. Sometimes grades indicate past failures of teachers to diagnose a learning disability or physical impairment. In comparison with the predicted or actual grade-level achievement as indicated through standardized tests, grades can also show a student's work as being above or below the tested level — indicating a need to review the program and the learning approaches with which the student is involved.

Teachers must remember that test results can show more than student achievement; teacher failure or achievement is also indicated. Perhaps the fault lies with the teacher's inability to present the material in an understandable fashion rather than with the student's inability to grasp and understand the concepts presented. Perhaps the test is inappropriate because the teacher is unaware of the student's level of development.

Teachers have a responsibility to understand each student in the class. This is best done through an ongoing research process. This research can be conducted, in part, through an investigation and understanding of the achievement tests that are a part of each student's permanent record. However, the facts and figures contained in such records cannot and should not be the only source of information. A collection of student work samples, dated and viewed in chronological order, can be a more concrete source of data—for teachers and parents as well as for students. Anecdotal records of students' social development through the course of a school year provide teachers with another framework for understanding students and programs. A student's journal of perceptions and feelings about self, school, family, and peers may be the most valid form of data about developmental progress through a year of education. All of these sources and factors must be included if the teacher, the parents, and the student are to have valid and useful data that can be used in making decisions concerning a learner and his or her education.

GATHERING AND USING DATA
IN THE EDUCATIONAL SETTING

An example of how numerous sources can supply information that leads to effective decision-making is in the area of evaluating certain curricula or textbooks. One of the authors (Heck) was recently asked to evaluate an individualized mathematics program. She perceived the teachers of the school to be the critical persons throughout this evaluation and formed a true partnership with them. Heck initially held individual conferences with each teacher who taught mathematics.

Working as a team, the teachers and evaluator developed the specific purposes of the mathematics evaluation project. These purposes were to review the mathematics curriculum used in grades one through eight, including textbooks and instructional materials; the instructional methods used to implement the mathematics program; the class schedule and time commitment to the program; the students' rates of progression through the various mathematics topics; and their retentions and applications of basic mathematics concepts. The project was also designed to make programmatic recommendations based on the data reviewed. Again, teachers had to be active in the decision-making process.

Five basic processes were to be used in gathering data: interviews, classroom observations, review of standardized test results, taped sessions of students' thought processes used in mathematics, and written comments from high school students who had completed the individualized mathematics program at the elementary school level. Detailed descriptions of the data collection process are provided here as a model of how a teacher can truly assume the role of a researcher or evaluator of any curricular program.

Interviews were held with elementary school teachers, high school personnel, and high school students. The purpose of these individual conferences was to better understand the program and to gather information about teachers' and students' perceptions of its strengths and weaknesses. Virtually all of the high school students interviewed were graduates of the elementary school where the individualized mathematics program was used.

Each of the teachers responsible for mathematics instruction was observed. The purpose was to observe the instructional program in action, the role of students in the process of learning, the role of the teacher in implementing the mathematics program, and the managerial logistics in administering the program. Follow-up conferences were held to give each teacher an opportunity to discuss and explain methods and instructional practices.

Both the teachers and the evaluator reviewed the standardized tests. The purpose was to analyze areas of strength and weakness and to see, by comparing a group of students as they moved from one grade to the next, if any general content area of weakness was evident.

The teachers who were responsible for teaching mathematics at the elementary school level gave a cumulative test to each child to determine his or her level of achievement in the individualized program. Following the adminstration of the test, preservice teachers under the guidance of the evaluator conducted taped interviews with all of the students in the school. The students were divided into groups of four or five for each taped session. The cumulative tests given by the teachers on the previous day were used in the sessions, and the elementary school children were asked to explain *how* and *why* they performed various mathematics computations in solving a problem. The primary purposes of this taped interview were to analyze problem-solving thought processes and to assess students' concept development as opposed to computational skills.

In the upper grades, students were also asked about their perceptions of the strengths and weaknesses of the individualized mathematics program. Those responses were recorded on audiotapes. The teachers then reviewed the transcriptions of the tapes. They commented frequently on how valuable these data were in understanding the progress of students. In addition to the tapes, a random sample of high school students was also asked to write perceptions of the mathematics program.

An evaluation of this nature offers numerous sources of data from which strengths and weaknesses can be reviewed. Those influenced most by the mathematics program—the students and the teachers— were involved actively throughout the evaluation. As the results of the study were analyzed, only the findings that appeared consistently across all sources of data were considered. For example, the comments of high school students as a single source of data were totally insufficient for making curriculum decisions; however, these comments, when verified through classroom observations of the same factors and through interviews with the teachers, became very important data. The data that consistently appeared from several sources were then summarized. These data served as the bases for recommendations. Again, teachers were involved in reviewing the data and in suggesting and verifying the recommendations. Having been an integral part of the research process, the teachers were not only willing but also eager to make the suggested changes. This type of inquiry into "what is" and "what could be" serves as a basis for bringing about meaningful educational change.

The emerging interest in qualitative research holds great promise for involving teachers as active participants in the research process. Furthermore, the holistic perspective of naturalistic inquiry overcomes some of the limitations of the narrow focus of some conventional research.

A study of a child from a more holistic perspective is included here. The narrative, prepared by a graduate student who was the child's teacher the previous year, reflects cumulative data about an individual child. The sources of data in this description are similar to those available to any teacher on a daily basis.

Ann is a fifth grader. Although the school year is only seven weeks old, there have been noticeable and significant problems with her behavior that have not been evident in previous years. The changes seem to be emotional in nature rather than academic. The causes of these problems must, I feel, be identified before Ann's emotional well-being and academic progress become adversely affected.

For this study, data about the student's personal and academic progress were collected from the following sources: interviews with family, school personnel, and peers; examination of work samples; review of the student's cumulative folder; and observations in the classroom, cafeteria, gymnasium, and on the playground.

Ann is ten years and eleven months old, four feet eleven inches tall, and weighs ninety-eight pounds. She lives with her mother, father, thirteen-year-old sister, and five-year-old brother. Her mother is employed, and her father is presently unemployed. Both mother and father are high school graduates, and the father has had two years of postsecondary education. Ann's sister is an honor student at the middle school and a first chair violinist in the school orchestra.

Ann's previous years of schooling were quite successful both academically and socially. She has maintained all "A's" since her first-grade days and has always been in the ninth stanine on standardized tests in reading and math.

Ann has studied the piano since she was five and is now also learning to play the clarinet. During third and fourth grades, she was involved in "City Enrichment Series," a program for gifted and talented students. Ann has received every award the school is able to present to its academically successful students. She has been involved in Girl Scouts for three years and is very active in a church youth group.

In reviewing the cumulative folder, I found a drastic difference in Ann's attendance and tardiness record from the first four years of school. In the past, Ann was absent no more than two days per year. This is contrasted to six days absent and three days tardy for the first seven weeks of this school year. Her records indicate excellent health with no physical defects. Her standardized test scores are all in the ninety-fifth percentile or higher.

The school librarian stated that Ann, in earlier years, had always checked out many books and had no trouble making choices. This year Ann has on many occasions lingered in the library after the rest of the class has left. Ann stayed longer under the pretense that she could not make selection decisions. The librarian said Ann indicated that no one bothered her, but she just enjoyed the quietness and orderliness of the library.

The nurse has seen Ann on three occasions this year because of upset stomach and crying spells. Each time, when nothing was found wrong, Ann would beg to go home because she said she hated school. The nurse was confused and shocked by this display of behavior because it was different from Ann's positive attitudes of the past.

Ann's mother and father were quite concerned about her change in behavior. Every morning it was a chore for them to get Ann to go to school. This was frustrating for Ann's parents because she had always loved school. The parents expressed disappointment that a conference with Ann's teacher was fruitless. Ann's sister was blunt about the situation and indicated that Ann hated the class because "it was so noisy and stupid." Ann's classmates disclosed that Ann was the smartest girl in the class, that everyone liked her, and that she didn't like the class because everyone was "so bad."

Ann's teacher was a substitute who was certified as a secondary physical education teacher. She had no experience as an elementary teacher and the only orientation she had received consisted of basic information about school rules and the daily routine. The substitute had been in the class for seven weeks. She knew nothing of the school's recently adopted reading program. The teacher was aware that Ann was very bright; however, to keep her from being bored, she was kept busy helping other children with their work. This approach was unsuccessful as all findings show that Ann was quite bored.

Classroom observations showed that whenever the class was completely out of control, Ann would either put her head down on her desk or ask to be excused to go to the restroom. She would remain at the restroom for at least ten minutes. When excused for instrumental music lessons, which was twice a week, Ann would almost run out of the room. During reading time Ann would constantly wear a frown and very seldom participated in discussion.

Ann was interviewed individually concerning her dislike of school. She was extremely uncomfortable with the noisy classroom and said she was glad school was so easy because she certainly could not concentrate. Ann said she hated reading class more than her other subjects because she had completed the text, workbook, and literature book last year with "A" work and was forced to do the same work over this year. Ann asked at the end of the interview if school was going to be like this from now on.

When we review the findings, a striking contrast can be clearly seen between Ann's behavior in grades one through four and that of the present school year. Ann's actions and attitudes toward school are very quickly changing from positive to negative. All observations and interviews indicate that Ann is having a terrible school year. Although her grades have not yet suffered, she is in danger of losing interest in school.

In the role of the teacher as researcher, the primary responsibility is to gather as much information as possible about each student. This narrative exemplifies the extensive sources of information about each pupil in the classroom that are available on a daily basis. A teacher's daily observations and interactions with a student, interviews with significant others who share the learning context with him or her, and a careful analysis of a student's cumulative record, with its variety of materials, results, and reports can be valuable sources of information. Used wisely and with training regarding the interpretation of the test results, these multiple sources of data can give the teacher a beginning— a foundation from which to adapt and tailor education to meet the individual needs and abilities of each student.

TOWARD BECOMING A RESEARCHER

Just as the art of observing is intrinsic to effective teaching, so too, observations serve as the initial step in the research process. Observations extend beyond merely watching students perform or evaluating the final outcome of a learning activity, and they should focus on the processes rather than the final product. During the course of a day, the entire spectrum of human drama unfolds: joys and frustrations; interactions and reactions; successes and failures; acceptances and rejections. The keen observer is aware of each of these events and their impact on the individual student. The keen observer is also a perceptive listener and questioner who must attend to the interactions students have with their peers and other adults, encourage questions, and note nonverbal communications.

These observations should extend to both the formal and informal settings of which students are a part. Often behaviors in the classroom differ from behaviors in the cafeteria or on the playground. Some students act differently in small group discussions. Some students work better independently while others need the support of their peers. Some students come to school rested while others seem exhausted. These are just a few examples of the factors teachers observe during the course of the day. One single factor, perhaps, is not very significant and may lead to an inaccurate or harmful conclusion. However, as teachers begin to accumulate or record data over a period of time, the interrelationships of these factors and the patterns that emerge become significant. It is important for teachers to arrange some systematic method of recording the information collected by these observations so that it can be stored for later reference.

THE ART OF OBSERVATION

Classroom observations are often restricted to an anecdotal accounting of an interaction between a student and a teacher, a student and the environment, one student and another, and so forth. Then, from the data collected, an observer attempts to draw conclusions and make decisions as to what actions might be taken. The information gained by such an observation is of course important. However, it is far from complete and cannot provide the basis for informed decision-making.

All behavior takes place within a context. It is this context that gives meaning and understanding to an observation. Thus, classroom observation must also include a moment-by-moment description of the dynamic context within which an interaction is occurring.

Most behavior is purposeful. That is, the person or persons being observed have reasons for their behavior. Thus, for observers to understand or explain an interaction, the subjects being observed must be involved — they should be questioned as to why they behaved as they did.

The data recorded in any observation are affected by the person who records them. A person observes a phenomenon through eyes that are influenced by what has been seen before, through the values that he or she holds. Thus, a classroom observation must contain information about the person doing the observing.

A classroom observation is influenced by the level of knowledge and understanding of both the subjects and observer. A person who has limited knowledge about classrooms, about the principles of good education, or about the developmental needs of learners will see and interpret information differently than a person who has such knowledge. It is therefore important to gather data concerning the student's development as well as data concerning the knowledge and understanding levels of the observer.

Observational data contain more than what is seen. They include that which is heard, smelled, felt, and "sensed." Such data are only useful when viewed from many angles. Just as one would not expect a doctor to reach a decision based on a single bit of information, neither should an educator use limited data in making decisions.

All persons perceive things as they believe them to be. They use these perceptions in making decisions. For most people, perceptions are constantly changing. As they gain new information (and this is always happening), their perceptions are changed and their decisions may be changed. Thus, any observation contains perceptions—perceptions of the observer and of the participants.

Classroom observation is very difficult and complex. It requires perseverance and rigor. Much of the data obtained through observation is subjective. Classroom observation is, however, a valuable educational resource for both those being observed and those doing the observing. It is, we believe, one of the best tools available for increasing one's knowledge about students and about teaching. It is a tool that can improve the quality of decision-making.

The following plan describes a series of steps that might be followed in observing classroom interaction. It is a comprehensive plan — one designed to provide understanding of the interaction and the many factors that affect it. This plan is not a model that should be followed slavishly. Rather, it is presented as a guide that can make classroom observations more meaningful and valuable.

Sample Plan for Observing Classroom Interaction

1. Identify the actors you wish to observe (a teacher and student, a parent and child) and position yourself where you are unobtrusive but have access to the most significant data sources (that is, you can hear conversations, see movements and expressions, and sense the emotional tone).

2. Describe the environment within which the interaction is taking place. Be sure to include both the physical and emotional environments. This description might include information about the number of people in the room, their location, the amount of noise in the room, or the feeling tone which seems to exist.

3. Describe the actors involved in the interaction—you might include information such as the approximate ages, their roles or relationships, their sexes and their appearances.

4. Describe your own past experiences, age, sex, interests, values, family status, education, and professional roles.

5. Briefly observe the interaction within the small group of persons. Prepare an anecdotal record (a running account) on everything that occurs between the participants or between them and the environ-

ment. Valuable information can be gained from one observation of five or ten minutes. However, more reliable information will be gained through a series (perhaps three or four) of such short observations.

6. Drawing upon all of these sources of information, interpret the observation in terms of *your own perceptions*. What do you think is happening? What is your reaction to what you observed? Are there factors about you and your background that might be influencing your perceptions?

7. Based on the information gathered, describe what might be the perceptions of the participants in the observations. How might they be interpreting the interaction? How might they be feeling about the situation? You will, of course, have no definitive information as to how the participants might be perceiving the interaction. You should therefore try to describe two or more possible alternative ways in which each participant might interpret the interaction.

8. From all of the data available, you are now able to make decisions that are more sensitive to the needs of learners and more responsive to the principles of sound educational practice.

Using this suggested framework for observing, the reader is encouraged to observe children in both formal and informal settings. The same framework could be used in analyzing videotapes, simulations, or written scenarios. Actual observations, of course, are much more valuable since the observer is able to obtain more first-hand information and to better assess the emotional context.

In an effort to help the reader develop the art and skill of a researcher, we have included a scenario that reflects actual data gathered about one child. Discussion questions, included at the end of the scenario, should help develop an awareness of the numerous ecological factors that influence each learner's growth and development. The account was written by a graduate student who tutors this child.

The child in this study is a nine-and-one-half-year-old girl. According to the information in her cumulative folder, her kindergarten adjustment was smooth and quite successful. On her grade card, every skill was accomplished at grade level, indicated by a check mark on the report card. There was no skill that she did not master. The teacher's only comment was that the student was very quiet at school.

The first grade report showed that the student was below level in reading skills. She could not read orally with fluency, and she lacked comprehension in reading. These were indicated on the grade card by blanks (meaning the skill is not yet achieved). Her grade card also indicated that she was very neat, that she completed all work on time, that she followed directions, and that she had no problems in arithmetic that was at grade level. The Metropolitan Achievement Test given at the end of the first grade showed her to be functioning at slightly below grade level in both reading and arithmetic. Her scores in language arts, science, and social studies indicated that she was functioning above grade level in these areas. The teacher recommended retention in first grade because of "weak reading skills." The parents refused to allow the child to be retained in first grade, so she was placed in second grade.

In second grade, this student's report card indicated that she was able to comprehend what she read, but she was not able to read orally with fluency. She was marked below level in reading every quarter. Her work habits were marked excellent, as were the categories "attitude" and "respect for others." Her arithmetic skills showed need for improvement ("N") in addition and subtraction facts. She was not able to complete the timed tests on the basic addition and subtraction facts in the given amount of time. The Basic Skills Test given in second grade, at the end of the year, showed her scores in reading and arithmetic to be slightly below grade level. Scores in social studies and science were above grade level. The second grade teacher recommended that the student be retained in second grade because of her lack of reading skills. The parents again refused, and she was placed in the third grade.

In third grade, the student received a plus indicating the skill was accomplished in all areas of reading except oral reading and answering questions orally. She was marked "at level" in reading. In arithmetic she received "N" (needs improvement) in subtraction facts (time tests of the subtraction facts) and an "N" in story problems. All other skills were accomplished at grade level. Her work habits were rated excellent ("E"). At the end of the third grade, she was given the Metropolitan Achievement Test in two forms: Form JS was given to the entire class, and Form F was given to the student by a tutor. On Form JS she scored below grade level in both reading and arithmetic. On Form F she scored above grade level in reading. The arithmetic was not administered a second time. The third grade teacher promoted her to fourth grade.

The cumulative folder also showed that the student has 20/30 vision, is driven to school by her parents, and has an exemption from required immunization. The student's father is a self-employed mason whose work is not very steady. Her mother is a homemaker. The mother underwent a mastectomy when the student was in the second grade. The mother has stated that the doctors have given her no hope as the cancer has advanced to the lymph glands. The mother cries frequently and often in front of the child. The mother said that she tries not to cry in front of the child but that at times she cannot stop crying. The mother also said that the girl gets a stomachache every morning before going to school if she has a test that day.

The girl has a sister who is twenty-four and a brother who is twenty-nine. They both spend time with their younger sister every week. Neither sibling has lived at the parents' home in the past six years.

Each one of this student's past teachers was interviewed. Every teacher agreed that she was a very hard worker, very conscientious and neat, and somewhat of a perfectionist. Every teacher observed that she did not have any close friends in the class. She was well liked by the class but did not play with anyone. She did not like recess according to her first and second grade teachers. These teachers also said the student's reading skills were very erratic.

The interview with the girl herself revealed that she "likes school but has trouble with timed math tests." She also stated that her teacher likes her but not her ideas. She felt her teacher does not listen to her or her problems. She said she is afraid to ask for help. She worries about getting good grades and said it is not quiet enough at school. Her favorite subjects are art and social studies.

An observation was conducted at the child's school during the beginning of the day. The teacher was doing boardwork with the class. The student sat upright in her chair; her eyes sparkled, and she smiled when she saw the observer. She moved around in her chair more and more as the lesson went on. She continually looked to the left and right at the other children near her. Her hands went back and forth across her desk once in a while. Her feet changed position as she would turn periodically in her chair. Her facial expression appeared relaxed at the beginning of the session, but later in the session, she pursed her lips and knit her eyebrows. She then began to twist her hands together. The teacher called on her. She thought for some time and said, "I don't know." As she said this, she quickly looked to the left and to the right. She then rested her head on her arm on top of her desk. Later, in a smaller reading group of five children, she sat silently and answered two comprehension questions aloud correctly. Later, she read orally in this small group. During seatwork time, she worked slowly but did a neat job. All of her answers were correct. She was the last one to finish. When the class lined up for gym, she walked slowly to the back of the line. She was by herself.

The child gave the observer two particular papers from her art and social studies classes, the two classes she "likes the most." She said she was proud of her work in these classes. She takes pride in doing a neat job but sometimes sacrifices too much time for neatness. She is a slow worker.

Having known and tutored this child for three years, the observer had access to a wealth of data that many classroom teachers would not have. The observer has seen her over a long period on a one-to-one basis and has been confided in by the mother many times about the child's problems. To understand all the data, one must first of all understand the child. She is a child born later in life to the family. She was surrounded by adults from early childhood. She lived the first seven years of her life on a farm excluded from neighborhood children. The mother has said that she did not want her child "playing with those other children." She was not permitted to ride the school bus for fear the other children might hurt her. When she first began to be tutored at seven years of age, she begged to play with the observer's two children instead of being tutored. She said she never had anyone to play with. Yet at recess, in school, she was afraid to play with the children because "they would make fun of her." Observation at school showed that she cared greatly about what the other children thought of her. Her mind was more on the other children than on her work. This was supported by the fact that at every grade level, first, second, and third, she did poorly in oral reading. She was afraid of making a mistake that other children would recognize. When she read orally, her eyes would dart to the left and to the right as she watched to see the other children's reactions. Consequently, she would often lose her place, repeat what she had already read, and lose all fluency. She did not seem to be able to separate her work from the influence of the children around her. This was also supported in the third grade when she took the Metropolitan Test Form JS. When she took the test in class with twenty-two other children, her scores in reading indicated performance below grade level. When she was given the Metropolitan Achievement Test Form F in a room all by herself, she finished the test before time with scores that were well above grade level. This student needs a quiet place to work, free from distraction, but she also needs to be exposed to other children so that she gets accustomed to working with others around her.

DISCUSSION QUESTIONS

1. What factors must the teacher consider in administering tests to this child and in interpreting their results?
2. What instructional implications are there for this child regarding small group, large group, or peer teaching?
3. In what way could the teacher capitalize on this child's favorite subjects of art and social studies?
4. What are the implications of the mother's physical illness in terms of the role of the teacher as understander of students' behaviors?

5. What recommendations might the teacher make to the parents regarding the child's need to make friends?
6. What factors might be considered in structuring a learning environment to meet this child's learning preferences?
7. What could the teacher do to help this child gain greater confidence in herself?
8. What could the teacher do to help facilitate greater acceptance of this child by other children in the classroom?

TEACHERS AS CONSUMERS OF RESEARCH

While not all teachers may be involved in producing an original scientific piece of research, because of the professional nature of teaching, all teachers must be consumers of research. Research findings should provide a rationale for the educational decisions teachers are continually making. Reading professional journals is a basic means of keeping informed. This is not an "extra activity" to be undertaken if and when time permits. Rather, teachers need to view professional reading as an essential ongoing preparation for teaching.

Teachers who are dedicated to excellence in education need to take the initiative for staying informed about important findings in today's knowledge explosion. It is essential that professional educators know and understand the research related to their disciplines if they are to participate in meaningful educational innovation and change. It is equally important to be aware of national and international issues and trends both in education and in all areas of human development.

Specific suggestions for helping teachers maintain relevance in their disciplines are given in chapter 1. The important factor is that teachers who are dedicated to excellence in education must also be dedicated to studying the results of research. They must be self-directed in their pursuit of new knowledge and theories. While membership in professional societies, attendance at professional conferences in which relevant research studies are discussed, and reading of professional journals all assist in providing relevant information, the teacher alone can use this information in a specific teaching-learning context. No one can "prescribe" what is best for a particular situation. Rather, as Eisner (1979) points out, research helps us to focus attention on aspects of classroom life that we might otherwise neglect. The major need is to be able to view situations from the varied perspectives that different theories provide and thus to be in a position to avoid the limited vision of a single view. Professional growth activities provide a repertoire of ideas from which the teacher can draw when a specific situation warrants it.

As consumers of research, teachers need to develop those skills necessary to critically analyze the validity and reliability of research results. Entire college courses are offered to help the reader critically analyze the scientific design of research in order to assess whether the results are reliable, consistent, and predictable. It is not our purpose to discuss the complexities involved in analyzing research; rather, readers are encouraged to locate one of the numerous research methodology texts available for this purpose. The reader needs to be aware that not all published articles meet the criteria of good research.

Criteria for judging good research differ according to the type of research being evaluated. In general, research can be classified as quantitative or qualitative. The mathematics research study described earlier in this chapter is an example of qualitative research. The major features of qualitative research, as summarized by Parlett and Hamilton (1972), are the following: the study focuses on the day-to-day reality of settings; an information profile is assembled from numerous sources such as observations, interviews, and documentary and background sources; issues are progressively clarified and redefined; alternative interpretations are continuously weighed in light of new information; and an effort is made to get a perspective of how events are regarded by different people.

Qualitative research is used when one wants to learn something about certain cases in depth without needing to generalize to all such cases. This approach is very valuable for classroom teachers who want to study their own unique classrooms and the specific school-community contexts.

A critical reader of qualitative research must examine several areas. He or she should examine the completeness of the data, that is, whether information on the perspectives of people involved in the significant multiple contexts has been gathered. The reader should be informed whether the findings reported were clarified and verified across various sources of data. For example, in our study of first-year teachers, it was extremely important to verify comments made by the principals through follow-up interviews with the first-year teachers, actual classroom observations, and a review of the videotapes of the classroom settings. Only findings that occur frequently, referred to as "patterns" by Patton (1980), should be reported as significant data. A single event does not provide significant information for making program decisions. Finally, because samples in qualitative research are usually quite small, the reader should be cautious not to generalize the data beyond the subjects being studied.

The major distinguishing features of quantitative research are the data collection procedures and the selection of the sample. In collecting data, researchers predetermine and carefully define the variables to be studied. The sample is larger than that required in qualitative research. In quantitative research, the reader should give particular attention to the description, selection, and size of the population from which the data were collected. Conclusions can be generalized only to similar representative groups. For example, if a questionnaire was administered to a group of six-year-old children in a rural community who are enrolled in a learning disabilities class, results can be generalized only to children with similar characteristics and not to all six-year-olds. It is critical that the sample be representative of the population from which it is selected. Random samples are much more reliable in terms of generalizing to similar situations or populations.

Teachers need to integrate their own experiential knowledge with the findings of other researchers. They should not accept all findings as "absolute truth," especially if these findings seem to contradict knowledge gleaned from daily experiences with students. Rather, teachers need to analyze, interpret, and select the findings that seem relevant to their own specific classrooms.

Another factor to consider in analyzing articles is the manner in which the data were collected. Teachers are in a key position to question whether the procedures were both feasible and comprehensive enough to provide a holistic view of the situation. If a locally prepared instrument or questionnaire was used, evidence should be presented to attest to the validity and reliability of the instrument. The purpose of research is to enable one to make recommendations; however, without the assurance that the results are both valid and reliable, it would be dangerous to make recommendations. Articles included in reputable journals are less likely to have faulty research designs.

No teacher can keep up with all of the literature in education or even maintain a thorough awareness in specific areas of interest. No other social science has had an information explosion rivaling that which has taken place in education over the last twenty years. If teachers are to provide the type of education that is needed by learners in the late twentieth century, they must become researchers—professionals who are always in search of theories and practices that will help them to become better teachers.

Chapter 7

The Teacher as Program Developer
A CREATING ROLE

> Implementation of curriculum changes is more successful if the users [teachers] have had something to do with design, writing, or choosing the curriculum philosophy and instructional materials. Large scale curriculum models developed in large educational communities such as district, county, state, or federal levels sooner or later fall into disuse. The professional growth that goes into developing curriculum may be worth more than actually using it. The single most important element in learning success may be the enthusiastic teacher using instructional designs and materials which she or he has developed. (Bailey & Neale, 1980, p. 75)

The role of the teacher as program developer can be discussed from two perspectives: involvement in the development of the general curriculum goals and policies and involvement in the specific curriculum decisions that need to be made on a daily basis. The latter perspective is discussed extensively in chapter 10. This chapter focuses on the teacher and significant others within the total school-community context who are or should be involved in general curriculum development.

The influence of the ecological context on the diversified roles of the teacher has been a major focus throughout this book. Again, the role of the teacher as program developer is influenced by political, cultural, technological, and social realities. For example, in the 1950s, the success of Russian space technology influenced curriculum goals, bringing forth a rebirth of interest in the mathematics and science curriculum. Millions of dollars were allocated to prepare teachers in science and mathematics. Curriculum materials were designed that focused on one common goal: the development of problem-solving skills that would be necessary for survival in an ever-changing technological society. Similarly, computer technology is now having its impact on the curricula.

The impact of the social context on curriculum development has for many years been recognized by progressive educators. These educators often criticized the separation of school programs from the realities and demands of life. Dewey (1900) wrote that the scheme of a curriculum must adapt to the needs of existing community life and must be selected with the intention of improving the life we live in common so that the future will be better than the past. Similarly, contemporary educators recognize that curriculum improvement cannot be accomplished without attention to the context of the school's community, culture, and organization. Historically, our schools have responded to changing societal demands. Tyler (1975) has emphasized that "responding to the need for the school to participate constructively and energetically in the reconstruction of the total educational environment in which children grow up will require new thinking, new planning, and new practices" (p. 13). Societal changes have made curriculum planning more complex. From his review of research and curriculum policy, Boyd (1978) has concluded, "If there is one proposition about curriculum politics that is clear, it is that the school curriculum becomes an issue in communities and societies that are undergoing significant change" (p. 48).

The advent of high technology, as exemplified by the use of hand-held calculators in the mathematics classroom, initially met with varying levels of success. The success, or lack of it, can often be traced to the communities in which such technology was introduced. In city schools, set in a community where new technology was in evidence in local businesses and industries, calculators became a fixture with relative rapidity and ease. However, in small rural schools, frequently isolated from the technology of the city both in attitude and in actuality, the use of a calculator was seen as taking time from the "essentials of education." Thus, acceptance and adoption were much slower.

The technology of television media and the advances in knowledge that came with that technology also had an impact on the curriculum. Many teachers found it necessary to compete in the classroom with the entertainment approach to learning that students were getting at home. The graphic realities of war that appeared on the television screen changed "the world of reality" and the values of those who live in that world. Students were no longer content to be preached at regarding "rights" and "wrongs" as seen through the eyes of historians in textbooks; they wanted to make their own judgments and were willing to question the truth and impact of history. Instead of "preaching" about the great American values, the curriculum began incorporating values clarification strategies that allowed a "questioning" attitude toward societal values. Simulations and role-play activities began to be used in many areas of the curriculum.

Traditionally, schools were charged with maintaining the beliefs and value structures of the community. As such, schools have transmitted middle-class values that are more or less conservative (Corwin, 1965). If schools are to meet the needs of our constantly changing technological society and are to present multifaceted and multicultural viewpoints without offending the community, there needs to be systematic involvement of the community in studying, questioning, and challenging the past. Without community involvement, programmatic changes often run counter to the school's culture and the community's expectations, values, and mores.

EDUCATIONAL GOALS:
A BASIS FOR CONTINUOUS PROGRAM DEVELOPMENT

If teachers are to become effective program developers, they need to broaden their definition of education beyond academic achievement. Kliebard (1972) has recognized the individualized nature of the curriculum. He has compared it to a route over which students travel under the leadership of an experienced guide and companion. Each traveler is affected differently by the journey since its effect is at least as much a function of his or her intelligence, interests, and intent as it is the contours of the route. This variability is not only inevitable but wondrous and desirable. Therefore, no effort is made to anticipate the exact nature of the effect on the traveler, but a great effort is made to plot the route so that the journey will be as rich, fascinating, and memorable as possible.

Curriculum objectives need to integrate academic achievement with personal and other social areas of development. The description of these areas presented here is not exhaustive but rather representative of the more holistic view of educational goals. Personal development includes the acquisition of knowledge, attitudes, and skills that enhance one's confidence in the dignity and worth of self and others. Personal development encompasses self-motivation and self-direction to assume responsibility as a "life-long learner"—a learner who is enthusiastic, curious, flexible, and open to new ideas. Social development includes the acquisition of knowledge, attitudes, and skills that reflect respect for cultural diversity, empathy for others, and appreciation for the people and events that have influenced our society. Social development also encompasses the self-motivation to become an actively involved citizen — a contributing member to society. Academic development includes the knowledge, attitudes, and skills required for problem-solving and critical decision-making. These include the analytical skills involved in research—skill in making observations and inferences and verifying knowledge through inductive and deductive methods of inquiry. Academic development is not static but dynamic and continues throughout life. The learner is aware of the tentativeness and continual reconstruction of knowledge. The learner is also able to apply knowledge from various disciplines to the study of human life and its ever-changing contexts.

If the goal of education is the development of the total student, then program development requires an integration of these personal, social, and academic goals. Once the educational goals are selected, teachers have the responsibility and must have the freedom to develop instructional activities that will help students achieve them. For example, if a program goal is "to develop the ability to see alternative points of view," then students need problem-solving experiences where divergent thinking is encouraged, where there is more than one answer or solution to a problem, and where many different views are discussed. Teachers need to communicate with parents about the relationships of various instructional activities to the general educational goals. Prior to implementing a unit of study, the teacher might send parents a description of the basic concepts to be achieved, a list of the instructional activities that will help students to achieve them, and the form of evaluation that will be used to assess whether the concepts have been developed.

PROVIDING LEADERSHIP IN THE COMMUNITY

As program developers, teachers should work with parents and other members of the educational community to acquaint them with curriculum goals that focus on the development of the total learner. For example, the exploratory research that is currently being done on learning and cognition may result in a need to look seriously at the arts in the curriculum. For some students, problem-solving skills might best be developed through the arts curriculum. The value of the arts in education has not been understood in terms of their influence on the development of creative problem-solving skills.

Teachers can play a critical role in informing parents about the need and value of the arts in education. Often the arts program is the first area of the curriculum to be cut when schools are facing a financial crisis.

Educators need to provide evidence for the community that the arts are at the core of learning, that they provide the means by which many students express themselves. The arts are an extension of the "self." The educational system must acknowledge its goal to develop the whole student by implementing a program through which students have an opportunity to express and communicate their sense of "self."

The arts are unique in that they are a comprehensive representation of the growth of society, past and present. Throughout history they have been an expression of and a means for attaining the best that resides in the individual and the culture. Aspiring, striving, growing, creative human beings need to develop talents for expressing feelings and ideas in positive ways. The arts are a reflection of the human mind at work. They provide a living record of contemporary attitudes, beliefs, and values that can be examined, studied, challenged, and questioned. Teachers in all disciplines can take the responsibility of demonstrating the ways in which the arts convey the foundation of any historical era. For example, the sculpture and the architecture of Greek and Roman history represent the love for beauty and the worship of human perfection. Shakespeare's work has preserved not only the language but also the attitudes and concerns of the Elizabethan period. Both historical and contemporary arts can teach as much about a culture as can any other mode of expression. Something as contemporary as the protest music of the 1960s has a valuable lesson to teach and presents an added dimension to students' understandings of the world as it exists today.

Dewey (1916) was a strong advocate of the arts. He felt that the purpose of education is not merely to make citizens or workers or fathers and mothers, but ultimately to develop human beings who will live life to the fullest. Goodlad (1979) has criticized current educational goals that do not emphasize these human qualities: "We should not be surprised to learn that success in school has not yet been shown to predict success in anything other than those clearly school-based activities for which instructional objectives are inferred. Good grades in school are generally representative of good grades in school but not much else—and certainly not those human qualities of compassion, happiness, appreciation of others, good work habits, and integrity" (p. 310).

Through a comprehensive arts program, significant changes of behavior—the hallmark of all learning—are facilitated. The most significant changes of behaviors are manifested in an attitude toward life where people are able to view their environment through the eyes of the artist, appreciate beauty in all its forms, and become artistic in all their endeavors. Curriculum programs that include discussions, field trips, talks with artists, examination of different media and styles, and learning the roles of artists in society help to encourage a more honest approach to learning about the nature of the arts and their place in the enrichment of our existence. No other area of the curriculum is with us so closely throughout our lives!

One way of convincing the community of the need for the arts is to be certain that accomplishments in this area are widely publicized and recognized. Displays of paintings, ceramics, and sculpture should be prominent within the school and in other appropriate areas such as libraries, hospital lobbies, and merchants' windows. Concerts, instrumental and vocal, should be known and available to the general public. Woodcraft projects should be placed where the public can view them and appreciate the craftsmanship involved. Sewing and culinary projects could also be featured in such a manner. An ideal setting for public viewing of projects that involve creativity is a systemwide "Night of the Arts." During a festival like this, projects from all areas of the curriculum could be displayed.

Another example of how changes in society might affect curriculum and program development is in the area of computers and related communication technologies. In his book *Toward Understanding the Social Impact of Computers* (1974), Amara describes the staggering growth of computer technology. The computer industry, which in 1950 was very small, is now the eighth largest industry in the United States. Experts speculate that by the year 2000, if not sooner, it will be the largest industry in the world. If education is to prepare people to live and participate meaningfully in an increasingly technological society, then the school curriculum needs to include, as a major educational goal, a greater understanding of the social and political ramifications of computer technology on our society. This awareness and understanding cannot and should not be limited to a course on computer literacy; rather, the influence of computers and related technology should be an instructional strand that is interwoven throughout each area of the curriculum. Accordingly, each teacher needs to understand the relevance and influence of computers on life itself. In recognizing the relationship between computer technology and excellence in teaching, Doerr (1979) indicates that "the computer *by itself* can never be as effective as a human teacher; an alliance of the two, however, creates a powerful teaching force. The computer, used creatively, has a multiplicative effect on the teacher's impact on his/her students. Far from threatening to replace *good* teaching, the computer offers a new arena with the opportunity for *great* teaching" (p. 12).

The need to integrate computer technology into all disciplines is already recognized by the many colleges and universities that require all students to have their own computers — a rule that probably will be as natural as requiring textbooks by the turn of the century. The impact of this rapidly changing world has significant implications for all levels of education. Some state departments of education are beginning to recognize these implications and are mandating computer courses at the elementary school level. While computer literacy is a plausible and necessary educational goal, to be truly significant it needs to be supplemented with a curriculum that reflects knowledge, attitudes, and skills of each discipline as they influence or are influenced by the advent of the technology.

The preceding discussions of the influence of the arts and computer technology on curriculum development are only two of many examples showing the importance of the role of teacher as program developer. In order to implement this role effectively, teachers need to be knowledgeable about societal and technological issues and trends; they also must understand current research related to various learning theories. Finally, teachers need to be open to new ideas; they must be willing to experiment and to integrate the results of good research into curriculum development and educational practices.

PROGRAM DEVELOPMENT:
AN INTEGRATION OF THEORY AND PRACTICE

Teachers as professionals possess specialized knowledge of various theories of teaching and learning. This knowledge provides the kind of comprehensive information on which valid programmatic decisions are made. In their preface to a book of readings entitled *Theory and Practice in the History of American Education* (1971), Hillesheim and Merrill strongly endorse the integration of theory with practice by saying, "Theory without practice is empty; practice without theory is blind. . . . Educational theories unless tested in experience degenerate into vacuous abstractions and practice — particularly educational practice — unless guided by systematic thought, degenerates into futile tinkering" (p. XVII). If teachers are to assume the role of program developers, they must study the theories and practices that constitute the development of American education and the fundamental principles that underlie educational processes. "Theories of human development and theories about the nature of knowledge each describe only a portion of the learner's setting, nature, and action. But used together, they constitute multiple curriculum criteria to aid the teacher and curriculum maker in planning and evaluating'' (Hass, 1974, p. 230). It is the knowledge of this curriculum criteria that adds to the significance and importance of the role of the teacher as program developer.

Rather than existing as two separate entities, theory and practice should interact dynamically. Furthermore, the context in which theory is translated into practice needs to become an integral part of the theory-practice paradigm. The ecology of the school community includes the institutional, social, cultural, economic, political, and personal forces of significant others. In addition to students, administrators, faculty, and supervisory personnel, the significant others include parents, community representatives, board of education members, and persons in the family and social contexts of which the teachers and students are a part. These influences were recognized by Foshay (1969), who concludes the section on curriculum in the *Encyclopedia of Educational Research* by defining curriculum as ''the operational statement of schools' goals. Since the goals of a school system are themselves the consequence of the *interaction* of the cultural and political traditions in a given place, tempered by the educational and political beliefs and perceptions of the people, it should not be surprising that the operations of the school, and especially the offering of subject matter for learning, are responsive to gross changes when they occur'' (pp. 278–79).

Perry (1980) attributes the lack of successful programmatic change to the lack of attention to these ecological forces. He concludes that the ''mismatch'' between the values inherent in the teachers' philosophy of education and those that underlie the behavior expected by board members, principals, the community, and other teachers may account for the lack of teacher involvement in curriculum development. Teachers who value and utilize individualized instruction and contracting for grades may find themselves in direct conflict with a principal who believes teachers should only lecture and test. In a strongly church-oriented community, a language arts teacher who chooses to teach the Bible as literature and who is disdainful of the religious implications for the students may find the community up in arms against an ''atheist.'' If pupils and parents are consumed with the importance of athletics, teachers may be expected—virtually required—to show interest in and to attend school athletic events. Teachers who feel that their principles are being sacrificed to such attitudes and demands may choose to avoid involvement in curriculum development; they do not want to, nor are they able to, fight the battle that they see in curriculum development.

Curriculum change involves risks. Unless the school environment is a supportive one in which teachers feel free to take risks, curriculum changes are not likely to occur. An underlying assumption of change theory is that if those who will be affected by the changes are involved in program-planning and decision-making, they will be more willing to make the necessary adjustments and commitments to implement planned change. Just as teacher involvement increases a "sense of ownership" of the change, so too, wider participation of diverse community groups in program development will assure that various needs are considered, thereby enhancing support from the community for implementation (Bennis, 1966; Berman & McLaughlan, 1976; Simon, 1966).

One of the initial ways to involve the community in program development, according to Eisner (1979), is to conduct community awareness sessions in which various orientations to schooling are discussed. This helps the members of the community to expand the options in curriculum planning. Often, community people are satisfied with the status quo ("What was good enough for me is good enough for our youth") because they are not aware of why changes in curriculum are needed; or perhaps they are not aware of changes that other school districts may have made. In many locales, the community is not aware of or responsive to changes in society. If students are to obtain the best education possible, teachers, as program developers, have a professional responsibility to help the community to understand why changes are necessary. What would happen if the members of the medical profession assumed the "what was good enough for me" attitude? Just as the medical profession is in a constant state of change and refinement based on new scientific knowledge, the teaching profession must be in a state of change that is based on sound research.

If an appropriate forum is not available to receive legitimate concerns, internal and external pressures for change are often subverted by individuals or subgroups. Goodlad and Klein (1970) studied one hundred fifty classrooms in sixty-seven schools and concluded that very little, if any, change had occurred in these schools over the previous fifteen years. They assert that below the level of intense criticism and endless recommendations for improvement, there is no structure whereby new ideas and models can be inserted and developed to the stage of becoming real alternatives. If professional knowledge and skill are to be combined to meet the educational challenge of developing and maintaining school programs appropriate to the needs of our ever-changing society, a systematic framework for continuous program review must become an integral part of the school.

INVOLVEMENT IN PROGRAM DECISION-MAKING:
A PROFESSIONAL RESPONSIBILITY

The role of the teacher as program developer is not well defined in the literature. Therefore, to provide insights into the process of program development, we contacted James Fox, a superintendent of schools who feels that successful program development and implementation require the full involvement of professional teachers. Some of his thoughts and concerns are included in the paragraphs that follow.

Educational programs must change to meet the needs of a rapidly changing world. Yet, change is often unsettling and difficult for the persons who are affected by it. True change involves the taking of risks. Reaching for the unknown is almost always accompanied by a fear of failure—even moments of terror. And in almost any effort to bring about change, there will be times when things won't work. However, these "failures" often result in creative thinking and important new knowledge. From this creative thinking and new knowledge an even better program can emerge.

Program development and change require the involvement of classroom teachers. As professional leaders, teachers are in an ideal position to evaluate current educational practices in relation to the developmental needs of pupils. Knowledge of these developmental needs is enhanced for teachers through their day-to-day contacts with students over a long period. This knowledge, in addition to an awareness of relevant research, is critical for making responsible programmatic decisions. In the roles of understander of the learner and of researcher, teachers serve as the most valuable source of information concerning the strengths and weaknesses of existing programs. Their professional knowledge and expertise is essential if effective programmatic decisions are to be made.

When teachers are involved in the process of program development, there will be better understanding of the program and the rationale that supports it. This understanding can enable teachers to make instructional decisions that will lead to successful implementation of the program. Because of this involvement and understanding, teachers are more likely to be committed to a program and to create an environment in which it can be successfully implemented. Teachers set the tone within which a classroom program takes place—if that tone is positive, the program is more likely to be accepted and supported by students, parents, and other members of the educational community.

Throughout this book, we have focused on the influences of the multiple contexts that affect the teaching-learning phenomenon. The acceptance or rejection of new programs is influenced significantly by the context of the school community. A climate for change must be established in that context. An understanding of the present program and the need for change are necessary if change is to be accepted. In their role as program developers, teachers have a professional responsibility to help parents and school-community people to understand not only ''what'' but ''why'' programmatic changes are in the best interests of students. Parents rely on the professional judgments of teachers in making curricular decisions. Because teachers are central to the classroom and school contexts, only they can provide the knowledge and leadership essential for change in the school or classroom program.

The concept of teacher and parents as partners is vitally important in the process of programmatic change. Broad-based decision-making responsibility is perhaps more important in today's world than ever before in the history of education. Public support for education is vital to our nation's future, and community involvement in decision-making is one of the best ways to assure community support. The complex problem of school finance, for example, cannot be resolved without involvement of the total community. It is this interdependent relationship that adds significantly to the need for broad-based participation in educational decision-making—participation that includes representatives from the larger school-community context.

Good programs are constantly developing and constantly changing. As a competent teacher implements a program, it is changed to fit the classroom or school context and the needs of the learners and the teacher. Program evaluation and development must also be an ongoing process. The school and classroom structure must have enough flexibility to encourage creativity yet enough stability and strength to maintain the program. The process of program development and change can and should be an opportunity for professional growth for teachers. It should provide a chance to share and test knowledge and ideas.

Truly professional teachers participate willingly in the process of program change. They realize that those qualities that define them as professionals—an understanding of human development and the process of education and an awareness of and sensitivity to the ever-changing contexts—provide them with the expertise to make meaningful programmatic decisions. These decisions address the needs of our world and of the learners and teachers who are a part of it.

Chapter 8

The Teacher
as Administrator
A PLANNING ROLE

As a student teacher, I got to experience first-hand the amount of administrative duties performed in the process of educating students.

Counts! Lunch counts, absentee counts, milk counts, state-federal-district counts. It seemed that I was always counting something. Of course, all those numbers had to be tabulated and recorded on the appropriate forms. There is a form for everything!

Grades! Here we are expected to condense six to nine weeks of a student's written work, participation, indeed his or her total school experience into one letter of the alphabet.

Plans! I spent hours planning, and trying to foresee anything and everything that could possibly happen with regard to those plans. I was constantly amazed at what was not foreseen, and at the amount of time I spent trying to fill out each two-inch-square block in my plan book.

Papers! Did I really cause all those papers to appear on my desk by the end of the day? How could I possibly check them all and write some sort of personal message on each one—by 9:00 the next morning?

Organization! Learning centers had to be made, bulletin boards changed, seating arrangements altered to best suit everyone. Remember to send Jimmy to speech class, Mary to the talent pool, Dan to the resource room, David and Jeanie to Title I, Karen to spelling—preferably, all at the right times. Remember the staff meeting before school, the parent-teacher conference after school, the meeting with the principal during break—and don't forget to make arrangements for the party next week! (Student Teacher in Ohio)

The role of the teacher as administrator relates to the other roles of the teacher. For example, in evaluating and reporting the progress of a student, the teacher as administrator becomes a researcher and adds to the information to be gained by other teacher-researchers. Without objective and ongoing evaluation, teachers are unable to communicate students' needs and abilities to parents, nor are they able to follow the necessary procedures for reporting those results. As teachers plan and schedule the course of study, they are also functioning as facilitators of the learning environment. All of these activities are selected on the basis of the teacher as an understander of children.

Our study of first-year teachers revealed that the greatest number of perceived stress-producing factors were administrative in nature. Based on the results of our study, the administrative duties of teachers can be broken down into certain functions that are common to those of anyone in administration. These functions or processes include planning, organizing, scheduling, reporting and evaluating, and communicating. The following sections deal with each of these administrative functions. Explanations, suggestions, and experiences of classroom teachers have been included. The intent is not to suggest that these particular methods are all-encompassing or that they will meet the needs of all teachers at all times; rather, we hope that these suggestions will help the reader realize the importance of each function and will generate the basis of a good plan —the key to the success of the teacher as administrator.

PLANNING

Although only a means to an end, planning is extremely important if teachers are to make the best out of the few short hours they have to spend with students each day. While all teachers need to plan, the nature and degree of planning depend on individual need. For some teachers, a simplified outline of goals and procedures suffices; for others, detailed plans, including a list of actual questions to be asked, may be necessary. Hoover and Hollingsworth (1970) recognize this and describe planning as a "personal invention." The amount and nature of planning depend on a variety of factors such as the type of lesson or topic, the number of years one has been teaching, and the personality and special skills of the teacher involved. For beginning teachers, a significant amount of planning is absolutely essential. Very seldom do beginning teachers—or any teachers—overplan. The actual process of thinking through the instructional plan can help teachers gain greater confidence in actually implementing the lesson.

Orlich et al. (1980) recognize the importance of planning but also emphasize that all plans are tentative. Plans are estimates of what ought to take place. What actually occurs may be quite different from the original intent. One of the greatest benefits of planning is that as teachers think through the lesson, they establish priorities of both what to teach and how to teach. The setting of priorities mandates a continuous set of decisions that only the teacher as a professional can make. Furthermore, these decisions differ from class to class since the needs of students differ.

Planning is a continuous process for teachers who must assess students' needs, abilities, and interests and address these variables in the classroom plan. Realistic scheduling and planning come with practice and require flexibility. Long-range planning for the school year—encompassing the goals represented by the curriculum—is an essential part of the teacher's role. Important, too, is the planning that is necessary for the day-to-day and week-to-week events of the classroom. Throughout the process, whether a plan is for long-term or short-term goals, the teacher plans not only for activities but also for flexibility.

Lesson plans, perhaps the most obvious type of planning that teachers do, reflect more than the activities that are to be accomplished in a given day. The planning of lessons—in varying degrees of detail—may reflect the teacher's ideas for a unit, for a week, or for a particular day. Initial plans, outlined before the first student enters the doorway of the classroom, reflect the general units and concepts that teachers expect to accomplish or may be expected to accomplish through the course of the year. From such an initial outline, teachers can anticipate the time parameters that may be required to develop concepts or units. However, once such parameters have been estimated, effective teachers will plan to accommodate the individual needs and abilities of the students. Such teachers know that plans are merely guidelines and will change according to the particular circumstances of the day or of the class.

The unit plan provides the basis for writing the weekly lesson plans that indicate the amount of material and the types of special activities that will be encompassed in a week's time. It is from such weekly plans that teachers can formulate detailed daily lesson plans that state specific objectives and activities and the assignments that should be completed both inside and outside the classroom setting. Again, any lesson plan serves only as a base or guide. From day to day or from class to class, teachers will discover that they have not allowed enough time or have allowed too much time for a particular lesson or activity. Flexibility and preparation are the keys here. A teacher may discover that a reading assignment that he or she had assumed would require a minimum of discussion has generated some real concerns and questions for the students. The answer is *not* to cut short the discussion because the time is not in the plans; instead, the teacher should be flexible enough to devote as much time as may be necessary to satisfy the interests and needs of the class. On the other hand, the teacher may have planned an entire class period around a single concept—a concept that is grasped readily and easily by the students. Rather then spend the scheduled time on the problem or activity, the well-prepared teacher will be ready and able to move on to a new activity or the introduction of an additional concept.

Sometimes students—either the entire class or part of the class— have difficulty with an assignment for which the teacher has allowed only a minimum of time. Once again, the teacher who is prepared with a variety of activities for the assignment and who can reach for supplemental material will be able to immediately retailor the lesson plans and activities to meet such needs. Following to the letter lesson plans that assume preconceived notions of ability, learning styles, and time required may result in a neat and predictable plan book; however, such inflexibility will also result in students who fall further and further behind, for they have not had the time or opportunity to grasp initial and basic concepts.

Long-term planning of units that is then developed into weekly and daily lesson plans allows teachers to establish an overview of materials needed, objectives to be met, and activities to be planned. As suggested in chapter 5, there is an incredibly wide range of outside resources available to classroom teachers, but these resources—from a special film to a guest speaker—must be scheduled and planned in advance. Teachers who plan only one week at a time may find that such resources are not available on short notice. Unit planning and semester or yearly planning allow teachers the time and opportunity to facilitate the use of educational media for all learning that takes place in a given time span.

Long-range planning also enables teachers to plan with others in the system. Continuity between the resource people in the district and the classroom teacher becomes a real possibility when unit planning is part of the approach. How much more valid a unit on folk tales becomes when it is taught to a fifth grade class at the same time the physical education teacher is having the students learn folk-dancing. The art teacher benefits too when the students who are studying Native American art in art class are reading about the historical importance of the American Indian in social studies. If the music teacher knows that students are studying the Christmas holiday from a multicultural perspective, he or she can teach them a variety of Christmas songs and dances from the different cultures and ethnic backgrounds about which they are studying. Integrating long-range plans with the aid of special resource teachers in the system can add new dimensions to lessons for teachers and students.

In addition to planning with special resource people, teachers must be aware of the plans of other teachers in the school setting and work with them. As suggested in chapter 2, teachers should not only inform other teachers of plans but also share special activities or resources with them. Many times, "human resources" may have ideas and facts that increase in importance and impact when they can be shared with others. If all of the fifth grade classes are studying ecology, a planned presentation by a member of the Park Service would benefit the entire fifth grade, not just that class whose teacher has arranged the presentation. If American history and American literature classes are taught concurrently, a dramatic presentation about Mark Twain could be integrated for both its historical and literary importance.

There are other circumstances in which both awareness and flexibility are important. If, for example, plans have been made for the second graders to have their hearing tested, the teacher should be aware of such plans—either through checking with the principal about any special activities or through being certain to read the weekly schedule that may be issued from the principal's office. Knowing in advance that such testing may interfere with the day's schedule and that small groups of students may miss class throughout the day, the teacher can plan for individualized or small group instruction that will not be affected by the arrival and departure of students.

Lesson plans can also be affected by such incidental events as fire drills or by such momentous occasions as closing school for an emergency. In either event, teachers should be flexible enough to allow for such events and to plan around them. A daily plan could also be tossed by the wayside by the arrival of a parent who has a real need to talk to the teacher at that moment. Teachers may find real benefit in keeping a file of "spare" activities for just such moments. Cards with "problem-solving challenges" or values clarification activities are valuable to keep for such circumstances. With a supply of cards with discussion questions that are applicable to books in the classroom library, teachers can know that students are active and are learning during an interruption. While the teacher talks to a parent or realizes that the fifteen minutes between return from a fire drill and the end of the class period is not the time to begin instruction in a totally new concept, the students can be engaged in worthwhile, enjoyable activities that have been prepared previously.

In planning for a possible interruption at the beginning of the school day, teachers may want to establish a standard "first thing in the morning" activity. Such an activity may be an elaborate math problem that is always written on the board when the students enter the room or it may be a standing assignment to write for ten minutes in the individual journals that students keep. Once the students realize that such an activity is *always* the first thing they do upon entering the room, teachers can talk to an occasional parent or to the principal, knowing that students are busy with an assignment.

Planning for the following day's classes is perhaps best accomplished during the "quiet time" of the day—after the students have left and before the teacher goes home. This is probably the ideal time to file papers, make copies of handouts to be used the following day, write assignments or special instructions on the board, and transfer anecdotal notes to students' folders. Also, this time of day gives teachers the opportunity to complete daily "housekeeping" duties such as straightening materials in a learning center or replacing books in the classroom library. Many times, the teacher who goes home with a messy desk and with plans to come in early to clean it up is the teacher who has to meet unexpectedly with a parent in the morning and who is off to a bad start because there is suddenly no time to complete those little tasks that make the day more organized.

The planning time of the teacher begins well before the first day of school—whether that teacher is a first-year or tenth-year teacher. Planning in such areas as the physical management of the room, the bulletin boards, and other physical characteristics of the room can begin as soon as the teacher knows the grade level or subject area in which he or she will be teaching.

The physical arrangement of the classroom can set the tone of the class and influence the type of instruction and its effectiveness. The classroom environment should be relaxing yet stimulating, and it should be structured so that the learning environment is appropriate for the students.

Teachers may find that some arrangements are better for some days than for others or that some arrangements are better for some activities than for others. Certain activities may prompt the rearrangement of desks so that students can work in small groups, on two-member team projects, or independently. The physical arrangement of the classroom should reflect the individual needs of the students as much as the choice of materials or activities.

When arranging the elementary school classroom, teachers should try to leave ample room for learning centers and other areas such as a quiet area, the play area, the library, a work table, and interest centers. It is also important to keep the height of shelves and tables suitable for the size of the students; ideally, the first day of class will be spent, in part, making certain that the students fit the desks to which they have been assigned. The room should not be designed with "quiet" areas near play areas. When the room is divided, partitions made of shelves, bricks, or plants are both functional as noise breakers and attractive.

The addition of carpet squares to the back of a bookshelf can cut down on the noise that may travel from one area of the classroom to another.

Before moving several pieces of heavy furniture, teachers should make a floor plan on paper for the desks, the bookshelves, and the learning centers. The teacher's desk need not be placed in the front of the room, where it often blocks the students' view of the chalkboard. It is also important that the arrangement of the room allow for a good traffic flow; this facilitates free movement for both students and teachers. Many high school teachers have found that placing students so that their backs are to the windows utilizes natural lighting and lessens distractions. However, some students—especially young children—may miss the distraction and the rested feeling that they gain from looking outdoors. The room arrangement should also facilitate a quick and easy exit; such considerations will eliminate panic during a fire drill and censure by a principal or fire marshal who sees a cluttered room design as nothing but a trap for students and teachers alike.

When four desks are placed together as a single unit, socialization and helping attitudes are encouraged. The seating arrangement should be changed regularly, perhaps every six to nine weeks. Students enjoy the change and have the opportunity to become better acquainted with other members of the class.

It is also necessary to set the stimulating tone of a classroom from the very onset of the school year. Perhaps one of the most obvious ways to set such a tone is through decorations which can reflect both a learning environment and the things that are to come as the year progresses. Bulletin boards can be used for such a purpose. Teacher-made bulletin boards that feature the units and/or the concepts to be studied are an important part of the initial impact that a student receives about a teacher and a class, whether the student is in kindergarten or a senior in high school. Once the year begins, however, bulletin boards can become a part of the students' activities. Such teaching aids can feature students' work, can become part of a learning project, or can illustrate the progress that students are making in a certain area.

Some of the best and most creative bulletin boards are the result of a joint effort by students and teacher. The teacher could begin the display, establishing the theme or content, and then allow the students to finish it with their own ideas, examples, and artwork or written work. Bulletin boards or wall displays may be used as interest centers by various students or by a class group that has a special project to display. The boards should be changed at least once a month so that they reflect changes in the seasons or in the material that is being studied; a change also allows all students to be involved in decorating the room.

In addition to the use of bulletin boards, other spaces for displays may include the doors, the walls, and even the windows of the class-room, as described in chapter 5. Once the teacher has checked with the custodial staff about the types of adhesives that can and cannot be used, almost anything goes. For example, one teacher carefully mounted on construction paper the poems written by each of her one hundred twenty freshman English students. These multicolored poems were then taped to the walls, forming a colorful border around the classroom and enabling all students to see their work on display.

Room decorations create a colorful atmosphere and may reflect holiday and learning themes, increasing both motivation and reinforcement for the members of the class. Especially for younger children, working bulletin boards with hands-on activities are very successful and welcome. Many times, these working displays can have a tactile as well as a visual dimension. Bulletin boards centered upon an object as simple as a map—local, national, or world—can provide opportunities for students to become aware of the events around them and the geographical locations of newsmaking occurrences. A study of current events can be facilitated when students clip and bring to class articles that interest them from both magazines and newspapers. Each student is then responsible for adding the article to the bulletin board adjacent to the correct geographical location.

Caring for a sick student is a problem that can face any teacher—grades kindergarten through twelve—and is an occurrence for which teachers must be prepared. A student who appears ill should rest his or her head on the desk while the teacher tries to ascertain the nature and degree of the illness. It may be necessary to have the student taken to the principal's office or the nurse's room; the teacher should send a note along. Often there will be a school nurse on duty, but if there is not, the office staff is usually prepared to handle such a problem. The teacher may want to confer with the principal about whether to send the student home. Teachers should remember that they are not authorized to administer any type of medication to students.

Whether at the primary or secondary level, teachers should keep a record—in the classroom—of students' medical histories. They may also wish to keep a record of the students' illnesses to watch for recurrences or particular patterns. Teachers should ask for and receive a list of those students who may have or have had medical difficulty. The response to a pupil whom the teacher knows is diabetic, for example, is quite different than the response to a student who is taking medication for the common cold. Before the class goes outside for a picnic, a teacher should know if there is a student who is allergic to bee stings; that teacher must know the correct procedure if the student does get stung.

ADMINISTRATIVE RESPONSIBILITIES
OF A SUBSTITUTE TEACHER

Planning is an administrative role that is also important for substitute teachers. Confidence in oneself is basic to success as a substitute teacher; being well prepared can help build self-confidence. Even substitutes who get called within a half hour of the beginning of class can go in prepared if they have done some preplanning. In this section, various practices and suggestions for substitute teachers are discussed.

When asked to substitute, the teacher should plan, if at all possible, to reach the school well before the students arrive. This may be the only time the substitute has to familiarize himself or herself with the schedule, the routine, and the curriculum to be followed for the day. It will also allow him or her to read over the instructions left by the regular classroom teacher. If at all possible, the substitute should speak to the regular teacher; this will give each the opportunity to ask and answer questions that may not be addressed in the written plans.

The substitute teacher should compile a resource packet—a supply of ideas and activities that can be easily carried to and used in a variety of teaching situations. One such activity is a file of various pictures—of people, of settings, or of events. The students could write about the pictures, and the only limitation on the story would be the grade level in which the writing is done. High school students in an English class and fifth grade students could easily be inspired by the same photograph, but inspired to write totally different compositions.

The substitute teacher's resource packet might also contain a good book to read to the students. Depending upon the length of the substituting assignment and the grade level of the students, any number of books of varying lengths and plots could be introduced. Again, the teacher may want to give the students only a "teaser" from a book and then ask them to write their own conclusions. Once the students have completed their own endings for the assignment, the teacher could read them the author's ending. Discussion could follow, especially if the students preferred their own endings to the original one. (Some short stories allow for this kind of exercise inherently—"The Lady or the Tiger" has no stated conclusion; readers must reach their own.)

An open-ended problem is a good activity for a substitute teacher to use. This can be a situation to which students respond—either through speaking or writing — that can prompt further class discussions about choices, values, or the decision-making process. The discussions could range from "What I Would Buy If I Had a Million Dollars" to "How Can Nuclear Energy Be Used to Serve Humankind?"

Another writing assignment that works well with students of any age

—and is especially useful for the substitute teacher who is settling in for a prolonged stay—is to have the students write autobiographies. This not only gives them an opportunity to write but also gives the substitute some knowledge and understanding of the class.

The substitute teacher could have the students develop their own discussion questions from books that may be available in a classroom or school library. Having given the students the opportunity to choose a book or having enlisted the aid of the school librarian in helping students select books, the substitute can ask the students not only to read but also to develop discussion questions that might aid other students as they read the book. The substitute teacher will find it truly advantageous to identify—as soon as possible—the students who can assume leadership responsibilities. These students might be called upon to take the lunch count to the office, to get the school nurse if she is needed, or to tell the substitute that Eddie is sitting in Johnny's seat and that Johnny is really the absent one. Identifying several leaders in the class—be it first grade or tenth grade English — can truly simplify the job of the substitute teacher.

Whether the assignment is for one day or one month, the substitute teacher will want to have some kind of activity for the students to complete while he or she takes care of the "bookkeeping" chores of the day (attendance, lunch count, morning announcements). One such activity could be an elaborate mathematics problem, written on the board before the students enter the classroom and established as part of the daily routine. Depending on the ages or the abilities of the students, such a problem could range from one long column of simple addition to the multiplication of two ten-digit numbers.

A good substitute leaves extensive notes describing exactly what was done and what was not done in the classroom during the time that the regular teacher was absent. When specific plans are left for a substitute teacher, and when those plans include papers that are to be completed and handed in during the day, it is only common courtesy for the substitute to grade them whenever possible. Although an essay test written by fifth grade social studies students may have to be left for the classroom teacher, spelling tests and true-false quizzes and math papers can be checked.

Perhaps the most important tool that the classroom teacher will leave for a substitute is the seating chart. Names are as important to students as they are to adults, and the ability to call students by their names can also affect the control the substitute may have. Also, pupils of any age are impressed by a teacher's willingness to learn names and to call them something other than "You in the third seat in the first row." It helps to have the students make name tags. A substitute who is hired for an extended stay should make this learning of students' names the first priority, for it can make a difference in the relationship and the experiences for both students and teacher.

ORGANIZING

For many people, the term *organization* denotes a mechanical process. While this may be true, it does not minimize the importance of organization. In fact, the major purpose of organizing materials, programs, and activities should be to give teachers greater access to all materials that they feel are educationally effective and professionally appropriate. Hoover and Hollingsworth (1970) compare organizing by teachers to that of lawyers who prepare legal briefs. Teachers need to organize their thinking with respect to teaching. Lawyers, like teachers, are unable to predetermine their entire strategy but their preplanned activities can be very useful in providing an organized framework consistent with their purposes. Similarly, teachers are unable to predetermine their entire instructional approach because of the need to be sensitive to the moment-to-moment influences on the students. With a basic plan, however, teachers are in a better position to adapt the plan to the situation than people who have no guiding framework for instruction. Teachers who are truly professional decision makers will be flexible enough to modify plans based on the unique situation.

The Annehurst Curriculum Classification System, designed by Frymier (1977), is an example of extensive organization and classification of curriculum materials. The system is based on the supposition that the teacher is the one person most capable of determining which specific curriculum materials might be most helpful to particular learners at any moment. The system, in fact, requires the teacher to assume more responsibility rather than less for decision-making about both materials and methods. The classroom teacher, as an understander of the learner, is the only person who knows enough about each student, the subject matter area, and the situation to make these decisions.

Organization of each aspect of teaching and the administrative duties involved with these aspects can do a great deal to facilitate the accomplishment of educational goals for students and for teachers. When organizing activities both within and beyond the classroom, teachers should be aware of any school policies that may affect these activities. Schools vary as to the nature and degree of written policies. In general, policies should not be viewed as absolutes or restrictions, but rather as guidelines that can be interpreted in relationship to existing circumstances. Mature professionals know whether to interpret policies according to the "letter" or the "spirit" of the law. Teachers should not use "policy" as excuse for decisions and actions.

As teachers organize educational activities for students, they should consider the school calendar. Planning special events around the holiday schedules can provide numerous opportunities for organizing projects. For example, a study of the Pilgrims that culminates the day before Thanksgiving vacation begins, and that allows the students to share their projects and their newly gained knowledge with others in the school, increases both the impact and the importance of such projects.

Organization of in-class projects or of special field trips should include more than the logistics of obtaining a guest speaker or of arranging for a school bus to transport students. These kinds of activities also provide an opportunity for organization of fellow teachers and of curriculum to meet the needs and accommodate the interests of far more than one classroom of fifth graders or one section of freshman English students. If a field trip or a guest speaker is scheduled well in advance, it is possible to team plan a unit or part of the curriculum to enable all of the fifth grade students or all of the freshman English students to participate in and profit from the special event.

Because they rely upon the freedom of students to move within the classroom and to work in small groups while the teacher is occupied, learning centers also require organization. As suggested in chapter 5, there are many ways in which learning centers can be incorporated to meet the needs and interests of students. Teachers also need to plan a management system and an evaluation system for the use of those centers.

First, teachers must instruct the students in the use of the centers, and this may be done in a number of ways. A small group may be shown the technique, and they in turn could instruct the other members of the class. Another way in which to organize the students would be through a class meeting; in this meeting, students could decide individually where to begin. When there are several centers from which to choose, students may rotate from one center to another as they finish a group of activities. The completed activities and centers may be recorded on a chart.

The "tap system" is another way of organizing rotation at the learning centers. At each center, a list of the students who should use that center is posted. When the first student is finished with an activity, he or she quietly "taps" the next person on the list. The list should be changed frequently so that the same student is not always first; the same students may appear on the same list every day, but the order of the names can be rearranged. These lists can be recycled and used over and over again throughout the year with various centers. When the centers have several activities, a small group of students could work—together or individually—on different activities. As one group finishes, the next small group may begin, or the members of the original group may rotate the activities.

The pacing of instruction to accommodate individual student differences requires organization on the part of the teacher. Organizing sufficient materials and information to reinforce a concept with which students have difficulty requires planning. The moment of learning may be lost when the teacher must spend several minutes or even an entire day finding and reproducing additional material. Time is lost, too, when students complete some aspect of the lesson, but the teacher is not prepared to go on to the next level of instruction. Pacing instruction requires organization and flexibility.

Teachers who have organized the routine daily activities of the classroom — milk count, lunch count, and attendance — find that such organization simplifies the routine and also allows teachers to spend more instructional time with students. Organizing a system of "student helpers" for these routine tasks and organizing a system through which the students perform their own lunch count can facilitate the work of teachers. A system in which students use tongue depressors on which their names are written and place them in either white milk or chocolate milk containers as they enter the classroom accomplishes the milk count very simply and also provides a record-keeping system of sorts for those students who may not recall which type of milk they ordered. Similarly, an attendance and lunch count system using clothespins on which each student's name is written can be used. The clothespins are placed on a board next to each student's name at the close of each school day. Every morning, students take their clothespins and place them in the box that indicates a school lunch or a brown bag (home) lunch. Both attendance and lunch count are accomplished simultaneously, for the clothespins that remain on the board are those of the students who are absent.

Organization within the classroom must often be coordinated with the availability of supplies. Activities that require supplies such as construction paper or paint depend upon the availability of these items. Teachers who have not obtained the supplies in advance may find that a student sent to the office to pick up supplies returns with the news that there is no orange construction paper to be found. In addition to an awareness of the supplies that may or may not be on hand in the building or in the classroom, teachers should make it a point to be aware of additional sources of supplies. Partial rolls of wallpaper, obtained from the local paint or hardware store, can often be used more effectively than construction paper, and newsprint may be less expensive when purchased from the city newspaper than when it is purchased from the art supply store. It is essential to organize supplies well in advance of a particular project.

One of the truest tests of a teacher's organization is his or her filing system. The filing of materials, worksheets, pamphlets, tests, and student papers can become an overwhelming task — one that approaches the impossible — if the teacher has not established some system. The teacher who has a system and who religiously files materials at the end of each school day will find that any system will work. Many times, there are no shiny, new, four-drawer filing cabinets available in the classroom. However, large cardboard boxes covered with fabric or contact paper can serve as student files—files to which the students themselves have access. Large plastic shopping bags, clearly marked on the outside, and plastic dish racks can serve as "file drawers" for unit-related materials and can be used to store appropriate instructional games and bulletin board materials as well as extra worksheets.

SCHEDULING

The administrative function of scheduling encompasses more than the classroom scheduling of subject matter; teachers must also consider planning their own time and the administrative responsibilities that must be met during that time. Scheduling time for others, resource people from the community as well as special service teachers, is another important aspect of this scheduling.

In developing a weekly schedule of classes, teachers should inquire as to whether any locally or state-mandated requirements exist regarding the number of minutes per week that must be spent on specific subject matter. For example, a fifth grade teacher may be required to incorporate health as a subject for sixty minutes per week; it is then the responsibility of the teacher to meet this minimum requirement when scheduling activities and lessons for each week. The schedule for the elementary classroom must also reflect the time demands of the special classes that may be a part of the curriculum—art, music, physical education. These classes, when scheduled with the help of the teachers responsible for them, can be incorporated and integrated with the remainder of the curriculum. Special classes should not be perceived as an interruption of the daily routine, rather, they are an ideal opportunity to truly integrate all areas of the student's learning.

Scheduling in the secondary school encompasses different considerations, for many of the specific topics and co-curricular responsibilities may be built into the schedule as it is adopted for the school year. Teachers are scheduled for specific blocks of time during which they may have a planning period or may be responsible for supervising a study hall. Since such scheduling is usually completed early in the spring of the preceding year, first-year teachers probably will not be able to adjust their schedules regarding nonclassroom responsibilities. However, it may be possible to rearrange within a department, producing a team effort for some subject areas or enabling two teachers to exchange, for example, sections of science when each has greater strength or ability in a different subject area.

Scheduling for special activities or programs requires not only planning on the part of the teachers involved but also may require accommodating the schedules of others who will be affected. Again, if such scheduling is done well in advance, and is done with the help rather than to the inconvenience of staff members, special programs can be a pleasure instead of a nuisance. It is also essential for teachers who are planning for something "out of the ordinary" to discuss those plans with the principal, scheduling the time and the date so that there is not a conflict with some other planned activity; they should also speak to the other teachers. The other fifth grade teachers may want their students to be part of a Thanksgiving play to be presented to the school, but they should be a part of the scheduling process so that the play does not conflict with the guest speaker scheduled for the same day.

Important, too, for teachers is the scheduling of time for resource people within the school to share their knowledge and understanding with both teachers and students. The librarian will probably welcome the opportunity to provide orientation for students — acquainting them with the physical layout of the library and with the types of information and services available. Guidance counselors are often neglected and yet have the means and ability to conduct group guidance sessions that benefit teachers and students. Aides have much to offer within the classroom framework, but their time and their responsibilities should be scheduled by the teacher. A classroom aide, with guidance and instruction, can assume many administrative duties for the teacher and can facilitate individual and small group instruction. Planning and scheduling enable these resource people to use their talents and abilities for the benefit of children and of the entire educational atmosphere of a classroom and a school.

Scheduling of parent conferences is a facet of the scheduling process that goes beyond those days set aside especially for conferences.

There is often a need for parents and teachers to meet and talk, without interruption, about the progress a student is making. Teachers should try to arrange a time that accommodates both teacher and parental work schedules.

Teachers also need to schedule time for themselves during the school day. They need a little time away from the bustle and the pressing concerns of the classroom, the students, and the other teachers. If possible, teachers should try to "get away" for lunch, leaving the building and the school grounds to go home or eat out. A break from the routine and from the responsibilities of teaching can be revitalizing. It is also valuable to schedule time to observe other teachers — to become aware of the things that others are doing. This type of observation can be the source of ideas and understanding for teachers, giving each of them the opportunity to grow professionally within the context of the school setting.

REPORTING AND EVALUATING

Reporting and evaluating as an aspect of the teacher as administrator gains importance in several ways. Primarily, the reporting of students' progress through the method adopted by a school system is viewed as the means by which parents are informed of their children's academic progress. However, the reporting facet of administration can function in a variety of other ways. As suggested in chapter 6, the grades and other notations that become a part of a student's cumulative record provide valuable data for other teachers and for the specialized personnel in the system. The reporting of academic or social progress—whether through a standard grade card or through informal communications with notes or telephone calls—is many times the link that dominates the role of teacher and parents as partners in education. Also, the reports made by teachers in daily grades, as well as on school-issued report cards, provide the students with knowledge of their own progress and their own needs in some area of the curriculum.

Reporting—to students, to parents, to peers, and to the principal—plays an essential part in the educational process. Records must be ongoing and accurate, for it is only through the various school records that progress can be recorded for the benefit of students, their parents, and others who will be a part of their school experience.

Considering the long-range use and effects of a pupil's cumulative record, teachers must assume the responsibility of reporting as one of the most important professional roles. It is a role that requires the continuous process of gathering accurate data from many sources, reflecting upon and analyzing the data, and arriving at some basic recommendations that have solid theoretical support in terms of what is developmentally appropriate for the students. The teacher, as a professional decision maker, needs to decide what information should be included, how it should be included, and what information should be left out of the cumulative folder. Criteria for making these decisions should include whether the information is important for future use and whether there is a danger that it will be misinterpreted or misused by future teachers. Great sensitivity and caution should be used when recording any data.

The first consideration is determining the reporting methods that have been adopted by the school system. Many variations exist from school to school; some schools utilize a Satisfactory/Unsatisfactory system; others mandate that letter grades—"A", "B", "C", "D", "F" — be recorded; still others may require that percentages be used to designate progress; some may prefer that notation of mastery of particular skills be the single factor reported to parents. A teacher should not feel limited by the reporting system adopted by a school and may add to or elaborate upon it. Teachers can add notations concerning specific involvement in various areas even though there is not a designated place for written comments on a report card. Such notations give parents, students, and other teachers a better understanding of the meaning and importance of any standardized grade. For example, a teacher may want to note that a student has shown marked improvement in social skills such as greater involvement in class discussion or improvement in getting along with classmates. These areas of improvement can be written on the card or noted on a separate sheet of paper that is sent home with the report card. Similarly, a secondary teacher may choose to add to a report card specific areas of improvement, such as attitude toward school, which might not be reflected in a change of grade from one period to the next.

It is important for teachers to keep more than standardized percentages or letter-grade notations on a student's progress. They may also keep descriptive data on that progress. Such data — statements about students' behaviors, attitudes, and achievements — should consist of specific rather than general comments such as "behaves well" or "is disruptive." Details in the record of a student's progress help teachers know which of the students might need a greater degree of encouragement and support in specific areas. This type of information, in the form of anecdotal notation, may be first recorded informally by teachers during the course of the school day or the class period. By maintaining individual classroom folders for each student and by transferring the anecdotes to the appropriate folder at the close of each school day, teachers maintain a current and specific record of the student's actions, reactions, and progress. Such data, accumulated throughout the grading period, are then available for parent-teacher conferences, for justification of grades, and for the teachers who will have those students in class the next grading period or the next year.

To supplement the standard grading system and maintain an on-going method of reporting and noting student progress, teachers may keep a "work sample" folder for each student. Such a record will provide teachers, parents, and students with a means of viewing academic progress. Through comparing a student's past and present work rather than by comparing one student to another, teachers are better able to discern the actual progress of each student.

The key to success in reporting students' progress is the ability of the teacher to "stay on top of" the collecting and filing of classroom materials. Once the folder has been established for each student and a specific place for those folders has been designated, teachers should make every attempt to file and record the day's work and events each day. When both the system and the procedure become habitual, teachers will find themselves with an up-to-date record for each student—a record that can be pulled at a moment's notice to share with a parent or a colleague.

One important type of reporting is that done directly to the students. Students are aware that they are being evaluated daily, and most want to know the results of the evaluation. This reporting of progress does not have to be done in a formal fashion; yet students often ask, "How am I doing?"

One way to inform students that they are doing well or are making progress is through "Happy Notes." These notes can take the form of a certificate for completing all of the assignments or the form of a brightly colored note pinned to a primary student, a note that may say, "I helped a friend on the playground today," or "I was the milk helper today, and I did a great job." As presented in chapter 3, such notes will also increase rapport between the home and school contexts. For older students, reporting of progress can be accomplished through comments on daily assignments. Simple, descriptive comments on assignments not only inform students of their progress but also show that the teacher sees value in their work, for he or she has taken the time to read or comment on the work done.

As teachers establish homework or class papers as a means of reinforcement for students, they also should consider the need for feedback to be as immediate as possible. Papers that are returned promptly not only provide students with knowledge of their progress but also provide the motivation to follow a model set by the teacher. If a paper is important enough to be completed, it is important enough to be graded or commented upon or corrected as soon as possible.

Teachers often send the formal report cards home at the conclusion of a grading period—either every six weeks or every nine weeks. Many schools also request that an interim report be sent home at a point halfway through the grading period. For the most part, such interim reports are predetermined forms that are completed in duplicate; one copy is sent home, and the other remains at the school and becomes a part of the student's permanent record. Usually, interim reports are required for students who are failing or in danger of failing a subject in that grading period. However, such reports do not have to be notes of failure; halfway through the grading period is an ideal time to inform parents, and therefore students, that the student is doing well in a subject or has shown marked improvement over past performance.

Another way to communicate progress or the lack of it is the telephone. By making a brief telephone call, teachers can inform parents that a conference is needed to discuss a pupil's work habits or simply that "Susie did a class presentation today and really did a super job." With a conscious effort to do so and with an established pattern— perhaps five parents a week—the effective teacher can open the lines of communication between parents and school and at the same time inform parents of their child's progress.

As the teacher reports student progress through the formal avenues adopted by the school, these reports become a part of students' permanent record folders. Such folders accompany students from their first day of kindergarten through the final day of high school. The permanent record, as suggested in chapter 6, becomes the location of and source for a wide variety of information. Usually, the permanent record folder contains yearly attendance and grade reports, standardized test scores, health information, anecdotal reports from previous teachers, a picture of the student, and any other information that will have lasting value in directing the student's progress through school. More extensive information about students may be contained in the plethora of records that are so much a part of the role of the teacher as administrator.

Health records are maintained in addition to academic records. These too are a valuable source of information and may answer teachers' questions about a student's academic or behavioral difficulties. Elementary teachers often use individual pupil record sheets to record pertinent information throughout the school year. These forms may include a record of daily attendance, the quarterly grades, and the most recent IQ scores. Individual record sheets are often kept by the classroom teacher during the school year, submitted to the principal at the close of the term, and temporarily transmitted to the succeeding teacher at the beginning of the new year. Subsequently, these records become a part of the cumulative folder.

Semester averages and attendance records for each year are entered on the permanent record card. This card is kept by the school for an indefinite period. The information on the card is then available for verification of attendance and achievement and serves as a source of personal data for the school, colleges and universities to which the student may apply, and prospective employers.

Report cards provide evidence of the various aspects of pupil growth and development and represent one constant form of communication between the school and the home. If a report card is to accurately and adequately reflect a student's progress, it must be given careful thought and planning. Teachers should endeavor to have the report card represent a true picture of the student's progress.

COMMUNICATING

Communication plays an important part in the development of the teacher's administrative role. By communicating not only with other teachers but also with administrators and parents, teachers can gain insight about the expectations that significant others have about their role. "Teachers must be impressed with the importance of positive school-community relations and must be encouraged to exert effort in this highly sensitive domain. . . . Because of an awareness of the importance of quality education, parental expectations for the schools continue to increase. Outstanding teaching is still the foundation of any school-community relations program" (Lipham & Hoeh, 1974, p. 331). Communication is especially important for the first-year teacher, for it is through this process that teachers gain new and different ideas about their roles and about the best way to incorporate and facilitate any suggestions that may be forthcoming.

As suggested in chapter 2, an important part of teaching is the existence of a solid support system between teachers. To begin establishing this system and, therefore, to begin understanding the administrative responsibilities of a teacher in a particular setting, teachers must begin with introductions. As teachers introduce themselves to fellow teachers, they become familiar with more than people; they start to understand the previous syllabi that were used, the curriculum guides that have been developed, and the procedures that are to be followed. To become effective administrators, teachers may find it essential to ask questions. Asking about the curriculum as well as asking for ideas and suggestions can simplify the role of the teacher as administrator.

The minimal effort necessary to speak to other teachers in the building reaps a wide range of benefits, for through such an effort teachers begin to share with one another the joys and frustrations inherent in the profession. Sharing leads to a developing support group among peers and provides an outlet and audience for emotional and professional concerns. Such a support group can only produce a more friendly and more stable environment for teachers and thus for their students.

Daily communication should encompass administrators and staff members in the building. The teacher who stops in the office each morning and makes it a point to speak to the principal starts the day on a positive note for both. A simple "Good morning" to a secretary or a custodian reminds that person that the teacher recognizes both the existence and the necessity of staff members in the operation of the school. Again, by making an effort to speak to and recognize the other people with whom they work, teachers begin to aid in the establishment of a strong system of support that ultimately affects the attitude of faculty, students, and the community toward school.

Written communication, even in a world that sometimes seems filled with memos, is a very effective manner of encouraging ongoing, two-way communication. A note to a parent regarding the positive progress of a child, an appropriate card or note to a colleague, or a written "Thank you" to the principal for help on some special project can work miracles. Such written messages not only remind the recipient, over and over, that the sender had something nice to say but also encourage response in like fashion. A building filled with teachers who express their appreciation for the work of others and a community filled with parents who not only receive but also return praise indicate a school setting in which all of the environmental factors are working toward the good of the pupil.

Oral communication serves a variety of purposes for the teacher. Each teacher should be concerned with oral communication as it affects students, community members, and colleagues and as it echoes or contradicts the nonverbal communication that may accompany it.

Oral communication to students from teachers takes its most obvious form in the dissemination of information and in the giving of directions or instructions. In both instances, teachers should take care not only to speak well and clearly but also to organize and explicate the information desired. Keeping in mind that some students are not auditory learners — and therefore may not comprehend oral instructions — teachers should make an attempt to relay the information in written form as well. Oral-verbal communication is also a valuable tool in the relationship between teacher and student when the teacher takes advantage of the opportunity to present oral positive reinforcement. This reinforcement could take the form of praise for behavior or for class work, but it is a tool that each teacher should use to some advantage.

Many teachers have opportunities to use their skills in oral communication as ambassadors from the school to the community. The teacher who can transfer the ability to speak to students to communication with civic and service groups as well as parents' organizations can provide public relations for programs and curriculum. A teacher who expends as much care and concern on public speaking engagements as on class preparation will present the school and its staff in a manner that encourages community support and interest. A knowledge of the community and the relationship between the school and the community can also ease the transition into the role of the teacher as administrator. Through attendance at meetings of the board of education and through involvement in other community-related activities, teachers can increase their effectiveness as administrators. Teachers also have the opportunity to address their colleagues—in situations ranging from committee meetings to faculty meetings or school assemblies. Again, with preparation as the essential element, this type of oral communication can be as successful as classroom communication.

As they communicate with others in their environment, educators should be aware that the nonverbal communication that accompanies words and phrases can be a powerful reinforcing or contradictory element. The tone of voice with which information is presented can affect the spirit with which information is accepted; a teacher whose tone portrays boredom or lack of interest can make even the most exciting event in history seem boring. By the same token, the teacher who can talk about a historical event with enthusiasm has gone a long way in instilling interest in the students. Gestures, too, reveal attitude and opinion and can convince an audience much more readily than words of the speaker's attitude. Teachers who are aware of their nonverbal signals and who are also aware of the nonverbal signals of the audience can dictate the tone and the reception of subject matter more effectively than teachers who do not recognize that their nonverbal communication speaks louder than words.

As suggested in chapter 3, a firm, well-defined system of interest and support between parents and teachers can and should be based on open and trusting lines of communication. Each teacher has a responsibility to communicate as often as possible with the parents of each student. This communication, which can be as simple and quick as a telephone call, cannot be reserved only for those occasions when there is difficulty at school. Far more rewarding for both teacher and parent is the telephone call made to inform the parent that a pupil has done an exceptional job on a homework assignment or is demonstrating marked improvement in social skills. When positive communication is the rule rather than the exception, parents and teachers can become better partners in the educational well-being of the student.

Frazier (1976) addresses the need for teachers to develop administrative skills in his book *Teaching Children Today: An Informal Approach*. He recognizes that although good organization and order will not ensure a program's success, if management of space, resources, time, and children is inadequate, a new program may not last long enough to make its virtues felt. If teachers are to be free to play a more interactive role with students, organizational skills become imperative. Similarly, Berliner (1980) emphasizes that teachers need to develop the administrative skills of executives if they are to manage effectively the complexities of today's classrooms. The examples cited in this chapter are not prescriptive but representative of the nature of the role of the teacher as administrator. As professionals, teachers must know their own need to develop those administrative skills that will ultimately free them to utilize their time to work more effectively with children.

Chapter 9

Transition
into the Profession
AN ASPIRING ROLE

In the professional life span of teachers, few periods of time compare in impact and importance with the first year of teaching. The beginning of a teaching career for some may be charged with excitement, challenge and exhilarating success. For others, the first year of teaching may seem to be confusing, uncontrollable, filled with unsolvable problems, and threatened by personal defeat and failure. For many, beginning to teach is a unique and more balanced mixture of success, problems, surprises and satisfactions. For all engaged in the educational enterprise, the first year of teaching has come to be recognized as a unique and significant period in the professional and personal lives of teachers. (Ryan & Johnston, 1980, p. 1)

For first-year teachers, transition into the profession may represent the single most difficult aspect along the road to becoming professional educators. The newcomer must simultaneously become an autonomous, responsible classroom teacher and be assimilated into the numerous school-community contexts consisting of other teachers, administrators, staff members, students, and their parents. These context-related concerns vary with the experiences of each individual teacher. Any career change involves a significant revision of one's life-style along with the inevitable stresses that are associated with such revisions. The first year of teaching includes three major characteristics that seem to be reflected in all career changes: (1) a change in the definition of oneself; (2) experiencing the novelty of a totally new situation; and (3) a major change in one's interpersonal support networks.

The change from being a student for sixteen or more consecutive years to being a teacher is an adjustment that many first-year teachers do not anticipate. Having had many successful field-participation experiences during their teacher preparation programs, they look forward to their first year of teaching as an opportunity to move right into the role of teacher with the same level of confidence, enthusiasm, and accomplishment. They do not expect their experiences to be stressful ones that involve such significant changes in responsibility. When problems inevitably occur, new teachers think that they are the cause of the difficulties they are experiencing.

In most cases, not only is the school a new environment for the teacher, but also the formal and informal expectations of the teacher are new. For many first-year teachers, entering the profession is concomitant with entering "adulthood." This change in self-perception involves restructuring thoughts, feelings, values, attitudes, and beliefs. This change implies the assumption of new roles and responsibilities.

The changes encountered during the first year of teaching often require first-year teachers to alter their relationships with others. Their most intimate friends and relatives, including spouses and family members, are often directly affected by the event. For example, first-year teachers need to restructure their daily schedules to accommodate the preparation required for class. The time required is often significantly greater than was ever required of them as students. New teachers may have less time available for household duties or personal time with friends than previously, and friends and family members are likely to feel disappointment and resentment. Unexpected and sometimes unwanted stresses and changes in relationships occur during the first year of teaching.

Our study of first-year teachers showed that the expressed concerns of beginning teachers are symptomatic of a larger problem than can be addressed with any single or simple solution. These context-related concerns varied with the experiences of each individual teacher. In their extensive studies of first-year teachers, Fuller and Bown (1975) also found that concerns experienced by beginning teachers were different for each individual. They found, however, that these concerns could be organized into three general areas: *self, task*, and *impact*. At first, new teachers' concerns focus on *self*. Once survival in the classroom has, to some degree, been assured, the teachers' concerns shift to the *task* of teaching and the establishing of an appropriate teaching environment. The final area of concern in this three-step developmental process is concern for the *impact* of teaching on the learning of pupils. These concerns are very real, and they should be shared with others if problems are to be identified and resolved in a manner that allows for the continuous professional and personal growth of the first-year teacher.

Greenberg (1969) has emphasized that teachers need help from colleagues in order to cope with their concerns about achieving "teacherhood." This colleagueship is important for the beginning teacher's survival.

Numerous studies have been conducted to examine the high attrition rate of beginning teachers. Holt and Uhlenberg (1978) conclude that first-year teachers may be so concerned with the issue of survival in the classroom that they are reluctant to try the innovative approaches often endorsed in their teacher preparation programs—approaches that could result in more successful teaching. By sacrificing these innovative methods and approaches, beginning teachers may add further stress to their position. Once established, this attitude of waiting to innovate in order to find the means and time to survive will dull the enthusiasm and idealism that are traits of beginning teachers.

The first year of teaching should be a confirmation of the excitement and enthusiasm that led a person to education as a career. Establishing a supportive collegial environment can often help the beginning teacher not only to "survive" but to maintain enthusiasm and idealism. The significance of a supportive environment and its relationship to teacher survival depends significantly on the people with whom a teacher has the greatest interaction, namely, students, parents, colleagues, supervisors, and principals. "A single encounter with another individual may tip the scales at an early stage in favor of staying in or dropping out of the profession. A mediocre teacher may last indefinitely in a mediocre school, while a bad teacher in a good school and a good teacher in a bad school may end up leaving the profession" (Pratt, 1977, p. 16).

Perceiving oneself as a professional teacher does not occur automatically upon obtaining a credential or even upon employment in a teaching position. In our study of first-year teachers, we found that new teachers did not perceive themselves as teachers until they had been in the classroom for several months. Yet, the realization of the transition to the role of teacher is very important. This attitude toward being a professional is pervasive and needs to permeate each step of the way in applying for, securing, and succeeding in a teaching position. Persons who truly believe themselves to be professionals convey this in many ways. They perceive themselves as adequately prepared and capable of assuming the professional challenge of teaching. They are enthusiastic about getting a teaching position. Their professional attitude is reflected in the written résumés of teacher applicants, in their letters of inquiry about job vacancies, in their preparation for job interviews, in the manner in which they conduct themselves at interviews, and in the numerous preparations required for the first teaching assignment. There are certain, identifiable steps in this transition to the role of teacher. Both the professional and mechanical aspects of each of these transitional steps are discussed in the following sections.

APPLYING FOR A TEACHING POSITION: AN INITIAL STEP

The résumé, a "written picture" of any job applicant, could be the means that determines the interview. It must present a neat, accurate impression of the prospective teacher. Typing errors, misspelled words, and inaccurate information may eliminate any chance the job applicant has of gaining an interview. A photostatic copy of a résumé is acceptable, but it must be a "clean" copy.

There are a variety of acceptable forms for the résumé. In general, it should include a statement of professional goals, educational background and experiences, work experiences, leadership roles assumed during both high school and college, and extracurricular interests and memberships in professional associations. The format should be consistent and should reflect a professional manner. Attempts at being "different" — using colored paper or an elaborate border — to attract attention often have an effect that is the opposite of the one intended. A résumé that is extremely unusual might be discarded by the reader as one that is *too* "different" to fit comfortably in the structured system of a school.

Just as the résumé is an indicator of the applicant, so too is the way in which that person completes an application. The neatness and completeness of the application can be a major determinant of whether or not the applicant reaches the interview stage. An application should always be completed in black ink and, if possible, should be typewritten. Prospective teachers should be certain that the information on the application and on the résumé is consistent and accurate. Many times, a school requires at least three references. Applicants should always receive permission from those people whom they want to list as references. Applicants should also remember that references should be people who are familiar with their teaching abilities, academic abilities, and general character. Relatives, friends, and acquaintances from religious or non-school-related affiliations are often of little value; former professors, supervisors, or cooperating teachers from student teaching and/or other field experiences are suitable and can give the employer some idea of the applicant's teaching ability and potential in the classroom. Whenever possible, applicants should hand-carry the completed form to the superintendent's office. This additional contact and indication of interest in the position may be advantageous.

There are many sources of information about possible teaching positions for both first-year and experienced teachers. The search for a job should probably begin with the placement office that is a part of most colleges and universities. Placement offices provide a variety of services to students—both present and past—who aspire to enter the field or to change positions. First, applicants should register with the office, completing the forms regarding personal data and compiling references from instructors. Through registration with such a placement service, applicants may receive a periodic newsletter listing openings about which the college or university has been informed. Applicants may also have an opportunity to interview with prospective employers who visit the campus. Placement files, along with transcripts, can be sent from the placement office to school systems or other places of employment to which prospective teachers may be applying.

Less formal than a placement service but equally informative is the "grapevine" system that exists in the field of education. Through contact with the system in which student teaching was performed, through communication with peers who have entered the profession, and through correspondence with former teachers and professors, prospective teachers may become aware of job openings before the general public learns of them. Many times, early contact with a system about a teaching position provides applicants with an advantage.

Teacher applicants should by no means feel limited to the above methods. Perhaps one of the most effective means of searching is through a self-instigated canvas of schools. Most states publish a directory of schools through the state Department of Education. This directory will contain the names and addresses of elementary and secondary schools in the state and often the name of the superintendent or personnel director who is responsible for the hiring of teachers. Although the résumé can be copied, the letter of inquiry should be a typed original, stating the applicant's interest in the system and requesting an application form from the school.

It is important that when applicants accept a position, they notify any schools that are maintaining active files on them that they have signed a contract. This notification can simply be a postcard on which is typed the information that John Smith has signed a contract and wishes to have his application removed from the active file.

INTERVIEWING FOR A TEACHING POSITION:
THE MAJOR STEPS IN SECURING A JOB

Just as the impression made by the résumé is important for the prospective teacher, so too, is the impression made when that applicant arrives for an interview. It is said that "first impressions are the most lasting." This should be remembered as applicants prepare for an interview.

Dress creates an impression, and teachers who look like professional educators create the feeling that they regard teaching as a profession. A person should use common sense in determining how to dress for an interview. Overdressing can be perceived negatively while the opposite can also be true. Conservative attire that is neat and clean goes a long way in creating a favorable, professional effect. Even though applicants know that the type of dress is not the critical factor for successful teaching, they must realize that teaching occurs in a context where the community sets general expectations and norms for teachers. Gum-chewing and smoking before or during the interview are both anathema. Taking along a "companion" can create the impression that the applicant is insecure or ill at ease.

Applicants who are late for the interview or who are not prepared do themselves a disservice. Prospective teachers should allow ample time to arrive at the interview location; ample time should encompass the possibility of getting lost, having to stop for directions, searching for a parking place, and needing help to find the right office in the right building. Applicants might want to take a trial run to the interview site prior to the date of the interview.

Having asked for and scheduled an interview for a position, prospective teachers must prepare for that interview. It is advisable to learn something about the community and the school system in which the position is available. A source as common as a state almanac will provide information regarding the population and size of the town or city and the principal industries. Possessed of some knowledge of the community, teacher applicants will be able to ask or respond to questions about the setting of the school.

In preparing for the interview, prospective teachers should also compile all information received from and sent to the school; this should include copies of the application and the résumé. Thus, applicants can familiarize themselves with the information held by the person conducting the interview. Often, the teacher applicant will be asked, "What is your philosophy of education?" The interviewer may expect either an oral or written response to this question. The best preparation for a question of this type is to sit down and write what one's philosophy of education is. Through having formally verbalized the answer to himself or herself, a prospective teacher will not be thrown into a panic by a question of this nature.

During the interview, a wide variety of questions may be asked. The following represent the type of questions to which an applicant may be expected to respond:

1. What do you want to accomplish most as a teacher?
2. How will you identify the needs of the students?
3. How will you go about deciding what should be taught in your classes?
4. What do you consider to be the most effective teaching approaches and techniques?
5. What are the most important things to do to maintain discipline in the classroom?
6. What would you do if a parent came to you and complained that what you were teaching his or her child was irrelevant to the child's needs?
7. What would you identify as your greatest strengths and greatest weaknesses?
8. What do you expect to be doing in five or ten years?

Applicants should ask questions as well; in fact, many interviewers expect and prefer that a potential employee ask questions about the position itself, the curriculum, and the specific responsibilities of the job. Well-thought-out questions denote an interest in the position and often reflect the interviewee's values and attitudes toward teaching. The interviewee should be very cautious, however, about asking questions of a political or religious nature. Questions that portray a lack of self-confidence or naiveté are often interpreted in a negative way. Questions regarding salary and fringe benefits should be of low priority and should perhaps not be asked during the initial interview.

Other questions interviewees might want to ask include the following:

1. Are parents encouraged to become actively involved in the school?
2. How would you describe the community in terms of the education levels of parents, interest in the school, and financial support for the school?
3. What are the primary businesses of the community?

4. What is the primary ethnic orientation and religious composition of the community?
5. What formal or informal opportunities are available to discuss professional concerns with the administrator?
6. Does the school district provide in-service programs for teachers?
7. Are teachers encouraged to make home visits prior to school in order to meet both students and parents?
8. Are teachers free to team teach if other teachers are interested in doing so?
9. Do teachers determine their own schedules, or are teaching units and times set by policy?
10. If pupils' needs warrant small group instruction, would this be allowed?
11. What are the specific responsibilities of the position aside from teaching?

The interview affords applicants an opportunity to discuss individual talents and abilities. A person interested in camping, for example, might inquire about opportunities to assist in outdoor education programs, even if the job opening is of a grade level that is not involved with environmental education. Similarly, a person with special talents in art, music, drama, or dance should inquire about the potential use of these talents beyond the individual classroom. Many employers are impressed by a candidate who has interests and capabilities beyond those of classroom teaching.

In many cases, especially at the secondary level, supplemental contracts may be involved. A supplemental contract could be as involved as coaching a basketball team or as simple as sharing the responsibility for a grade level money-making project. Prior to interviewing for a position, future teachers should consider how much time they may be able to devote to extracurricular activities. Often a teaching position may be contingent upon the willingness or ability of applicants to assume such duties. Under such circumstances, it may be wise to ask for the name of the person who has been responsible for the activities in the past; by contacting that teacher, applicants may gain an in-depth understanding of the time and the effort involved before agreeing to a supplemental contract.

At the conclusion of the interview, applicants should ask when they will hear from the interviewer regarding the position. If there is no specific answer ("We will call you by next Wednesday"), applicants should ask if they may call to inquire in a week's time. When applicants have interviewed for more than one position in more than one system, it is important to know the time schedule for the interviewing and hiring process; this allows teachers the opportunity to schedule other interviews and the freedom to accept or reject a job offer while other possibilities are pending. Interviewees should not hesitate to inform interviewers they are being seriously considered for a job in another school district. Often this serves not to jeopardize but rather to enhance the chances of being offered a job. However, such information must be completely accurate—applicants must not mention another position unless there is a bona fide offer. Also, such information must not be used as a way of forcing a decision on the part of the potential employer — such a scheme usually produces negative results.

After being interviewed for a position, teacher applicants should send a follow-up letter to the superintendent or the personnel director by whom the interview was conducted—a letter merely thanking the interviewer and restating interest in the system. Such a letter indicates interest in the school and the position, and it reminds the interviewer of an exceptional applicant.

PREPARING FOR THE REALITY OF TEACHING: THE PROFESSIONALLY CHALLENGING AND REWARDING STEP

Once hired for a full-time position, teachers must begin the process of preparing for the first day of school and for the entire school year. This process begins long before the first week of the school year or the first teacher work day prior to the opening of school. The building principal is usually on duty preparing for the beginning of a new year a month before the beginning of school. This is the time for a teacher new to the system to become acquainted with the building, the procedures, and the many other teachers and staff members who will also be in evidence around the building.

The days before school starts can also be used to learn more about the multiple educational contexts of the school and community. The more familiar teachers are with facts regarding the attendance area, the more effective they will be in communicating with parents. The following teacher's journal illustrates the numerous administrative functions that need to be considered during the first few months of teaching. Data in the journal were compiled by participants in our study of first-year teachers.

Journal of a Beginning Teacher
July 1–December 28

July 1. Today, I received an appointment to teach third grade at Washington Elementary School—an inner-city, low socioeconomic area. I called the principal, Mr. Smith, and requested an interview with him—it is set for July 12.

July 12. On the drive to Washington Elementary School, I noted that the area was not going to be very conducive for taking students for walks in the neighborhood. The school is situated between two heavily traveled streets. Field trips will have to be arranged using school buses.

Mr. Smith welcomed me to Washington School and gave me a copy of the *Teacher's Guide,* which explains school policies and procedures. He also gave me the third grade curriculum guide, which had just been completed. Mr. Smith explained that the students do not have textbooks for science and social studies, but that there are many resources available to teach these subjects. An in-service meeting is scheduled for August 17 to explain the use of the kits that are available to teach science using the process approach. Mr. Smith told me that the language arts textbooks the students will be using are outdated, but that they are still useful. He explained that he encourages his teachers to use the basic texts, but he also likes to see them supplement the texts with a variety of learning activities. But, he added, be prepared to state the purpose of the activity! A new classroom management program is in its second year of implementation at Washington School. Mr. Smith gave me a brief overview of the program and a booklet that details this plan. He mentioned that there is a movie available on this plan if I cared to view it. I obtained the cumulative records of the students I will be teaching—there are twenty-eight!

Mr. Smith then gave me a tour of the building, pointing out the areas with which I would especially need to become familiar. We ended up at room 108—my classroom! Mr. Smith told me to call him if I had any further questions. My classroom is very large with a restroom area, a sink, and much wall space that can be used for displays. There are plenty of cabinets and storage areas with shelves above them. The height of the shelves will not be a problem for setting up learning centers. A steel file cabinet is next to the teacher's desk. One area is carpeted—this will make a nice reading center. Overall, I am extremely pleased with the classroom and most anxious to bring it to life.

July 15. I have finished reading the cumulative folders on my students. This class is certainly going to be a challenge! It appears that these children need strong reinforcement in the area of self-concept. Many of the students are shy and withdrawn. I am going to spend the first two weeks of school on self-concept-building through the use of learning centers. Luckily, I have an idea file, from my college field experiences, which contains many ideas for establishing learning centers on self-concept and self-awareness. I will also need to collect music materials to include in this unit. I will check the Media Center to see what films are available.

July 30. The unit entitled "Learning about Yourself" is now complete. The learning centers are ready to be placed in the classroom, a film is reserved for September 12, and I have a list of children's books that I will need for implementing this unit.

August 1. I have studied the curriculum guide, and I can see where many areas will lend themselves to an integrated unit of study. I called Mr. Smith to discuss this matter with him; he cautioned me to take into account state-mandated minimum time schedules. With that in mind, I will attempt to integrate our units of study. I have charted the units to be studied under each subject heading — this will enable me to keep abreast of future topics to be studied. This is a helpful aid when perusing professional literature or when I am just browsing through magazines. I may come across a new idea that I might want to include in a unit of study. I can also plan ahead for any resource materials I will be needing during the year.

August 14. I have completed the bulletin board displays that I will be putting up in my classroom the first week of school. I had no idea it would take so long!

Today I met with Susan, another third grade teacher, and we decided to plan our first day of school together. It's fun and encouraging to plan this experience with a colleague. We're making name tags for each student and will also put each student's name on his or her desk. The textbooks that the students will be using will also be on their desks. I will keep a copy of the students' names and the numbers of the books assigned to each one.

Susan and I agree that it is important to establish a clear set of expectations with the students on the first day of class. I have decided to have each child introduce himself or herself and share one thing about himself or herself. If my students are too shy to participate, I won't force them to comply. I too will introduce myself and tell the students something about myself. Next, I will discuss classroom management procedures by introducing routines and expected behaviors. I will ask the students to help establish a list of classroom rules. Knowing that I will need to enforce the rules on a consistent basis, I will guide the students to make rules that are very reasonable and fair—rules that can be enforced.

Next, the pupils and I will discuss classroom jobs and make a chart of jobs and students' names. The chart will be changed weekly. I will discuss the daily schedule with the students. After the students have a break, we will have a music and/or art activity, followed by the film "Winnie the Pooh on the Way to School," which stresses safety precautions and courtesy procedures. As a follow-up activity, the children will discuss some of the concepts presented in the film.

I will then introduce the students to the learning centers in the room and explain when and how they may be used. Before the closing activity, the students will be given an opportunity to ask any questions they may have. Each student will be given a personal letter to take home to his or her parents. This letter will briefly outline the goals for the coming year, include the school's phone number, and encourage parents to call whenever they would like to talk about their child. The letter will encourage parents to visit the school before open house. It will include a form on the bottom portion where parents can list their jobs or professions. Then, when help or materials are needed for a special project, I can scan the list and choose the parents most likely to be able to help.

That's my plan for the first day of school! It looks good on paper, but it will be interesting to experience it first hand, knowing that each class of students is different. It was fun to plan with another teacher, and we want to get together on a regular basis to plan our lessons and share ideas.

August 17. The in-service meeting concerning the teaching of science is scheduled for today. Each teacher received a list of kits to be used in developing a particular concept. In the curriculum guide I will note the kits I need next to the concept to be taught.

August 25. Today I met the faculty of Washington Elementary School. Everyone seemed very friendly and willing to help me become better acquainted with school policies and routines. Mr. Smith gave us a calendar of the school year, pointing out the days for in-service meetings, parent conferences, and holidays. He also gave us a roster of teacher duties. We rotate every week serving playground supervision and cafeteria duty. I spent the remainder of the day organizing the classroom. The steel file came in very handy as it had dividers in it with tabs across the top. I changed many of the headings to fit my own purposes. I arranged the learning centers so that they are at a child's level and so that I did not have a quiet center next to a game center.

September 2. I am getting very nervous and anxious! I had lunch with a fellow teacher today, and we went over last-minute details.

September 7. The first day of school is over! I feel drained and yet very stimulated. The students were, indeed, shy! One little guy got sick and had to be sent to the nurse!

September 11. The end of the first week of school! We are making progress in many areas such as "respecting the property of others" and "being courteous." The students are beginning to trust the classroom atmosphere and are beginning to open up more in class discussions. I am charting the behavior of different groups of students on a daily basis. I select the students that I will chart at the beginning of the day and record my comments at the end before something interferes with this task. On Fridays, I will send home a note to five different parents informing them of their children's accomplishments. I will also mention any ideas I have that parents can use at home to help children with a particular skill.

September 25. OPEN HOUSE! I will be meeting many of the students' parents for the first time tonight. A brief formal meeting will be held in the school gym at which time the principal will introduce the faculty members. Each teacher is requested to talk briefly about himself or herself and his or her goals for the school year. Then we will go to our classrooms and await the arrival of the parents. I have displayed a sample of each student's work somewhere in the classroom along with the daily chart I have been keeping on each child. The textbooks we are using will be readily available for the parents to see. I remember how frustrated I have personally felt at an open house when one parent attempts to monopolize a teacher's time; therefore, I will suggest scheduling a conference within the next few days with any parents who seem to want a lengthy discussion about their child. I am eager to meet all the parents who come into my classroom.

October 12. Columbus Day—no school! My third grade colleague and I are meeting today for a two-hour session on "self-evaluations."

November 15. In another week, grade cards will be sent home. Students will be assigned a letter grade in language arts, math, and science and an "S" or "U" in all other subjects. I will be evaluating each student on an individual basis for the next week by scheduling five-minute conferences with each of them. I am preparing a list of anecdotal notes to include on the grade cards and also to have in hand for parent conferences.

November 18. The fall testing results have just arrived. I will study them closely and place them in the students' cumulative folders to be readily available for conference day.

December 3. PARENT–TEACHER CONFERENCE DAY! Fifteen parents have requested a conference with me. I have each child's folder at hand along with a note indicating those things I want to talk about.

Samples of the student's recent work are also at hand. I am prepared to explain to the parents the results of the fall testing program. The parents and I will sit at a round table at the back of the classroom rather than my sitting at the teacher's desk and the parent sitting at a student's desk. This ought to help the parents feel as though we are equals and help put both them and me more at ease. I will remember to say something positive about each student at the beginning of the conference.

December 23. CHRISTMAS BREAK BEGINS TODAY! The students are busy taking down the decorations and wrapping their presents to take home to their parents. I was very touched by the presents the students brought in for me today. I need to buy a package of thank-you cards!

After the children left for Christmas break, I found myself reminiscing over these beginning months of my teaching career. I have learned a lot. I also feel confident that the children have learned a lot! What was the secret to my success? I was well organized in my role as an administrator! This included such things as planning lessons within a realistic time frame; planning the physical environment of the class; organizing a good management system for filing materials; scheduling classes around the state-mandated minimum time schedules and around the special classes such as physical education, music, and art; communicating effectively with parents, peers, and the principal; reporting and using the school's adopted grading system; coordinating the services of teacher aides; and deciding on appropriate instructional activities.

As illustrated in the journal entries, the two or three weeks before school opens are the ideal time for the new teacher to become acquainted with other teachers on a one-to-one basis. An open classroom door should be an invitation to stop and say, "Hi! I'm Susie Smith, the new first grade teacher. I'll be in the room next door." Openness and friendliness often must come from the newcomer; meeting with and talking to other teachers prior to the new teachers' orientation will make that introduction to the entire staff much less overwhelming.

New teachers should remember that they are "new kids on the block" and, as such, responsible for asking questions and introducing themselves to others in the system and the building. By introducing themselves to the secretaries and the custodians, new teachers will know the sources of information and help. The secretary will know where the construction paper and other supplies are kept and the procedure to follow for obtaining them; the custodians will be able to tell the new teacher what can and cannot be placed on the walls and what can and cannot be done in the classrooms. Again, these people must be asked for their help, but having been asked, they will often be happy and eager to share their knowledge. As stated in chapter 2, everyone who works in a school is there for one purpose — good education for each pupil. The cooperative efforts of all are needed to assure the best education possible for all students.

The weeks before the opening of school are also the time to become knowledgeable about the textbooks and curriculum. New teachers should read and study the information available; then, if there are questions, they should try to get answers. Many "old hands" are pleased to share their knowledge and materials with a new teacher; the principal, too, can be a source of information about previous years and methods.

As teachers learn about the materials, texts, and units to be covered during the first few weeks of the school year, they can begin to plan and organize the classroom. This "quiet time" before the students arrive is ideal for rearranging desks, assembling interest centers, and decorating the room. The closer one comes to the opening day of school, the less time there seems to be for such preparation.

Once initial curriculum decisions are set, teachers have other decisions to make. What kind of classroom management system will be used? Are there school rules concerning classroom or school discipline or are teachers at liberty to use a system that they feel is best or with which they are most comfortable? What kind of schedule are teachers expected to follow? At the elementary level, the schedule — with the exception of recess and lunch—may be left to the discretion of teachers or may be predetermined by the principal. At the secondary level, the master schedule of classes is usually determined the preceding spring. Regardless of the level or the schedule, beginning teachers should learn what that schedule is and find a convenient place to note times, special classes, and/or room changes.

This is the time, too, for the teacher to plan activities for the first day of school—for that first sight of students pouring into the room, students who may be just as uncertain of the teacher as he or she is of them. How will the teacher introduce himself or herself to the class or the classes? How will the pupils introduce themselves to the teacher and to each other? What textbooks, if any, will be distributed on that first day or during that first week? At the intermediate and secondary levels, how will the teacher communicate—in a fifty-five-minute period—the expectations for the students?

Similarly, the elementary teacher will need to know which buses go in what direction and will need to answer questions from students about the bus that they are to ride home. The intermediate or secondary teacher will want to be able to interpret schedules that may confuse students and give directions regarding the locations of classrooms and lockers. In fact, for one of the teachers in our first-year teacher study, the most frustrating aspect of the first day of school occurred when her first graders got on the wrong buses to go home. The numbers of the buses that brought them to school differed from the numbers of the buses departing from school. While the experienced teachers were able to put this situation in perspective and laugh about it, the first-year teacher took it personally and blamed herself for not inquiring about the bus departure procedures. This same first-year teacher often remarked that her principal was very receptive to answering any procedural questions; the problem was that she often did not anticipate certain concerns and therefore did not know what questions should be asked. The bus situation exemplifies this point very well. Perhaps first-year teachers need to reflect step-by-step upon the total schedule and routine of the first school day in an effort to formulate questions that need to be answered.

Many times, the first day of school will be filled with special forms to be completed by the teacher or sent home to parents. There may also be the technicalities of fire drill and tornado drill to be covered as well as in-depth attendance reports to be completed. Organization of forms and procedures and compilation of a *list* of the tasks to be accomplished can be the most valuable tools for a teacher facing that first day of school.

SUBSTITUTE TEACHING: A CHALLENGING TASK

Teaching is difficult, but substitute teaching is even more difficult. Whereas new teachers experience a traumatic career change at the beginning of the school year, substitute teachers go through a series of such changes. While they are unaware of the individual needs of each specific group of children, they do possess general knowledge of how children learn, of education, and of schools. It is this general knowledge that helps substitutes to truly assume the role of professionals. Substitutes must not perceive themselves as "only" substitutes but rather as "teachers"—the professionals to whom the pupils have been entrusted. Just as regular teachers influence the students, either consciously or unconsciously, so too, substitute teachers influence the students. The role of a substitute teacher is different but not inferior to that of the teacher who works with the same children over an extended period of time.

We noted in chapter 8 that substitutes who arrive at the school prepared are in a better position to set a tone of professionalism and self-confidence. One way in which substitutes can come prepared is by developing a unit that can be adapted to various grade levels. This unit may relate to the teacher's area of expertise or to specialized knowledge and interest. A slide program, for example, that illustrates one's travel experiences can be used and adapted to various grade levels. A slide show on Japan focusing on dress and customs is as interesting to first graders as one focusing on the political and cultural forces that helped shape the Japanese economy may be to high school seniors.

The regular classroom teacher often does not have the time or the opportunity to prepare lesson plans that can be followed by someone who is unfamiliar with the material or the textbooks. Substitutes should not feel helpless if there is no lesson plan nor should they feel totally bound by lesson plans that are left. Substitutes who perceive themselves as teachers will take ownership of the plans and the situation and feel confident to adapt plans to meet the needs of the students as well as their own.

Teacher colleagues serve as great resources to substitute teachers. One of the first things substitutes should do is to introduce themselves to other teachers, especially those who are teaching at a similar grade level or whose classrooms may be adjacent. If at all possible, substitutes should familiarize themselves ahead of time with the various school communities where they might be teaching.

The initial period that substitutes spend with students is often vital to what happens throughout the day. Substitute teachers should consciously set a tone of professionalism, confidence in self, and interest, concern, and caring for each student. They should introduce themselves to the class as a first step in establishing the fact that they are people, professionals, and concerned individuals. Students are curious about the new people in their lives, and they will want to know something about this "stranger" before they get down to work. Substitute teachers should share personal information with the students — not just their names, but perhaps where they attended school, if they have children, and unique interests and experiences such as travels, hobbies, interests, and other jobs.

As teachers prepare to enter a classroom as substitutes, they must remember their impact can have far-reaching consequences. Being a substitute teacher in a school system could open the door (or shut one) to a full-time teaching position in that system. Substitute teachers who are prepared, professional, and work well with students do much to increase not only their own value but the worth of the experiences of the students in that classroom.

While orientation to the profession may seem overwhelming, to say the least, a good helping of common sense can go a long way. A useful guideline to measure common sense is a simple question such as, "If this were my child, how would I want the teacher to react?" or "If I were the principal, parent, or another teacher, how would I react?" The premise throughout this book is that the numerous decisions made in teaching cannot be prescribed. Using common sense in making decisions takes into consideration both the professional knowledge and the numerous past experiences of the teacher. Just as students learn through experiences, the past experiences of teachers can serve as a valuable base of information for making some commonsense decisions.

As suggested in chapter 1, new teachers need to be aware of the value of having interests and activities outside of the school setting. Especially during the transition period, it is easy to become so committed to preparation, grading, and students and school that teachers find themselves with no time for any other activity. Dedication to the profession is essential; overwork to the point of excluding other people and activities can lead to extreme stress and even "burnout." Teachers should schedule time to devote to family and friends outside the school setting and to nonschool activities. Through maintaining these contacts, teachers allow themselves to establish continually different perspectives —perspectives about people and the world in which they live.

Whether new teachers obtain full-time positions or serve as substitutes, the transition from the role of a student to that of a teacher is significant. Many of the initial anxieties experienced during this transition are very natural feelings that might accompany any career change. To help in this adjustment, beginning teachers should avail themselves of one of their greatest resources—teacher colleagues. Beginning teachers must also be realistic in terms of the expectations they place on themselves. They must accept the fact that they will make mistakes. Learning from these mistakes is part of a teacher's continuing professional development.

The Teacher
as Decision Maker
A PROBLEM-SOLVING ROLE

The instructional level of making curricular decisions is one to be guided by more than teacher intuition if any systematic implementation of society's expectations for schooling is to occur. Decisions may be made by default through letting the textbook become the curriculum or by thoughtless acts of commission. But decision-making through omission or commission cannot be considered adequate for helping students build the kinds of skills, attitudes, and knowledge they need now and in the future. (Klein in Goodlad, 1979, p. 188)

Teaching is decision-making, and decision-making as a process is similar to that of conducting research. In general, decision-making includes those abilities outlined by Dewey (1916) for effective problem-solving. These include perceiving, collecting, and making inferences about data; drawing conclusions from the data; hypothesizing about what might be done by selecting from among alternatives; hypothesizing potential cause-effect relations; and using knowledge within a given context.

Similar characteristics and qualities necessary for decision-making are summarized by Netzer and Eye (1979). They maintain that knowledge that provides a wide-ranged vision is necessary if the decision maker is to anticipate the outcomes of any major decision and the impact of that decision in other related areas. The decision-making process focuses not only on the use of former knowledge but also on the creation of new knowledge. This requires openness and awareness of various alternatives. If teachers can see only one particular way of doing something, they are not in a position to be aware of or to select from among the many alternatives that are usually available. Many people do not see decision-making as the opportunity to *choose* from among a number of ways of doing things. Entirely too often, decision-making is looked upon as the process of seeing a problem, thinking it through from a predetermined viewpoint, and arriving at a conclusion. But the thinking-through process, if it is valid at all, must be the process of looking at the various ways of accomplishing a purpose.

TEACHERS ARE DECISION MAKERS

During the course of the day, teachers continually make decisions that affect the lives of students—decisions that range from minute ones to those of much greater magnitude. What types of decisions do teachers make on a daily basis? During a seminar, a group of teachers was asked to reflect upon a day's happenings in terms of the types of decisions they had made. A summary of the decisions that were commonly revealed includes the following: which discipline approach to use in a specific situation; how to evaluate the students; how to individualize instruction; when to be flexible; how to evaluate curriculum; how to organize time; how to deal with trauma and stress in students; how to choose correct student placement and appropriate learning activities; how to select the teaching method for use at a specific moment; how to communicate with parents, peers, and students on specific issues; how to distribute classroom responsibilities; how to design the physical arrangement of the class; when to give homework; how to deal with one's own personal evaluations; and how to separate personal values from professional life. These examples are only illustrative of the hundreds of decisions teachers may make during the course of a single day.

In addition to the everyday instructional decisions that teachers make, they need to be involved on a cooperative basis with the total school and the community in programmatic decisions. Such involvement is described extensively in chapters 4 and 7. These chapters emphasize the need to discuss and evaluate the viewpoints of administrators, teachers, parents, pupils, and community residents in order to identify alternatives for effective educational decisions.

One difficulty in making decisions is that most of them need to be made spontaneously. Spontaneous decision-making is both an art and a skill that requires the ability to consider simultaneously the many variables associated with the personal and educational needs of each individual student. In order to act upon these variables, teachers must become extremely sensitive receptors of data; they must be aware of the moment-to-moment context that they share with the student as well as the separate contexts within which the teacher and each pupil function. As effective decision makers, teachers need to constantly gather data about each student, about themselves, and about the interdependent influences in the total ecological context. Teachers must develop the ability to spontaneously sort and evaluate these cumulative data. The ability to consider the numerous juxtaposed variables distinguishes the teacher as professional from the teacher as technician. The latter transmits information or acts as some outside source (a textbook or a professor) instructs him or her to act. The technician assumes, too, that all students at all times are ready for and receptive of data that are presented in one certain manner. The professional educator, on the other hand, is knowledgeable and keenly aware of the context and is able to combine this information with professional judgment in choosing from available alternatives.

Effective decision makers need a repertoire of alternatives or solutions to problems from which they can choose. This requires both a breadth and depth of knowledge. Teachers must possess a deep understanding of the discipline being taught, a comprehensive knowledge of human development, ability to apply this knowledge, and a thorough understanding of and appreciation for the importance of education in a culturally pluralistic society.

Teachers need to have the autonomy necessary to make decisions. They also need support from colleagues and administrators — support for making decisions and in developing decision-making skills. The inner resources and strengths of a teacher are not developed when teachers are expected to implement the decisions of others. The teacher's own self-competence, understanding, and ability are denied when decisions are imposed upon him or her by peers or administrators. John Dewey (1900) considered his teaching staff to be professional decision makers who had the right, obligation, and responsibility to make choices regarding an appropriate course of action. His teachers were not merely consulted; they made the decisions. In his school, Dewey did not dictate a specific discipline model or method of presenting curricular material; he expected teachers to select whatever they felt was best for each specific situation.

Since any teaching-learning process—whether formal or informal—takes place within a given context, realities within the context of the classroom create effects that are multidimensional, simultaneous, and possibly unpredictable. These effects often leave teachers little time to reflect before reaching a decision and acting on an event. In spite of this limitation, professional decision makers must be able to consider the many variables existing at a specific moment before they act. They must be able to assess not only where the student is in the cognitive process but also where the student is developmentally (Elkind, 1976; Piaget, 1973). Professional decision makers need to learn how to orchestrate instructional approaches within a developmental plan—approaches that are intended to move learners along, both individually and systematically, from their present levels of achievement toward higher goals. Technicians, however, simply respond to learners as a group without making any attempt to study the individual contexts of each student.

Professional decision makers must realize and recognize that the specific needs of learners may change over time; pupils are continuously growing, and their needs are ever-changing. The existence of these dynamic variables makes it impossible to provide prescriptive solutions to the problems teachers encounter each day. Rather, teachers need to develop the art of making decisions that are responsive to a precise moment and to a specific context. Solutions to problems in one context might not be acceptable in other contexts. In fact, a solution may be desirable for one student but not for another in the same classroom.

Teachers as decision makers must develop the ability to see a problem from the students' viewpoints as well as their own, taking into consideration all of the factors that come into focus from both perspectives. The differing backgrounds of both teachers and students contribute to this variance. Furthermore, what one teacher perceives as a problem may not be a problem for another. Often, the decisions that teachers make, either consciously or unconsciously, reflect their perceptions of the problem. These perceptions are often based on their values about the teaching-learning process. Some factors that might influence teachers' values include their views about students, about schools, and about the society in which students live. For example, teachers who feel that society needs people who are self-motivated, divergent thinkers will make academic decisions that will help pupils acquire these characteristics; conversely, teachers who view the role of students as one of conformity to established, traditional values are likely to require unquestioning conformity to rules and regulations.

Students' views of problems also differ according to background, values, and personality. For example, a teacher confronted by student dissatisfaction with a particular rule or regulation must first be aware that the student might view that rule as unnecessary; he or she may see a rule as just one more way in which teachers try to control students and not as something that is important to student health and safety. "No running in the halls" may translate differently for students than it does for teachers. It is the mental review of these possibilities that brings one finally to the selection of a particular decision.

Another important factor to consider in decision-making is the tone in which a decision is made and transmitted to the student. A difficult or demanding decision made in a supportive, optimistic environment will be more likely to achieve a higher degree of success than a good decision made in a negative, emotional manner. Students are more likely to accept a decision if they have been involved in discussing alternatives or if they are provided with an explanation of why that decision was made. They also need to understand that decisions are often made for different reasons. Some decisions require a quick, definitive answer, such as those made when physical safety is involved. Others are made on a moral or legal basis; some are made in adherence to local or state policies. Openness on the part of teachers leads to openness and candidness on the part of students. When the tone or atmosphere in the classroom is warm, accepting, trusting, and open, students will feel that they are not being judged but are being seen and treated with respect and trust. They will be more likely to view the teacher as someone who is nonmoralizing and nonpunitive—someone who is willing to listen to and to accept what they have to say.

Teachers must also realize that not every decision is safe. Even when they are sensitive to the moment-to-moment context, risk-taking is involved in making decisions. In fact, teachers are often required to make decisions that go beyond the absolute safe level, that is, they may not be able to predict the single best answer. Sometimes, teachers need to risk making decisions that they know are best for the students but might not be approved wholeheartedly by their principal, colleagues, or the parents.

Unless the developing teacher understands that meaning is derived from context and is context-related, it is not possible for him or her to become an effective professional decision maker. Therefore, teachers should constantly evaluate the results of all decisions and thus provide data for future ones. This evaluation will also help them to gain greater confidence in making decisions that involve risk-taking. "By becoming aware of the decision being made, and by being able to review the way the decision interfaces with a given context, the knowledgeable educator can make wider and more effective decisions" (Williams, Neff, & Finkelstein, 1981, p. 95).

TOWARD BECOMING A DECISION MAKER

Table 1 presents a framework for thinking through and analyzing situations that require decision-making. Some basic steps involved in problem-solving are included in the framework. These steps include

TABLE 1. The Decision-Making Framework

Statement of Problem	Context of Problem and Possible Ecological Influences	Some Acceptable Solutions	Rationale	Some Less Desirable or Totally Unacceptable Solutions	Rationale
Two boys have not completed their work in the allotted time. They have been playing and looking around the room and out the window.	Both boys are perceived by the teacher to be bright and capable students.	Conduct an individual conference with each child to find out the students' reasons for not completing the assignment. During the conference, set individual goals for completing the work.	Conferences can help teachers gain greater insight into the student's developing thoughts and feelings and the possible causes of the problem. Conferences also demonstrate the teacher's interest in the child as a unique person.	Placing their desks on either side of the teacher's desk.	Could denote mistrust on the part of the teacher and thus encourage the "self-fulfilling prophecy."
		Assess the level of difficulty and appropriateness of the assignment.	Since the teacher diagnosed the boys as being bright, their lack of motivation may be due to boredom.	Isolating the boys for long periods.	Allowing the boys to sit where they want may be more beneficial since often students who share a social context apart from school develop certain expectations about each other that importantly influence their behavior in the classroom.
		Offer options in the learning assignments.	Each child learns selectively and according to his or her own learning style.	Constantly reminding the boys to get busy.	Reinforces inappropriate behavior; takes away quality time the teacher should be giving the reading group with whom she is working directly.

identifying the problem; noting relevant and irrelevant data; being sensitive to the variables in the multiple learning contexts that might influence the decision; and generating alternative solutions that have theoretical support. The ability of teachers to integrate their knowledge of development with the knowledge of the many variables existent at that particular moment is important to the decision-making process. The more decision-making is practiced, the more it will become a very natural part of individual performance. For example, the beginning swimmer is at first very conscious of individual aspects such as movements of the hands and legs, the types of strokes, and body positions. After much practice, the individual gains the facility to swim without being conscious of the various body movements. So too, the art and skill of decision-making can become a very natural part of the teacher's actions.

The use of simulations, videotapes, or scenarios of actual classroom environments can provide information for use in developing the skill of decision-making. In *The Making of a Teacher* (1975), Travers and Dillon point out that in studying scenarios, the reader must think about how their modes of expression would be called into play by the particular situation and how they would incorporate the role of decision maker through the medium of their own teaching styles and philosophies. For example, a teacher who has incorporated in the classroom a management system that utilizes a class meeting as one form of problem-solving may list such a class meeting as a viable solution to a problem. Another teacher, one who has adopted Dreikurs's (1972) social discipline model for classroom management, may find that determining a student's goal—attention, power, revenge, helplessness—and punishing inappropriate behavior with some logical consequence is a more realistic solution to a problem.

It should also be noted that what one teacher identifies as a problem may not be a problem at all for another; this too is dependent upon the experience, attitudes, and understandings that each individual brings to the teaching-learning situation. For example, one person may have difficulty with the fact that kindergarten students forget to remove their street shoes and put on their tennis shoes without being reminded every morning. Another person may view repeatedly reminding the children of this rule as merely a part of the day's work in dealing with very young children.

In his essay "Talks to Teachers on Psychology," William James states that "we gain confidence in respect to any method which we are using as soon as we believe that it has theory as well as practice at its back" (Hillesheim & Merrill, 1971, p. 217). He goes on to suggest that teachers gain this confidence as well as independence and interest in decision-making when they are able to view each student from a two-dimensional perspective—treating him or her with tact and insight while recognizing the individual nature of internal motivations, attitudes, and values. Such a complete knowledge, for which every teacher ought to strive, is required for effective decision-making.

The remainder of this chapter includes scenarios of actual classroom situations that have been submitted by experienced teachers. Using the decision-making framework presented in table 1, the reader is encouraged to examine these scenarios. Discussion questions are provided to help the reader become aware of the many factors involved in decision-making, to identify problems of decision-making issues, and to explore possible solutions based on the individual's orientation to the teaching-learning context.

The first scenario is taken from one day's experiences of a third grade teacher. In reading this scenario, the reader should be able to identify several points at which the teacher acts as decision maker. Although there are other aspects of teaching and decision-making that function within this scenario, the discussion questions focus on self-discipline and prejudgment.

Scenario 1

At 8:45, I began my day with my students by taking attendance, lunch count, and milk money. While I was doing this, each child was writing a page about autumn for our class book.

By 9:00, the principal had made the announcements and played the national anthem, and we had recited the pledge of allegiance. I began giving the students directions for their morning work but was interrupted by a knock at our door. It was the coordinator of the learning styles project; he gave me a set of learning styles inventories to complete. It was a new form, so he stayed and explained the procedure to use when administering it. While the coordinator was in the room, one of my students went to the resource room for learning-disabled students, and two boys from the other second grade came to me for reading. My students were working on their morning work. The coordinator finally left, and I finished giving directions to my class.

At 9:20, I called my first reading group. While we went over new words, the rest of the class stayed busy. The reading group started writing their new words, and I helped with spacing, letter formation, and reversals.

Around 9:45, I called my next reading group. As we were going over the new words orally and writing them, several children from the first reading group were finishing their work and taking various learning games to different parts of the room.

At 10:15, the children who had finished their work were excused for recess. Those who had not finished stayed inside to work. There were two boys who, I was certain, would not finish their work. Their desks were on either side of mine. Even though they were that close to me, they looked around, played at their seats, or looked out the window. I was constantly saying their names and reminding them to get busy. I was so tired of their not doing their work that I wondered if I should just accept whatever they had finished at the beginning of recess. Both boys are bright and can do the work; it is very frustrating for me when they do not complete it.

At 10:20, I received a telephone call from a teacher at another building who has had one of my former students move into her building. She wanted to know about him and about his work habits. As my class came in from recess at 10:30, I waved them on to the music class because I was still talking on the phone. When I got back to my room, I saw that the two boys about whom I am concerned had done nothing while I was gone. While the class was at music, I made a quick trip to the lounge for a cup of tea.

My class returned from music at 11:00. I sent four of my students out for Title I reading, and a girl from our primary unit came to me for reading. I met with a child whom I have on an individual program for reading and language arts to see how he was doing and to give him new assignments. While the third reading group was writing their new words, the rest of the class was working on an art project to accompany a poem they wrote earlier in the morning.

At 11:30, I sent five of my students to Title I reading as the first four returned. I then called my last reading group. This group also went over their new words and wrote them. While the group was writing their words, I set a timer for one student to help keep him on task. This method worked, and he finished writing his words. I set the timer for twelve minutes, and he also finished his poem.

Around 11:50, we began cleaning up and getting ready for lunch. It took the students quite some time to get the floor and desks clean because of our art project. We had time to sing a song before we left for lunch.

One of the many goals of teaching is to help students to develop a level of self-discipline so that success may occur both in social and in academic skills. If a student lacks the self-discipline to remain on task, learning is hindered and disruption of others often occurs. In this scenario, two boys have not completed their work due to inappropriate behavior.

DISCUSSION QUESTIONS

1. What kinds of behavior seem to be exhibited by the two boys who did not complete their work?
2. What teacher behaviors may have affected the behavior of the boys?
3. What steps has the teacher taken to alleviate the problem?
4. What is the teacher's attitude toward these two students?
5. How might this teacher's attitude hinder any progress in their behavior?
6. If the teacher does decide to "just accept whatever they had finished at the beginning of recess," how might this affect the students' future behaviors and the behaviors of the rest of the class?
7. In what ways might parental involvement be utilized here?

Prejudgment of students can influence the approach teachers use and their expectations of students and can eventually influence the academic success of individuals. The controversy over IQ scores and their relationships to teacher expectations is but one case in point. Although information about a student's previous experiences can be of value, care must be taken lest a so-called low achiever not be challenged or a pupil be labeled as a behavior problem throughout his or her educational experience. In Scenario 1, the teacher received a call from another teacher requesting information about the study habits and abilities of a transfer student.

1. What kinds of academic information might be given to assist the teacher?
2. Do you feel that a teacher who provides another teacher with information about the behavior patterns of a child is fair to the student?
3. Under what kinds of circumstances would previous knowledge of a child's behavior be vital to the teacher?
4. How might preconceived ideas about a student affect teaching methods? How might these expectations, in turn, affect the student?

Scenario 2 recounts the Friday morning of a sixth grade teacher. Her decisions and the factors at work in one short morning were many and varied. The teacher is shown in several of the roles that exist within the context of teaching as a profession; she reveals both the joys and frustrations that can occur in a relatively short period of time. Initially, the reader may want to focus on the decisions made regarding the effects of the home context on the student and on the mainstreaming of learning-disabled students. These factors are considered in the discussion questions that follow the scenario.

Scenario 2

Friday began with an early morning teachers' meeting. As I entered the hallway, my principal stopped me to ask about Andy, one of my students. Andy had injured his hand in an unsupervised home carpentry accident three days before, and a neighbor called the school this morning to ask if we felt that she should take him for medical attention since his mother was gone and she was caring for him. The principal asked me to check Andy's hand upon his arrival and then send him to the school office. I entered my classroom and wrote preliminary instructions on the board for any early-arriving students. (Often times, teachers' meetings run late, and the students will already be in the classroom when I return.)

Most teachers were on time for the meeting. My principal asked that I "volunteer" for a committee to redraft a reading inventory card for those students entering fourth grade. Such a record is invaluable to teachers when selecting supplementary reading materials for classrooms —it avoids duplication of materials. This committee is chaired by the reading supervisor of our building. As the meeting continued, memos (regarding amended playground rules, cafeteria dismissal, and workbook fee collections) were explained. Further into the meeting, our coordinator of the talented and gifted program distributed information that concerned students who had been identified as potentially gifted. Each teacher received lists of test scores, referral sheets, and identification outlines for any other child in his or her classroom who may, in the teacher's opinion, qualify for the talented and gifted program. The coordinator asked if I would spearhead a committee for the compilation of a resource list of learning activities that might be implemented at school this year. I found myself thinking, "Wow, two committees in one meeting plus going to graduate school!" The meeting was adjourned; it had run longer than planned. Most children were in their rooms, and I was hurrying to my room. A student who arrived on a late bus asked me about the scheduled band concert; I directed him to the band room.

My class was waiting in the room and seemed to be ready for art class at 8:50. All band members who remembered have left for the band room for the sixth grade concert. One student who had forgotten the concert time scurried from the room. Several students waited at my desk with book money, change for book money, workbook money, notes concerning their absence from school (we've had a siege of flu), and late assignments. Andy was there to show me the injury to his right hand. I collected the money quickly, asked the students to file their late work (some are still learning the mechanics of our sixth grade room organization), stapled notes to the attendance sheet, and realized that because of the late teachers' meeting and the band students' absences, I was not able to take attendance and lunch count. Consulting the remaining students about who was or was not in the room today, and considering the menu, I guessed about the lunch count.

With the remaining minutes left until art, I motioned Andy closer to my desk and inquired about his hand. He immediately informed me that a neighbor was taking him to the doctor today because his hand hurt. Andy moaned a little for me and offered a grimace. I comforted him and assured him that the principal and I would like to see him as soon as I took the class to art. Andy seemed pleased that he was going to see the principal. He had been in the principal's office at other times during other school years, and had not always enjoyed a positive reception.

On Thursday, Andy had given me a hastily scribbled note from his mother telling me that she would be out of state for a week and that she was glad I would be there for Andy when he needed help. She was aware of his injury before she left. His parents were not at home when he injured his hand. A neighbor had been called by Andy's teenage sister to administer first aid to the wound. As Andy handed me the note, he blurted out that his parents were "splitting up." His sister had chosen to live with her mother, and he would remain with his father. Andy's parents are educated people of middle-income level. His sister was a student in my class several years ago, and I know the family fairly well.

Thursday after school, the guidance counselor had asked me for a conference concerning Andy. In her office, she began to relate facts learned from other sources concerning the problems surrounding Andy. In the past, Andy discussed his home problems with the guidance counselor, and she had a sympathetic interest in this case. She asked that I send Andy to her any time I felt he needed to talk.

After my students were in their Friday art class, I saw the principal concerning Andy's hand. He agreed with me that it appeared to be healing but that it should have a covering during outside activities. We both realized that Andy's concern about his hand was his way of telling us that he needed attention and affection during these most trying times in his life. The principal placed a call to the concerned neighbor to relay our opinions concerning medical attention for Andy.

As I left the principal's office, the secretary informed me that I had another phone call. A parent was calling to get assignments for her child.

The child, according to the parent, was quite sick. I assured the parent that I would help the child with her assignments when she returned to school and that her daughter should rest and concentrate on getting well. By this time, planning period was over, half my class was in the room (back from band), and the remaining few were still in art class. We took a morning restroom break and rounded up the art room crowd. Finally, we were all together! I rechecked my attendance and lunch count and proceeded with the morning activities.

When the teacher is trying to gain an understanding of the academic, social, and behavioral aspects of an individual student, the influence of home factors should not be taken lightly. The amount of parental attention, types of physical surroundings, number of siblings, and types of parent-child relationships can affect school performance, socialization, and overall self-concept. The experiences a student has at home before coming to school in the morning may emotionally hinder or enhance any academic learning that is to take place that day. The teacher in this scenario discussed one student, Andy, and his home life, revealing factors that could be affecting school performance.

DISCUSSION QUESTIONS

1. What evidence mentioned indicates that Andy had experienced a history of trouble in school? How might this history affect Andy's self-concept?
2. How might a teacher's knowledge of this history affect teacher expectations and, in turn, Andy's behavior?
3. How might this visit to the principal's office influence Andy's future attitudes toward the principal and the act of going to the office?
4. What factors presented indicate a low level of adult supervision at home? In what ways might this affect Andy's school performance?
5. What types of behavior might the teacher expect to observe in Andy as a result of his parents' divorce?
6. In what ways might the teacher help Andy through this family crisis?

The third scenario, an account written by a fifth grade teacher who teaches in a rural area, reveals a variety of situations in which the teacher must function as decision maker. Students' feelings of acceptance by the teacher and their need for various instructional methods to meet individual needs are two of the areas presented in this scenario. Again, the reader should consider the decision-making framework; what acceptable solutions are there to these situations and what are the criteria for reaching these solutions? What unacceptable solutions may be evident in the scenario itself?

Scenario 3

It seems as though the first question that most people ask me when they discover that I am a teacher is, "What do you teach?" I know they mean, "What subject or what grade do you teach?" But I generally answer, "I teach children." I want them to realize that children are the center of *any* teaching that takes place in my classroom.

I have thirty-two students in my fifth grade class this year. There are three fifth grades at our building. We have tested and placed the children in three levels for math. I have the middle math group. We change classes for reading, also. The students have their own art, physical education, music, and band teachers.

The children entered the classroom around 8:45. (I have six students that walk to school; the remainder ride the bus.) Most of the students came straight to my desk to eagerly share the events of the night before. Some of the boys are on the football team, and they wanted to talk all at once. Two apples and four cucumbers were placed on my desk. I smiled and kept listening. The boys, having told me about last night's game, left to play football on the playground. It is the girls' turns. Three of my girls are making "fun books" to send to their friends. They shared these with me. I wrote myself a reminder to write a thank-you note for the cucumbers. A verbal "Thank you" will suffice for the apples.

The 8:55 bell rang. The students were in their seats. Announcements were made from the office over the PA system. The student chosen as class secretary took the attendance and lunch counts, and the messenger took these to the office. I read a chapter from the book *Knee Knock Rise* aloud. We had some time left for sharing. Football team members cheerfully announced that practice had been cancelled and that they would be able to attend the fifth and sixth grade skating party tonight. A cheer was raised.

It was 9:15 and time to change classes for reading. The students had the weekly assignment sheets that I handed out on Monday. I worked with the students on one reading level until 9:30; I helped those in another level until 9:45. Some students were taking clothespins from my desk to go to the library. (The pins have my name on them and are used as passes.) Others were curled up on the rug in the reading corner. I held individual conferences until 10:05. I read orally from *Mrs. Frisby and the*

Rats until 10:15. The last fifteen minutes of my class were for silent reading.

At 10:30, the students returned to their homeroom. From 10:30 to 11:00, I gave individual help with spelling workbooks. My students went to music and physical education from 11:00 to 12:00. While my students were gone, I worked on next week's lesson plans, decided what lesson my teacher education student from a local college would teach next Tuesday, and talked with a parent on the phone.

The student who is my audio-visual director showed a filmstrip on American Indians. We also discussed four pages in our social studies book between 12:00 and 12:30.

My lunch period was from 12:30 to 12:50. I had recess duty from 12:50 to 1:15. It was my lucky day! There was only one disagreement with which I had to deal. The two boys who had argued are from my homeroom. I asked them to please stand in different locations for five minutes, and then I permitted each of them to share his side of the story while the other listened. During recess, I also had some interesting conversations with my students from last year.

At 1:15, we changed classes for math. We're working on place values. After contemplating several alternative ways of explaining this concept, I found that what works for one student does not work for the next. That's the way it goes! A teacher always needs an alternate route.

We had another recess break from 2:10 to 2:30. I had duty again, but this afternoon there were no major problems.

The last period of the day is reserved for either health or science. Today we are studying health.

At 3:20, we prepared to leave. The desk inspector checked for paper on the floor. Around the room I heard, "Do we have any homework?" "Are you going skating tonight?" "Will you be there?"

Good-bye class. I really enjoyed working with you today. See you tonight!

From 7:00 to 9:30 P.M., I attended a skating party with five other teachers and approximately one hundred seventy students and some of their parents. It is nice to have the opportunity to talk with parents in a neutral location.

It was 10:30; I was almost exhausted. I went to sleep, remembering that tomorrow is Friday.

Students' feelings of acceptance by their teachers can have a major impact on their attitudes, motivations, and academic achievement. Students are often anxious not only to *receive* acceptance from their teachers but also to show *their* appreciation. This can be done through the simplest smile and verbal compliment or the writing of a congratu-latory letter. Whatever its form, the importance lies in the students' knowledge that their efforts are appreciated. The teacher in this scenario received gifts from some students in the form of two apples and four cucumbers.

DISCUSSION QUESTIONS

1. How did the teacher immediately let the students know she liked their gifts?
2. What problems might arise from writing a thank-you note to one student and not to another?
3. What other ways might the teacher have expressed thanks?

If teachers are to help students master academic skills, they must understand that students learn in different ways. Educators must recognize the differences among students and plan teaching to best fit those individual differences. In teaching a lesson on place value, this teacher found it necessary to use different explanations.

1. What are some of the various ways in which the teacher might have explained the place-value concept?
2. In what ways might the math group (which has evidently already been "ability-grouped") be further organized to meet individual learning needs?
3. React to the teacher's statement that "a teacher always needs an alternate route."

The final scenario occurs in an eighth grade language arts class and encompasses an entire day. With the change of students for each of this teacher's four classes, the role of decision-maker takes on additional importance. The ability to consider the multiple contexts that affect each student and the need to respond to each student as an individual become more complex; meeting with and teaching almost one hundred students each day presents additional variables that the teacher must consider. The reader should consider the types of negative behaviors observed by this teacher and the decisions she made about dealing with them. The reader should again consider both acceptable and less accept-able solutions to problems and the rationale that may prompt either type of solution.

Scenario 4

Monday, September 28, dawned bright and chilly. I arrived at the middle school shortly after 7:25 A.M. My briefcase and book bag contained graded papers and lesson plans for my four eighth grade language arts classes.

Nancy met me with her cheerleading top. I had to alter the top to fit her better. I couldn't carry all these items, but somehow I managed to get to my classroom and unlock it.

I hung up my coat and sorted through the papers on my desk. I had noted on my way in that the principal was not present, so I circulated in the hallway until the homeroom period began.

The bell for homeroom rang at 7:45 A.M. The students came to class. I took attendance quickly before the morning announcements were made. I made a mental note that one girl who is a ringleader in a "hood group" was absent for the third day.

The announcements were made, and we stood for the pledge of allegiance and "The Star Spangled Banner." I had positioned myself near the front of the room (the flag is in the rear) before the patriotic ceremonies. I did this to keep an eye out for possible disturbances. No trouble occurred today.

With the attendance slip in one hand and the spelling masters in the other, I went to the office after the first period bell rang. I ran off the spelling papers and picked up the three-hole punch. I had twenty minutes before my first class.

To facilitate the scheduling of time, I wrote an outline of the day's activities on the board. Today's work included work on book reports, spelling, grammar, literature, composition, and listening. I reviewed the story I am working on for today and braced myself for the first group of students.

At 8:23 A.M., twenty students entered my classroom. I tried to briefly describe the events scheduled by running through the outline. Few students seemed to need the time for book report work, so I handed out the spelling. I explained the directions for each section of the spelling worksheets. All three pages would be due tomorrow. I walked around the room to assist any students who were struggling with the directions.

The noise level was rising due to talk, so I moved on to the next subject. I assigned grammar groups and reassigned seats. This effectively squelched the talking. Some students required ten minutes to finish the grammar; others required twenty minutes. I interrupted the class to explain "Raymond's Run," the story that they were to read. I tried to build some interest in the reading. There were questions to answer following the reading.

The composition assignment is a continuation of journal writing that we began the week before. I put, "Do you know who you really are?" on the board as a stimulant for today's writing. The time went quickly, and I decided that changing seats had been beneficial. I will change the next class's seats before work begins.

It was now 9:35 A.M., and I began my next class — consisting of twenty-four students. By rearranging seats immediately, I avoided some noise problems. Since quiet work seemed to enhance reading, I assigned the literature story first for those who did not need the time for book reports. I watched the class to see if any problems existed. Satisfied that "all was well," I began grading the first class's papers.

After about twenty minutes, most students were either finished, restless, or both. I handed out the spelling, went over the directions, and told them that the papers would be due Tuesday. During my discussion of the spelling directions, one student put a key ring on his finger. It got stuck. When I was finished with the directions, I took it off his finger. He winced with pain (?), but the ring was easily removed.

I then assigned grammar groups and began working with individuals. My attention was distracted by two boys. These young men had not read the story I had assigned, so they were threatening a young lady in their group to "give us the answers or else." (Remind me to give them an "F" on the assignment.) My thoughts were, "Aren't the ignorant demanding?" I also began thinking of methods I might use to make my classroom more fair.

To snap me back to the grammar, a girl asked me about the work her group had been doing. I devised an alternative quiz so I would not have to repeat the information. If she achieved a "C-minus" or better, she could be assigned to a new group.

The day was flying by. It was time for me to send this group to study hall. Four students did not finish their work and asked if they could stay to finish. This time is supposed to be my preparation time, but I allowed them to stay and finish their work. Before the students went to lunch, I found out that one of the boys involved in the harassment of the young lady was kicked out of the house the night before. The other boy is failing algebra. One never knows what is going on in those little heads and hearts.

After lunch, I had a twenty-minute study hall. The students were a little noisy, so I limited library privileges for those who were not quiet. I also wrote journal assignments for the last week so those students who were behind could fill in their blank spaces.

The third class, with twenty-six pupils, began at 12:12 P.M. I again rearranged seating first to relieve some unwanted alliances. In this class, I tied the seating arrangement to the grammar groups.

I assigned the story, as I had done for the second class, and gave students the option to work on the book report. Much more work was done during this class period. I strolled about the room to observe why this was occurring. Actually, this class simply had more conscientious students than the other classes. I also believe that no matter how you plan, each class is different for varying reasons.

In a weaker moment, I let a student go to the restroom to put wax on his braces. He actually went to his locker (against all school rules) to get a science book. I realized this after he returned, and I congratulated him on being a "sly dog." He was really amazed that I caught him. There was the bell. Another class was over.

The fourth class has twenty-eight students. My time was terribly cramped. I had several grammar grouping problems to solve. I also needed to separate some battling students. They had more difficulty with the spelling directions, so I took more time with the spelling sheets. This group had the most potential and the least ambition.

I decided to use this group as my project group for developing the learning styles program. They are dependent on my help and approval to survive in the room. I had four to six students at my desk and two by my side when I walked about the room.

Ah — the day has been completed. I paused to review the day and made several conclusions. From reading this account, it seems that I had given much more attention to detail in my first two classes. My third and fourth classes were mentioned in more of an affective realm. I believe I went through a burnout period about one o'clock. The afternoon students were much more demanding emotionally than those in the morning. I believe these circumstances were significant when reviewing my decisions and methods of teaching.

Any grade level may present a variety of discipline problems with which the teacher must deal successfully to ensure the continuance of instruction and learning. Methods used in responding to these situations, however, will vary from grade level to grade level due to differences in maturity, socialization, and development. The *types* of behaviors displayed may also contrast greatly from one of these levels to the next. Therefore, it is vital for middle school teachers to have a workable understanding of the behavior patterns, socialization levels, peer influences, and maturation levels of students if effective discipline techniques are to be found and utilized.

Discussion Questions

Throughout the scenario this teacher observed a variety of behaviors.

1. Cite instances where the teacher approaches the day and her classes with both positive and negative expectations. How might her attitude have influenced the students' behaviors?
2. How might the teacher's circulating in the hallway be viewed in a *positive* manner by the students?
3. How might the teacher's labeling of the girl who is a ringleader in a "hood group" reflect the teacher's attitude?
4. What did the teacher do during the patriotic ceremonies in an attempt to prevent possible disturbances?
5. How did the teacher deal with a rising noise level? What may be some reasons for the increase in noise? What other methods might she use to discourage noise and excessive talking?
6. The teacher stated that "after about twenty minutes, most students were either finished, restless, or both." What might this say about her lesson plans? What might she do to prevent restlessness?
7. How might one deal with the two boys who told the girl to "give us the answers or else?" If this incident were ignored by the teacher, what possible occurrences might result?
8. Respond to the teacher's comment, "Aren't the ignorant demanding?"
9. What other factors mentioned might have contributed to the behavior of these two boys?
10. How did the teacher deal with students who were noisy in study hall? If that method did not alleviate the noise problem, what other approaches might the teacher have used?
11. Do you feel this teacher successfully dealt with the boy who misused his restroom privileges? Why or why not?
12. Discuss the possible relationship between this teacher's one o'clock "burnout" and the afternoon students who are "much more demanding emotionally."

The role of the teacher as decision maker is ongoing throughout all that a teacher does. The fact that these daily decisions must be made instantaneously and spontaneously adds both complexity and importance to this role. To function as decision makers, teachers need to consider the ecological factors that affect both students and teachers and to review all of the possible alternatives presented by each individual interaction with students. Through consideration of both acceptable and unacceptable solutions to decision-making situations and through practice in decision-making afforded through the scenarios in this chapter, we hope that each prospective teacher will become a professional rather than merely a technical decision maker.

Chapter 11

The Teacher as Professional Leader
A CHALLENGING ROLE

A critical quality of any leader is that he is profoundly convinced that his vision of what ought to be or could be has a dramatic significance for the lives of those for and with whom he works. He is caught up with the drama and excitement of what he and his subordinates are doing, and he communicates and shares them with subordinates. When speaking of educational leaders, we must add to the above quality, a continuous, lived experience of learning, in which the educational leader shares with his subordinates his own zest for expanding his own understanding and appreciation of the human epic. (Starratt, 1973, p. 13)

The ultimate goal of all teachers who are professional leaders is to unleash the human potential of each student entrusted to their care, demonstrating a sense of confidence in the ability to influence positively and significantly the lives of others. This confidence is developed, in part, by the specialized knowledge that teachers possess about the teaching-learning phenomenon. A basic understanding of the complex roles of the teacher forms a part of this specialized knowledge. Knowledge alone, however, does not assure professional leadership. Leadership is multifaceted and, as such, must encompass both personal and professional qualities.

Through the integration and interdependency of personal qualities and professional competence, instructional leadership is enhanced. For example, the teacher's own enthusiasm and love for living and learning provide a sense of purpose to his or her roles as professional leader and facilitator of learning. "Leaders bring to their jobs a sense of vision and purpose which adds rich meaning to their lives, the lives of others, and the activities of the school" (Sergiovanni & Carver, 1980, p. 325).

Combs (1982) has written extensively about the integration of the personal and professional dimensions of leadership and the importance of this integration for successful teaching. The essence of this thinking is reflected in the following quotation: "Teacher effectiveness is a function of how teachers use themselves and the world in which they live. The skillful use of self and the creation of conditions for significant learning is truly professional achievement" (p. 74). A similar view has been expressed by Van Hoose and Hult (1979): "Once the aspiring teacher realizes the importance of using himself or herself as an instrument to promote student growth and development, the careful acquisition of a repertoire of dramatic and social as well as academic skills can begin. Teachers need to become effective facilitators of learning, motivation, and guidance. On occasion this may require the teacher to be an information giver, disciplinarian, counselor, advisor, or referral agent" (p. 37). It is students' needs that should determine what teachers do. Responsive, sensitive teachers will be aware of the ever-changing needs of the students, assuming the contextual awareness discussed throughout this book—a perspective that accommodates the influences inherent in the total context within which students reside.

THE INTEGRATING OF ROLES

In reflecting on the teachers who most influenced our lives, we have identified a number of important leadership qualities. Some of the common personal characteristics of these teachers include optimism about the future; authenticity; concern; belief and trust in human potential; enthusiasm; confidence; high ethical standards; willingness to admit errors; a sense of spontaneity and emotional involvement; and an innate drive to achieve. Many of these qualities parallel those characteristics identified in leadership studies. A leader is one who "dreams dreams" and who is successful in translating these dreams into reality. Both as researchers and as consumers of research, teachers gain a broader vision of alternative possibilities and are in a position of "translating" dreams into programs that meet the individual needs of students.

While each chapter in this book focuses on a specific role, the complex roles of the teacher operate simultaneously and function interdependently. This complex and integrated structure might be compared to the construction of a mosaic in which the artist has an overall vision of how each part will relate and contribute to the total picture. The artist is well aware that the completed mosaic will be far greater than the sum of the individual pieces. It is this awareness that enables him or her to make the thousands of decisions for selecting specific colors, shades, and shapes. Similarly, it is the teacher's overall perspective of the teaching-learning phenomenon that helps him or her to see how the roles are related and to make decisions concerning which role may need greater emphasis at any specific moment. This type of holistic decision-making is where the "art" of teaching differs from the mere "knowledge" of teaching—where education differs from schooling. It is here, too, that the teacher chooses to initiate rather than to maintain—to actively lead rather than to passively follow.

While the complex roles of the teacher are integrated throughout the total teaching-learning phenomenon, the degree to which a specific role is emphasized differs in accordance with each unique situation. The degree to which one role is emphasized over another indicates a teacher's sensitivity to the moment-to-moment context. Based on the individual needs of the pupils, for example, the role of the teacher as facilitator of learning may be called more into play than the role of the teacher as program developer; at other times, however, the latter role may be more dominant. As the competent teacher gains greater knowledge of self and of each learner, he or she can almost intuitively select the role that best meets the needs of each individual student at any given moment. This intricate interdependence of the various roles of the teacher is recognized by Travers (1979) in his statement, "Effective teaching is not a set of distinct acts, each isolated from the other, as the proponents of the theory of distinct competencies would have us believe. The work of the plumber can be described in that manner as a succession of distinct competencies which collectively define the trade of the plumber. Effective teaching does not consist of a parallel chain of social competencies" (p. 14).

UNDERSTANDING THE LEADERSHIP ROLE
OF THE TEACHER

The following scenarios are included to help the reader examine the complex, interrelated roles of the teacher. The discussion following the scenarios reviews the various roles of the teacher and shows their intricate interdependency. One scenario reflects a day in the life of a third grade teacher as seen by that teacher; the other describes a morning in the life of a high school teacher through that teacher's eyes. While each scenario reflects the interdependency of the roles of the teacher, the difference in degree of emphasis of one role over another is evident.

Scenario 1: A Day in the Life of a Third Grade Teacher

The children came into the classroom bringing various supplies from home. Many brought shoeboxes and articles for a science project. There was some consternation among the children who had not remembered their supplies. I did not rush the children out to the playground. I observed them as they interacted, and I responded as they showed me their things. I hoped that this would create an interest in the project. As the children came into the classroom, each child took the tongue depressor with his or her name on it and placed it in one of three containers (labeled "white milk," "chocolate milk," or "no milk"). Slowly, they went out for recess before school started.

When the children came in from recess, we immediately had to go to art class. I wanted the children to get ready quickly, but I didn't want to create confusion. I think the children are rushed too often and sometimes show a feeling of frustration. I allowed the children to get their materials and to get into line as they were ready. I want them to learn to take care of their materials and prepare for changing subjects in an orderly manner.

As the children returned from art, I reminded them to put their supplies away quietly. I complimented them on their art projects. It was necessary for us to discuss controlling the noise in the room while they put their things away. I am striving for self-discipline within the children.

We began our opening exercises by changing "helping hands" (the chart used to assign work responsibilities in the classroom). Two girls began arguing over the job of helper. We discussed what had happened, and I then asked that one of the girls choose something else from the helping hand chart since we wanted to take turns at each job and she had already had that job. This appeared to satisfy both girls. I wanted them to feel that they were treated fairly. We then had "sharing time," which we have daily. I feel that the children need time to express themselves in a relaxed atmosphere. Also, they need to learn to be courteous and attentive listeners. During the busy schedule of the day, it is often difficult to take individual time to listen to the children's comments.

It was necessary to discuss sending five children to listen to a speaker from the newspaper. It was explained to the class that students should volunteer to participate only if they were interested and if they were willing to be responsible for work missed. Since many children showed an interest, it was necessary for me to choose the representative from our class. I did this on past teacher assessments of potentially gifted children and also on how the student had been performing in my classroom. I chose one on art ability, hoping that he would do drawings for the school newspaper.

During the reading groups, the children at their seats were working quietly and seemed excited about their science projects. I decided to lessen the amount of paperwork I gave. This would allow more free working time for science. I did not want the children to lose their enthusiasm. After reading, I called several children up to correct their papers. I felt that they had made too many mistakes and that they needed individual help to better understand the subject.

The remedial reading teacher had asked me to send for testing any children whom I felt needed extra help in reading. Two children were having trouble in the classroom, so I decided to send them.

As the class and I were watching an educational television show, one child began to cry. He said the show was upsetting him. I took him out of the class and talked to him. The real problem was that he had forgotten his lunch money and was worried about it. I reassured him that he could charge his lunch and that I would never let him go without eating. He seemed reassured and happy again.

It was then time to change classes for mathematics. As we were lining up, there was a problem. One boy let another boy in front of him. We discussed the problem and decided that both children should go to the end of the line if they wanted to stand together.

During math, I decided to move a child from an isolated desk to one located among the group. He had been having trouble concentrating and was bothering the other children. I want him to learn to function as part of the group. It seemed that isolating him did not improve his behavior; it only called more attention to him and gave him a chance to be noticed. I talked to him privately and told him that I was confident that he could do his work without causing a problem. He worked better today. Also, during math it was necessary to discuss when it is appropriate for children to leave their seats to sharpen a pencil or get a tissue. I wanted them to know that they are free to move around the room as long as they are working independently and are not interfering with other classroom activities.

On the playground, it was necessary to correct several children who were not following the rules. The children appear to be very concerned with themselves, and they do not always consider the rights of others. I am striving in my classroom to make the children more aware of people around them and to be more observant of their environment.

After we returned from music class, it was time to prepare to go home. The children cleaned up the room as I handed out the corrected papers. I want them to be responsible for the room. The children lined up to leave.

FOCUSING ON EDUCATIONAL PRACTICE

The effective and successful teacher is a person who possesses the human qualities of caring, loving, respecting, trusting, and understanding. In this scenario, the teacher expressed the concern that children are often rushed and sometimes feel frustrated because of it. She also recognized the need to be a good listener to each child. She was reassuring and comforting to the child who had forgotten his money for hot lunch. She talked privately to the child who was disturbing the class; she told him she was confident that he could do his work without bothering the other children. The role of the teacher as person is reflected throughout the scenario. Similarly, the role of the teacher as decision maker is basic to all of the roles.

Teachers must remember that they function only with the help and guidance of many other staff members. Administrators, secretaries, and teacher aides need to feel that they too are a part of the community that exists within the school; they need to be included in activities and projects. Working with colleagues is a very important part of teaching. Nowhere in the schools is there a better resource for ideas and suggestions. One example from the scenario that illustrates this cooperative role of teacher as colleague relates to establishing the schedule for the day. For this to occur, it would obviously be necessary that there be thoughtful planning with the art teacher, the music teacher, and the remedial reading teacher.

Both parents and teachers need to understand students and the environmental influences that affect them. Teachers serve as resources to parents in providing information about pupils' performances in school; parents serve as resources in providing information about their children in various other contexts. Often information about how students act and react in both the home and school contexts can help determine the solution to problems they are experiencing at home, at school, or both. Close communication between home and school is critical in developing a partnership between parents and teachers. In this scenario, the teacher might discuss with the parents the reasons why she feels a child should be placed in the remedial reading program; there should then be close communication with the parents regarding the student's progress both socially and academically. This will be very important as the teacher reevaluates the decision to place the student in the reading program. While the teacher in this scenario recognized the need to discuss the child's progress with the remedial reading teacher, discussion with the parents is equally important. Furthermore, the teacher could provide suggestions to the parents regarding how they might reinforce reading skills in the home environment.

The role of the teacher as understander of students' behavior includes an understanding and awareness of the developmental needs of learners and the specific moment-to-moment influences that affect them. This knowledge and awareness are necessary if teachers are to facilitate a learning environment that is both adaptive and responsive to the students' individual social, emotional, intellectual, and physical needs. In the scenario, there was evidence that the learning environment was adaptive and responsive to the students' individual rates of cognitive development. The teacher had divided the students into several reading groups. She used the services of the remedial reading teacher. Individual instruction was provided for several pupils who had made numerous mistakes in their reading assignments. The teacher was also aware of the affective development of learners. The daily "sharing period" provided an opportunity for students to share some of their values and inner feelings with classmates. The teacher remarked about the need for children to express themselves in a relaxed atmosphere. She felt that "sharing time" was particularly important because of the busy schedule that often made it difficult to take individual time to listen to the students' comments. In solving the argument over the job of "helper," the teacher gave each girl an opportunity to discuss the problem. The teacher remarked that she wanted each of the girls to feel that she was treated fairly. These are just a few examples from the scenario that illustrate the role of the teacher as understander of students.

To create the best possible learning situations, teachers must be able to adapt and tailor instruction to the specific needs of students on a particular day. Teachers should encourage and value the self-expression of each student. This requires an environment characterized by a proper balance between control of student behavior and the freedom necessary to allow learning. This scenario reflects a relaxed yet orderly classroom environment. The teacher said she wanted the pupils to know that they were free to move around as long as they were working independently and were not interrupting other classroom activities. As the students entered the classroom both at the beginning of the day and after art class, the teacher was there to greet them and reinforce them (for example, she complimented them on their art projects). Her respect for and awareness of the needs of the individual helped to create a very supportive, nonthreatening learning environment.

This scenario contains several examples of disagreement among the students. Two girls argued over the job of "helper"; one boy let another boy in line in front of him; and several students did not follow the rules on the playground. In each of these cases, the teacher involved the students in resolving the problem. She also recognized that isolating a child who had a problem was not an effective solution to that problem. The teacher talked to him privately and told him that she was confident that he could do his work without causing a problem. She then brought him back into the group.

While viewing the educational television program, one child cried and said the show was upsetting him. The teacher was aware of the need to discuss this with him and took him out in the hall to do so. The real problem was that the child had forgotten his lunch money and was worried about it. Instead of scolding him, the teacher reassured him that he could charge his lunch, and, furthermore, that she would never let him go without eating.

The supportive interactions and communications with children, involvement of students in discussing problems and their solutions, recognition of children's efforts, and awareness and acceptance of their varying learning rates are just a few examples of how this teacher created an environment conducive to fostering a positive self-concept— an important component of the role of the teacher as understander of students and the role of the teacher as a person.

As a facilitator of learning, the teacher worked with small groups in reading; she also worked independently with two or three students who were encountering some difficulties in reading. She involved the students in science experiments. Educational television was used for one class. Students were engaged in a creative arts project. The role of the teacher as understander is critical to the role of the teacher as facilitator. The teacher's knowledge of how children learn is important in making those decisions about the learning environment.

One of the major goals of the teacher as a facilitator of learning is to promote independence and self-direction. While the teacher was working with a small reading group, she expected the other students to work independently. She made reference to the fact that she was striving for self-discipline in the children; therefore, she discussed the noise problem that occurred during the change of classes. She focused on each person's responsibility in this regard. The teacher also assigned daily tasks for cleaning the room and stated that she wanted the students to be responsible for care of the room.

Another characteristic of the teacher as facilitator of learning is the ability to be flexible. Although the teacher did not describe the science project in detail, she referred to the fact that the children brought in shoeboxes and articles for a project. She recognized that the children were excited about the science project and therefore decided to decrease the reading assignments.

In this scenario, there was evidence that the teacher played the role of a researcher by gathering data about the children as a basis for her decision-making. A representative from the newspaper was at school to speak as part of the gifted program, and each teacher was asked to send only five students to listen to the speaker. However, since many children showed an interest in participating, the teacher needed to choose the representatives. She commented that she did this on the basis of past teacher assessments of potentially gifted children and also on the basis of how these children had been performing in her classroom.

The role of the teacher as administrator is evident in this scenario. The teacher had made preliminary plans for the day so that she was free to greet the children when they came in that morning. She acknowledged that it was important to have this time to observe and interact with the students. While the teacher worked with the small groups in reading, the other children worked independently on instructional activities that she had preplanned.

The teacher's schedule included not only the daily schedule in her own classroom but an integrated schedule that was coordinated with that of special programs—the art class, the music class, the gifted program, and the remedial reading classes. She also coordinated routine responsibilities in the classroom—a chart used for assigning responsibilities for classroom cleaning helped to facilitate this. The teacher acknowledged the importance of having the children develop responsibility for the care of the room.

From this discussion of the scenario, the reader can readily see how all the roles of the teacher are interdependent and woven into each moment of the school day. While some of the roles are enacted almost intuitively, others call for conscious deliberation. Furthermore, depending on the moment-to-moment context, some roles may be more dominant than others. This dominance of one role over the other is evident in the next scenario, which describes a morning in the life of a high school teacher. While all the complex roles are evident, the roles of the teacher as administrator and colleague seem to permeate the scenario. The scenario was written by an experienced secondary English teacher who has taught nine years in a rural school district where a strong spirit of camaraderie exists among the teachers. Discussion questions are included at the end of the scenario in order to help the reader synthesize and better understand the complex roles of the teacher.

Scenario 2: A Day in the Life of a High School Teacher

7:20—As usual, I arrived at school early; this is my favorite time of the day—it sets the tone for the rest of the day. I filed the graded assignments and quizzes that I had completed last night. I also cross-checked my materials for the day with my lesson plans. Did I have the handouts, quizzes, transparencies, and textbooks that I needed for the day? This is also the time to exchange a few words with the custodian who comes down each morning to sweep the floors and clean the chalkboards in the rooms in the lower hallway.

I gathered my gradebook, my attendance folder for first period study hall, a textbook we are thinking about adopting, and my file on the new course of study.

On my way to the office, I detoured through the library. There I chatted with our media specialist before completing the equipment request forms for the film projector I needed in the afternoon.

I stopped at the office to check my mailbox, said "Good morning" to the office secretary, and wandered into the principal's office. He wanted to know if I had chosen the date for the theater trip I was planning for my junior American literature students. Since I had not been able to find a good date, we looked at the calendar together. There were two possible dates that would not conflict with any athletic, music, or community events. We marked both dates, knowing one or the other would have to go because of conflicts with buses scheduled by teachers in the elementary or intermediate buildings.

Now, it was on to the teachers' lounge—again, setting the tone for the day. One of the other early arrivals had already made our first pot of coffee, and over that coffee we spoke about all the things that occupy teachers: students, curriculum, assemblies scheduled for the week, and upcoming parent-teacher conferences. Other staff members wandered through the lounge as we talked—and before the day actually began, almost everyone who teaches in our building had been in and out. Too soon, it seemed, it was time to "face the kids."

7:55—I went to my first period study hall, held in the cafeteria. Study hall is not too bad this year—I have approximately one hundred twenty students, but at least thirty of them a day go to the library instead of coming to study hall. Since they know what I expect of them, and they also know what to expect of me if they do not follow the rules, first period can be pleasant and rewarding. Arriving in the cafeteria early gave me an opportunity to check on the students who were absent yesterday and to make certain that they had been to the attendance office.

8:10—The bell rang to begin first period. I read the morning announcements (we have found that having each individual teacher read them to his or her class is far more effective than having them read over the PA system), took the lunch count, and began to take attendance. There is no truly simple way to check the attendance of one hundred twenty students, but with an accurate seating chart and cooperative students, the task doesn't take all period.

Attendance taken, I got to work on my revisions for the course of study. (The beauty of study hall where the students do study and where they study quietly is that I get work done, too.)

9:00—The bell rang, and I joined the sea of people moving toward various classrooms for second period. My creative writing class and I met in the library again today. There were not very many students from study hall in the library this period, so we took a corner to ourselves. This room —with carpeting on the floor and with those nice round tables—makes writing of any kind easier. I also like the peer tutoring that goes on informally when the students share thoughts or dictionaries. That kind of sharing occurs more often when they are sitting in groups of four or six. Of course, the small class—only ten students—helps. I may not be quite so lucky next semester.

We began the period by writing in our journals. The journals serve several purposes for the students as well as for me. We use the journals just to warm up, as practice for expressing our emotions on paper, and as "inspiration" for later writing assignments.

I began the cyclic story for the day. It was my turn to begin, so I wrote the first paragraph. Each student added to the story, and by the end of the class period, everyone had added to it. The last writer tied it together with a conclusion. They do enjoy this exercise, and I must say that we end up with some very strange combinations at times. We began another writing exercise of observing various students and then describing their unique characteristics. Too soon, there were only five minutes left in the period.

9:55—I was not looking forward to this class today. Normally, I enjoy it as much as I do my others, but we had a problem. Several people copied the homework that they turned in yesterday. I cannot decide whether they think I never read what they turn in but just give them credit for handing in a paper (although they should know I read papers from the comments and corrections I make on assignments) or if they think that I cannot remember that I have read exactly the same thing —word for word, misspelling for misspelling—once or twice or three times already. I got on my "soapbox" and addressed the entire class about the problem. Because this class of juniors is very adept at reading my nonverbal signals, I avoided looking directly at those involved. Having gone through my explanation of the problem and my disappointment with those who allowed others to copy, I asked the students for their solutions. Some students were ready for me to proclaim the names of the offenders for public humiliation, but I knew that that solution was no solution at all. After everyone who wanted to speak had had the opportunity to do so, we decided to give those who committed the "crime" a second chance. They will not receive credit for the assignment until it is done again. Even those who, I think, did the work originally and gave it to others to copy agreed with the solution. We also agreed that if it happens again, both parties would receive a zero for the assignment. Satisfied that we had reached a reasonable solution, we got on with the class.

This is a good class, but it is one for which I have had to do a great deal of preparation. It is a nine-week course entitled "American West," and the combination of ability levels in the class coupled with my own lack of knowledge has meant that I have had to really scramble to find enough materials for everyone—including myself.

We began by discussing the story I had assigned for today. It was written by an American Indian about the traditions and the signs and symbols of the Indian culture. The material from the text was a natural lead in for a discussion not only of the folklore and religious beliefs of Native Americans but also of our own dependence on signs and symbols.

As the students began to work—in groups of three—on a list of symbols and their meanings in our own culture, I was able to speak to one boy about a special project he was beginning for me. Brad is almost an addict of the Old West. He has read more and knows more than I do about the cowboy culture of the Old West—Jesse James, Annie Oakley, the Dalton brothers. We have agreed that he will teach part of that unit, and we are setting goals for both his unit and for him. He was ready for me and had brought several of his own hand-drawn illustrations to be used in the bulletin board introduction to the unit. Our only point of contention, thus far, was his desire to bring to school an old-fashioned revolver that he had assembled. I think he finally understood that he cannot bring a gun to school; we agreed on photographs instead.

10:50—My planning period began. Ideally, I would be able to spend this period in my classroom, but the health classes must have some place to meet, and mine is the only classroom that is free this period. I collected the papers and materials I would need and waited for the teacher to arrive. She wanted to know how her volleyball players were doing; the athletic eligibility sheets that go out each week do not give her enough information about the academic progress of the students. (She wants to know *more* than whether or not they are failing subjects.) None of the players I have are having difficulty academically, behaviorally, or socially; she is as relieved as I am — we have a big game coming up, and she wants them ready and eager to play.

On my way to the lounge, I stopped in the guidance office. I could not understand why one of my freshman boys was being so difficult in class, and I wanted to check his permanent record. I was surprised to discover that I must sign out the file — date, time, and reason for pulling the file must be recorded as well as the time that the file is replaced. It was interesting to note, though, that not many of the faculty have spent any time at all with the records. I was dismayed to realize that Mike, my "problem student," has superior standardized test scores; he has not been my best student. (Perhaps he is just too bored to do the work that I have assigned him.) I spoke to the counselor and got both times and dates that would be convenient for him to have a conference with Mike's parents. Then it was on to the office to call Mike's mother. Once I had assured her that Mike is not in terrible trouble, we made an appointment for a three-way conference. I hoped that his mother, the counselor, and I could establish a course of study for Mike that would enable him to do the kind of work of which he is capable.

I headed for the lounge. It was past time for that cup of coffee, and I really wanted to take a closer look at the American West papers.

11:40 — Already it was time for lunch. The lounge filled rapidly. The first lunch group, of which I am a part, was planning to establish Friday as "Goody Day," and there was great discussion about a schedule. Who was responsible for *this* Friday? What kind of goodies do we want? The laughter covered, temporarily, the insistent knocking at the door. In spite of the groans and the comment that we were to have "thirty uninterrupted minutes for lunch," I answered the door. The student, a little disbelieving that teachers giggle as much as students do, asked for the math teacher. In the midst of cheers from the others, the math teacher went out into the hall with the student. Although the sign on the back of the lounge door reads, "If it won't fit under the door, we don't want it," there are only two or three people on the entire staff who are *not* glad that the students search us out when they have problems — from "I don't understand the problem," to "Will you be judge for the Pep Rally?" or "Jack just told me he doesn't want to go steady any more."

The bell summoned me to my afternoon class.

DISCUSSION QUESTIONS

1. Leadership has been discussed in terms of sensitivity to the needs of those who are led. Teachers who are professional leaders must be aware of the unique needs of their students. They need the ecological perspective that accommodates the influences inherent in the total context. This teacher examined the academic background of a particular student; how can this information begin to aid her in addressing his needs? Cite other examples, from this scenario, in which the teacher shows concern for the problems of particular students.
2. The sign of a true leader is "the ability to unleash human potential." This teacher understood that one member of her American West class had a real knowledge and interest in the course material — perhaps knowledge and interest that surpassed her own. How did she deal with this student's interests? How did her understanding enable this student to attain more success than he may have had within a more structured environment?
3. A leader possesses the ability to be challenged by complex events and to face a variety of risks. In this scenario, the teacher accepted the risk of confronting the students with the problem of copying homework assignments. How did she solve this problem? How did she involve the students in the decision-making process regarding the problem of cheating? What other actions could have been taken? Provide a rationale for other acceptable solutions.
4. The teacher who is truly a leader has a sense of confidence in his or her ability to influence positively and significantly the lives of others. In this scenario, the teacher recognized the need to provide assistance to Mike, who was having difficulty in class. She recognized the need to develop a partnership with the parents in helping Mike and therefore scheduled a conference with the parents. In preparing for this conference, what type of information would you gather?
5. The responsive, sensitive teacher will use several methods and approaches to facilitate student motivation and learning. What teacher behaviors did you observe that could foster a positive self-concept? The creative writing class in this scenario meets in the library rather than in the classroom. How does this different setting facilitate the teacher's objectives for the class? What other evidence was there that the learning environment was adaptive and responsive to the students' individual rates of cognitive development?
6. A leader is a source of support for others. This requires an appreciation and understanding of the feelings and special sensitivities of others. The teacher in this scenario functioned often in her role as a colleague; she made it a point to join the other staff members in the

teachers' lounge and was certain to stop in the library and the principal's office in the morning. What other evidence is there of the teacher's involvement in this role as colleague? What factors did you observe that have the potential to reduce teacher stress?

7. One of the qualities of a leader is enthusiasm toward living and learning. Cite examples from the scenario that demonstrate this leadership quality.

8. The role of the teacher as an administrator includes such processes as planning, organizing, communicating, evaluating, and reporting. This role is extremely important if teachers are to make the best out of the few short hours they spend with students each day. In this scenario, the teacher was involved extensively in the role of administrator. Cite various examples that illustrate how the teacher functioned as an administrator. How was the role of the teacher as administrator integrated with other teacher roles described in this scenario?

Throughout each of the scenarios it is evident that teaching is leadership. The effectiveness of teachers as leaders encompasses the integration of the numerous roles described throughout this book—roles that ultimately lead to unleashing the human potential of each student. The teacher who is truly a leader is committed and dedicated to teaching as a helping profession. He or she is a person who welcomes the challenge of providing a learning environment in which each student has the opportunity to grow as a total person. Thoreau once said, "To affect the quality of the day is the greatest of arts." Similarly, to affect qualitatively the lives of students through teaching is the greatest of arts. Teachers, as understanders of students, can make a difference in the lives of these students. The degree of difference often depends on who the teacher is as a person. The influence teachers have is strengthened as they work cooperatively and supportively with parents, colleagues, and teacher educators. Efforts to become involved as researchers and program developers will ultimately enhance the role of teachers as administrators and facilitators of an enriched learning environment. All of these roles orchestrate to help teachers become those professional leaders who affect the lives of learners.

References

Alexander, W. M., & George, P. S. *The exemplary middle school.* New York: Holt, Rinehart & Winston, 1981.

Allport, G. W. *Pattern and growth in personality.* New York: Holt, Rinehart & Winston, 1965.

Almy, M., & Genishi, C. *Ways of studying children.* New York: Teachers College Press, 1979.

Amara, R. *Toward understanding the social impact of computers.* Menlo Park, Calif.: Institute for the Future, 1974.

Applegate, J. H., Flora, V. R., Johnston, J. M., Lasley, T. J., Mager, G. M., Newman, K. K., & Ryan, K. *The first year teacher study.* Columbus, Ohio: Ohio State University, 1977. (ERIC Document No. ED 135 766)

Bailey, W. J., & Neale, D. C. Teachers and school improvement. *Educational Forum,* 1980, *45*(1), 69–76.

Bennis, W. G. *Changing organizations.* New York: McGraw-Hill, 1966.

Berliner, D. C. Using research on teaching for the improvement of classroom practice. *Theory into Practice,* 1980, *19*(4), 302–308.

Berman, P., & McLaughlan, M. W. Implementation of educational innovation. *Educational Forum,* 1976, *40*(3), 345–370.

Berne, E. *Games people play.* New York: Grove Press, 1964.

Blau, P. M., & Scott, W. R. *Formal organizations: A comparative approach.* San Francisco, Calif.: Chandler, 1962.

Bloom, B., Englehart, M. D., Furst, E. J., Hill, W. H., & Krathwohl, D. R. *Taxonomy of educational objectives: The classification of educational goals. Handbook 1: Cognitive Domain.* New York: Longman's Green, 1965.

Blosser, P. E. *A study of the development of the skill of effective questioning by prospective secondary school science teachers.* Doctoral dissertation, The Ohio State University, 1970. (ED 052008)

Blume, J. *It's not the end of the world.* New York: Bantam Books, 1972.

Boyd, W. L. The changing politics of curriculum policy-making for American schools. *Review of Educational Research,* 1978, *48*(4), 577–628.

Breidemeier, M. E., & Breidemeier, H. C. *Social forces in education.* Sherman Oaks, Calif.: Alfred, 1978.

Britton, J. Their language and our teaching. *English in Education, 1970, 4*(2), 5–13.

Bronfenbrenner, U. *The ecology of human development.* Cambridge, Mass.: Harvard University Press, 1979.

Brophy, J. E., & Good, T. L. *Teacher-student relationships: Causes and consequences.* New York: Holt, Rinehart & Winston, 1974.

Brown, F. Study of the schools' needs of children from one-parent families. *Phi Delta Kappan,* 1980, *61*, 573–580.

Cartwright, D. P., & Zander, A. *Group dynamics: Research and theory.* New York: Harper & Row, 1968.

Chandler, L. A. What teachers can do about childhood stress. *Phi Delta Kappan,* 1981, *63*(4), 276–277.

Chilman, C. Some angles on parent-teacher learning. *Childhood Education,* 1971, *48*(3), 119–125.

Colgrove, M. A. *Stimulating creative problem solving: Innovative set.* Doctoral dissertation, University of Michigan, 1967. Ann Arbor, Mich.: University Microfilms, No. 67-15, 607.

Combs, A. W. *A personal approach to teaching: Beliefs that make a difference.* Boston: Allyn & Bacon, 1982.

Corwin, R. G. *A sociology of education.* New York: Appleton-Century-Crofts, 1965.

Cruickshank, D. R. What we know about teachers' problems. *Educational Leadership,* 1981, *38*(5), 402–405.

Culver, C. M., Shiman, D. A., & Lieberman, A. Working together: The peer group strategy. In C. M. Culver & G. J. Hoban (Eds.), *The power to change: Issues for the innovative educator.* New York: McGraw-Hill, 1973.

DeVault, V. (Ed.) *Research development and the classroom teacher: Producer and consumer.* Washington: Association for Childhood Education International, 1970.

Dewey, J. *The school and society.* Chicago: University of Chicago Press, 1900.

Dewey, J. *Democracy and education.* New York: Macmillan, 1916.

Doerr, C. *Microcomputers and the 3 r's: A guide for teachers.* Rochelle Park, N.J.: Hayden, 1979.

Dreikurs, R., & Cassel, P. *Discipline without tears: What to do with children who misbehave.* New York: Hawthorn, 1974.

Eisner, E. W. *The educational imagination.* New York: Macmillan, 1979.

Elkind, D. *Child development and education: A Piagetian perspective.* New York: Oxford University Press, 1976.

Erikson, E. *Childhood and society.* 2nd ed. New York: Norton, 1963.

Foshay, A. W. Curriculum. In R. L. Ebel (Ed.), *Encyclopedia of educational research.* New York: Macmillan, 1969.

Frazier, A. *Teaching children today: An informal approach.* New York: Harper & Row, 1976.

Frymier, J. *Annehurst curriculum classification system: A practical way to individualize instruction.* West Lafayette, Ind.: Kappa Delta Pi Press, 1977.

Fuller, F. F., & Bown, O. Becoming a teacher. In K. Ryan (Ed.), *Teacher Education: Seventy-fourth yearbook of the National Society for the Study of Education.* Part 2. Chicago: University of Chicago Press, 1975.

Galloway, C., Steltzer, M. C., & Whitfield, T. Exchange and mutuality: Growth conditions for teacher development. *Theory into Practice,* 1980, *19*(4), 262–265.

Genishi, C. Young children communicating in the classroom: Selected Research. *Theory into Practice,* 1979, *18*(4), 244–250.

Glasser, W. *Schools without failure.* New York: Harper & Row, 1969.

Goodlad, J. I. An ecological version of accountability. *Theory into Practice,* 1979, *18*(5), 308–315.

Goodlad, J. I. The school as workplace. In G. A. Griffin (Ed.), *Staff development: Eighty-second yearbook of the National Society for the Study of Education.* Chicago: University of Chicago Press, 1983.

Goodlad, J. I., Klein, M. F., & Associates. *Behind the classroom door.* Worthington, Ohio: Jones, 1970.

Goodlad, J. I., & Tyler, L. L. The personal domain: Curricular meaning. In J. I. Goodlad (Ed.), *Curriculum inquiry: The study of human practice.* New York: McGraw-Hill, 1979.

Goodson, B., & Hess, R. D. *Parents and teachers of young children: An evaluative review of some contemporary concepts and programs.* Palo Alto, Calif.: Stanford University Press, 1975.

Gordon, I. J. Parent involvement in early childhood education. *National Elementary Principal,* 1971, *51*(1), 26–35.

Gordon, T. *P.E.T.: Parent effectiveness training.* New York: Wyden, 1970.

Gordon, T. *T.E.T.: Teacher effectiveness training.* New York: Wyden, 1974.

Greenberg, H. M. *Teaching with feeling: Compassion and self-awareness in the classroom today.* New York: Macmillan, 1969.

Greene, M. *Landscapes of learning.* New York: Teachers College Press, 1978.

Hamachek, D. E. *Encounters with the self.* New York: Holt, Rinehart & Winston, 1971.

Harris, T. A. *I'm OK, you're OK: A practical guide to transactional analysis.* New York: Harper & Row, 1969.

Hass, G. *Curriculum planning: A new approach.* Boston: Allyn & Bacon, 1974.

Heck, S. F., & Cobes, J. *The creative classroom environment: A stage set design.* New York: Pergamon Press, 1978.

Hillesheim, J. W., & Merrill, G. D. (Eds.) *Theory and practice in the history of American education—A book of readings.* Pacific Palisades, Calif.: Goodyear, 1971.

Hinely, R., & Ponder, G. Theory, practice, and classroom research. *Theory into Practice, 1979, 18*(3), 135–137.

Holt, L. & Uhlenberg, D. Dropout factors in the process of influencing classroom change through teacher education. The University of Utah. Washington, D.C.: Educational Resources Information Center, 1978. (ERIC Document 155141)

Hoover, K. H., & Hollingsworth, P. M. *Learning and teaching in the elementary school.* Boston: Allyn & Bacon, 1970.

Hunt, S. L. Stress without distress. *The Educational Record,* 1983, *19*(2), 38–42.

Hunter, M. The teaching process. In D. W. Allen & E. Seifman (Eds.), *The teacher's handbook.* Glenview, Ill.: Scott, Foresman, 1971.

Hunter, M. Teaching is decision-making. *Educational Leadership,* 1979, *37*(1), 62–67.

James, W. Education as habit formation. In J. W. Hillesheim & G.D. Merrill (Eds.), *Theory and practice in the history of American education—A book of readings.* Pacific Palisades, Calif.: Goodyear, 1971.

Jarolimek, J., & Foster, C. D. *Teaching and learning in the elementary school.* (2nd ed.) New York: Macmillan, 1981.

Jersild, A. *When teachers face themselves.* New York: Teachers College Press, 1955.

Kimmel, D. C. *Adulthood and aging: An interdisciplinary, developmental view.* New York: Wiley, 1974.

Klein, M. F. Instructional decisions in curriculum. In J. I. Goodlad (Ed.), *The study of curriculum practice: Curriculum inquiry.* New York: McGraw-Hill, 1979.

Klein, N. *Taking sides.* New York: Pantheon, 1974.

Kliebard, H. M. Metaphorical roots of curriculum design. *Teachers College Record,* 1972, *73*(3), 403–404.

Kohlberg, L., & Turiel, E. *Research in moral development: The cognitive developmental approach.* New York: Holt, Rinehart & Winston, 1971.

Languis, M., & Kraft, R. Hemispheric brain function: What it means for you. *Ohio Council of Elementary School Science,* 1975, *7,* 14–28.

Lewin, J. Behavior and development as a function of the total situation. In L. Carmichael (Ed.), *Manual of child psychology.* 2nd ed. New York: Wiley, 1954.

Lieberman, A., & Miller, L. The social realities of teaching. In A. Lieberman & L. Miller (Eds.), *Staff development: New demands, new realities, new perspectives.* New York: Teachers College Press, 1979.

Lightfoot, S. L. Toward a conflict and resolution: Relationships between families and schools. *Theory into Practice,* 1981, *20*(2), 97–103.

Lipham, J. M., & Hoeh, J. A. *The principalship: Foundations and functions.* New York: Harper & Row, 1974.

Lortie, D. *Schoolteacher: A sociological study.* Chicago: University of Chicago Press, 1975.

Mann, P. *My dad lives in a downtown hotel.* New York: Doubleday, 1973.

Maslow, A. H. Some basic propositions of a growth and self-actualization psychology. In A. W. Combs (Ed.), *Perceiving, behaving, becoming: A new focus for education.* Washington, D.C.: Yearbook of the Association for Supervision and Curriculum Development, 1962.

McCarthy, M. A., & Houston, J. P. *Fundamentals of early childhood education.* Cambridge, Mass.: Winthrop, 1980.

Michael, D. Tomorrow's sources of actualization and alienation. In R. R. Leeper (Ed.), *Humanizing education: The person in the process.* Washington, D.C.: Association for Supervision and Curriculum Development, NEA, 1967.

Netzer, L., & Eye, G. *Strategies for instructional management.* Boston: Allyn & Bacon, 1979.

Orlich, D. C., Harder, R. J., Callahan, R. C., Kravas, C. H., Kauchak, D. P., Pendergrass, R. A., Keogh, A. J., & Hellene, D. I. *Teaching strategies: A guide to better instruction.* Lexington, Mass: Heath, 1980.

Outland, B. A. Parent education can significantly affect pupil achievement. *Phi Delta Kappan,* 1977, *59*(2), 132.

Parlett, M., & Hamilton, D. Evaluation as illuminations: A new approach to the study of innovative programs. Occasional Paper No. 9. Edinburgh: Center for Research in the Educational Sciences; University of Edinburgh, 1972.

Paterson, K. *The Great Gilly Hopkins.* New York, N.Y.: Crowell, 1978.

Patton, M. Q. *Qualitative evaluation methods.* Beverly Hills, Calif.: Sage, 1980.

Perry, R. The organizational/environmental variables in staff development. *Theory into Practice,* 1980, *19*(4), 256–261.

Persell, C. *Education and inequality: A theoretical and empirical synthesis.* New York: Free Press, 1977.

Piaget, J. *Genetic epistemology.* New York: Norton, 1970.

Piaget, J. *The child and reality.* New York: Grossman, 1973.

Pratt, D. Predicting teacher survival. *Journal of Educational Research,* 1977, *71*(1), 12–18.

Purkey, W. W. *Inviting school success: A self-concept approach to teaching and learning.* Belmont, Calif.: Wadsworth, 1978.

Raths, L., Harmin, M., & Simon, S. *Values and teaching.* Columbus, Ohio: Merrill, 1966.

Raths, L., Wasserman, S., Jonas, A., & Rothstein, A. *Teaching for thinking: Theory and application.* Columbus, Ohio: Merrill, 1967.

Rich, D. The relationship of the home learning lab technique to first grade student achievement in the Archdiocese of Washington, D.C. Schools. Doctoral dissertation, The Catholic University of America, 1976.

Rogers, C. R. The interpersonal relationships in the facilitation of learning. In R. R. Leeper (Ed.), *Humanizing education: The person in the process.* Washington, D. C.: Association for Supervision and Curriculum Development, NEA, 1967.

Rowe, M. B. Wait, wait, wait . . . *School Science and Mathematics,* 1978, *78*(3), 207–216.

Ryan, K., & Johnston, J. M. *Research on the beginning teacher: Implications for teacher education.* Occasional Paper. Columbus, Ohio: Ohio State University, 1980.

Ryan, K., Newman, K., Mager, G., Applegate, J., Lasley, T., Flora, R., & Johnston, J. *Biting the apple: Accounts of first year teachers.* New York: Longman, 1980.

Sarason, S. B. *The culture of the school and the problem of change.* Boston: Allyn & Bacon, 1971.

Sartre, J. P. *Search for a method.* New York: Knopf, 1963.

Schutz, A. Making music together. In A. Schutz (Ed.), *Collected Papers II: Studies in Social Theory.* The Hague: Niihof, 1964.

Scriven, M. The necessity for evaluation. In A. D. Calvin (Ed.), *Perspectives on education.* New York: Addison-Wesley, 1977.

Sergiovanni, T. J., & Carver, F. D. *The new school executive: A theory of administration*. New York: Harper & Row, 1980.

Sergiovanni, T. J., & Starratt, R. J. *Emerging patterns of supervision: Human perspectives*. New York: McGraw-Hill, 1971.

Shields, J. S. Mini-calculators and problem solving. *School Science and Mathematics*, 1980, *80*(3), 211–217.

Simon, H. A. *Administrative behavior: A study of decision-making process in administrative organizations*. New York: Free Press, 1966.

Simon, S. B., Howe, L. W., & Kirschenbaum, H. *Values clarification: A handbook of practical strategies for teachers and students*. New York: Hart, 1972.

Smith, F. *Comprehension in learning*. New York: Holt, Rinehart & Winston, 1975.

Snygg, D., & Combs, A. *Individual behavior: Perceptual approach to behavior*. New York: Harper, 1959.

Starratt, R. J. Contemporary talk as leadership: Too many kings in the parade? *The Notre Dame Journal of Education*, 1973, *4*(1), 13.

Stevenson, H. W. Learning and cognition. In J. N. Payne (Ed.), *Mathematics learning in early childhood: Thirty-seventh yearbook of the National Council of Teachers of Mathematics*. Reston, Va.:National Council of Teachers of Mathematics, 1975.

Taylor, M. D. *Roll of thunder, hear my cry*. New York: Dial Press, 1976.

Travers, R. M. Training the teacher as a performing artist. *Contemporary Education*, 1979, *51*(1), 14–18.

Travers, R. M., & Dillon, J. *The making of a teacher: A plan for professional self-development*. New York: Macmillan, 1975.

Turner, P. H., & Durrett, M. E. *Teacher level of questioning and problem solving in young children*. Washington, D.C.: Department of Health, Education, and Welfare, 1975. (ERIC Document, Research in Education, 105997)

Tyler, L. L. Meaning in education: A personal view. *Educational Forum*, 1981, *45*(3), 375–376.

Tyler, R. Reconstructing the total educational environment. *Phi Delta Kappan*, 1975, *57*(1), 12–13.

Van Hoose, J., & Hult, R. E. The performing artist dimension in effective teaching. *Contemporary Education*, 1979, *51*(1), 36–39.

Webb, N. L., Moses, B. E., & Kerr, D. R. Developmental activities related to summative evaluation. Technical Report No. 4, Mathematical Problem-Solving Project. Bloomington, Ind.: Mathematics Education Development Center, 1977.

Williams, C. R., Neff, A. R., & Finkelstein, J. H. Theory into practice: Reconsidering the proposition. *Theory into Practice*, 1981, *20*(2), 93–96.

Wolfgang, C. *Helping passive and aggressive pre-schoolers through play*. Columbus, Ohio: Merrill, 1977.

Wolfgang, C., & Glickman, C. *Solving discipline problems: Strategies for classroom teachers*. Boston: Allyn & Bacon, 1980.

Index

Almy, M., 41, 42
Amara, R., 121
Annehurst Curriculum Classification System, 137
Applegate, J. H., 8

Bailey, W. J., 116
Berliner, D. C., 149
Berne, E., 16, 68
Blau, P. M., 16
Bloom, B., 79
Blume, J., 32
Bown, O., 2, 151
Boyd, W. L., 117
Breidemeier, H. C., 50
Breidemeier, M. E., 50
Britton, J., 59–60, 63
Bronfenbrenner, U., xiii, 50, 58, 59, 74

Cartwright, D. P., 16
Carver, F. D., 16, 21, 188
Cassel, P., 67, 174
Chandler, L. A., 32–33
Chilman, C., 30
Classroom environment, 32–33; discipline in, 64, 67, 68; emotional aspects of, 63, 66; management of, 164; physical aspects of, 64, 132–133. *See also* Context; Learning environment
Cobes, J., 85
Colgrove, M. A., 78
Collegiality: with other staff, 27, 147, 193; among teachers, 6–7, 14–17, 21–25, 146–147, 152. *See also*

Communication; Professional development
Combs, A. W., 4, 51, 189
Communication, 146–149; between teacher and parents, 28–30, 34–36, 42–43, 49, 99, 193; between teacher and principal, 22–23. *See also* Collegiality
Community, 116–118, 121, 125–126; communication with, 148, 169; providing leadership in, 27, 119–122; role in program development, 118, 125; support for education, 126
Concept development, 63, 75
Context: of classroom and decision-making, 170–171, 172; of home, 28–29, 33; moment to moment, 2, 51–53, 64, 172, 196; multiple, 2, 9, 28, 53, 58, 64, 65–66, 68, 97, 98, 126; of observation, 107; -related concerns, 150–151; societal, 50–51, 116–117. *See also* Classroom environment
Cruickshank, D. R., 7
Cultural diversity of students, understanding, 30, 51, 53–55
Culver, C. M., 21
Curriculum: Annehurst Curriculum Classification System, 137; changes in, 123–124; hidden, 55; objectives of, 118–119; social context on development of, 63, 121. *See also* Program development

Data. *See* Research

Decision-making: developing skills
     of, 172–174; holistic, 190; parental
     participation in educational, 36–37;
     process of, 168; teacher involve-
     ment in programmatic, 125–126; of
     teachers, 143, 169–172
DeVault, V., 94
Dewey, John, 73, 95, 117, 120, 168,
     170
Dillon, J., 174
Discipline. See Classroom environ-
     ment
Doerr, C., 121
Dreikurs, R., 67, 174
Durrett, M. E., 76–77

Educational practice, 68, 193–197.
     See also Classroom environment
Eisner, E. W., 113, 124
Erikson, E., 57
Eye, G., 168

Finkelstein, J. H., 172
Foshay, A. W., 123
Frazier, A., 149
Frymier, J., 137
Fuller, F. F., 2, 151

Galloway, C., 14
Genishi, C., 41, 42, 61
Glasser, William, 67
Glickman, C., 35, 67
Goodlad, John I., ix–xii, 16, 26, 27,
     74, 120, 124, 168
Gordon, I. J., 28, 29, 30, 36–37
Greenberg, H. M., 1, 5, 8, 14, 152
Greene, M., 3, 83

Hamachek, D. E., 18
Hamilton, D., 114
Harmin, M., 68
Harris, T. A., 68
Hass, G., 123
Heck, S. F., 85
Hillesheim, J. W., 122, 174

Hinely, R., 96
Hoeh, J. A., 26, 27, 146
Hollingsworth, P. M., 128, 137
Holt, L., 152
Hoover, K. H., 128, 137
Houston, J. P., 40, 42
Howe, L. W., 79
Hult, R. E., 189
Hunt, S. L., 8
Hunter, M., 60, 64

Interaction. See Communication
Interdisciplinary instruction, 82–86

James, W., 174
Jersild, A., 2
Johnston, J. M., 150
Jonas, A., 74

Kerr, D. R., 78
Kirschenbaum, H., 79
Klein, M. F., 168
Klein, N., 32
Kliebard, H. M., 118
Kohlberg, L., 61

Leadership role of teacher, 188–193;
     in community, 119–122
Learning: active involvement in,
     75–76; development of total learner,
     56–64. See also Learning environ-
     ment
Learning center, 89
Learning environment: facilitation of,
     85–87; home as, 33; ideal, 60–61.
     See also Classroom environment
Lesson plan. See Planning
Lewin, J., 28
Lieberman, A., 15, 21
Lightfoot, S. L., 29
Lipham, J. M., 26, 27, 146
Lortie, D., 8

Mann, P., 32
Maslow, A. H., 60

13.38

McCarthy, M. A., 40, 42
Merrill, G. D., 122, 174
Miller, L., 15, 21
Moses, B. E., 78

Neale, D. C., 116
Neff, A. R., 172
Netzer, L., 168

Observation, 97–106, 107–113; data
   from, 107–108; of interaction,
   108–109; of other teachers, 12–13;
   by parents in classroom, 39; of
   students in multiple contexts, 53,
   97, 98; suggested framework for,
   108–109
Organization, 137–142. See also
   Reporting
Orlich, D. C., 128

Parents: conferences with teachers,
   42–43; as partners in education, 28,
   34–44, 126; as teachers, 33–34
Parlett, M., 114
Paterson, K., 79
Patton, M. Q., 114
Perry, R., 123
Persell, C., 54
Personal development: encouraging in
   students, 119; of teachers, 1–3. See
   also Self; Collegiality
Physical development, 57, 59, 62
Piaget, Jean, 58, 59, 74, 171
Planning, 128–134; lesson, 129, 131;
   long-term, 130; unit, 129–130
Ponder, G., 96
Pratt, D., 152
Prejudice. See Cultural diversity
Principal: communication with,
   22–23; and teachers as colleagues,
   21–25
Problem-solving, 72–82, 168; creating
   environment for, 73–74; developing
   conditions for, 74–76, 78–82; facil-
   itating, through questioning, 76–78;

skills of, 73, 76, 80, 81
Professional development: continuing
   process of, 10–13; establishing
   climate for, 17–21; nuturing, 12–13,
   116. See also Collegiality
Program development: educational
   goals as a basis for, 118–119;
   integration of theory and practice
   in, 122–124; role of community in,
   124; role of research in, 124;
   teacher involvement in, 125–126,
   169. See also Curriculum
Purkey, W. W., 34, 66

Questioning: facilitating problem-
   solving environment through,
   76–78; importance of divergent, 77;
   levels of, 76–77; process of, 76; by
   students, 77–78

Raths, L., 68, 74
Reinforcing influences, 7, 87–88
Reporting, 142–146; health records,
   134, 145–146; report cards,
   142–146; system for, 143–145; work
   samples, 144. See also Organization
Research: basic principles of, 95; as
   basis for improvement, 94; collecting data in, 97–106; criteria for
   judging, 114; qualitative, 103,
   114–115; quantitative, 115; using
   classroom for, 95–97; utilizing,
   101–106, 113–115
Rich, D., 40
Rogers, C. R., 4, 5, 72, 74, 75
Rothstein, A., 74
Rowe, M. B., 77
Ryan, K., 21, 50

Sarason, S. B., 6
Sartre, J. P., 1
Scheduling, 140–142
School environment. See Collegiality;
   Classroom environment
Scott, W. R., 16

Self: -acceptance of student, 56; -actualization of student, 60; -actualization of teacher, 5; -concept of student, 34, 60; continuous development of, 1–2, -encounter, 5; perceptions of, 3–4, 51

Sergiovani, T. J., 14, 16, 21, 188

Shiman, D. A., 21

Simon, S. B., 68, 79

Smith, F., 73

Snygg, D., 51

Social development, 51, 57; encouraging, 119

Starrat, R. J., 14, 188

Steltzer, M. C., 14

Stevenson, H. W., 81

Stress: in family, 31; helping students cope with, 32; on teachers, 6–10, 87–88, 167

Students: academic development of, 119; affective emotional characteristics of, 57; conferences with, 61; discipline of, 64–68; environment of, 51; influence of family on, 30–31; interacting with, 98–99, 106; personality development of, 72, 118; physical development of, 57–58, 62; as problem-solvers, 78–82; self-concept of, 61, 65; social development of, 118–119; stress on, 30–33; teacher observation of, 28, 53; testing of, 100; total development of, 56–60, 119; work samples of, 99

Substitute teachers, 165–167; administrative responsibilities of, 135–137

Support system. *See* Collegiality

Taylor, M. D., 79

Teacher, first-year: human qualities of, 4–6; involvement in program decision-making, 125–126; professional relationship with principal, 21–25; as substitutes, 135–137, 165–167

Teacher educators, as partners with teachers, 26–27

Teaching position: applying for, 153–154; interviewing for, 155–158; sources of information about, 154

Technological change, influence on curriculum, 116–117, 121–122

Tests, 100–101

Travers, R. M., 174, 190

Turiel, E., 61

Turner, P. H., 76–77

Tyler, L. L., 33, 74

Tyler, R., 74, 117

Uhlenberg, D., 152

Unit plan. *See* Planning

Values, of students, 30, 51, 53–55

Van Hoose, J., 189

Wasserman, S., 74

Webb, N. ., 78

Whitfield, T., 14

Williams, C. R., 172

Wolfgang, C., 35, 67

Zander, A., 16